PLAN
DE LA VILLE DE
LOUISBOURG
EN LISLE ROYALLE
Avec les Emmences qui l'avoisinent, leur
distances Entr'elles ainsi que de
La Fortiffication, Ensemble
les ouvrages d'attaques de
l'ennemi et celles de deff.ces
de la part des Assiegé
levé et dessiné sur les lieux
par le Sr Lartigue
M.DCC.LVIII
Batterie de la
Grave
on DAuphin
Bastion Maurepas
Hopital du Roy
Batte Nouveau
depuis 1748
Cimetière
Place
D'Armes
Pte de Rochefort.
Bastion de la Reine
E
R A I S

LOUISBOURG: KEY TO A CONTINENT

THE AMERICAN FORTS SERIES
as planned by Stewart H. Holbrook

GUNS AT THE FORKS
(Forts Duquesne and Pitt)
by Walter O'Meara

LOUISBOURG: KEY TO A CONTINENT
by Fairfax Downey

★ ★ ★

Other Subjects in Preparation

SUTTER'S FORT
Oscar Lewis

FORT LARAMIE
Remi Nadeau

VINCENNES
August Derleth

FORT NIAGARA
Robert West Howard

THE FORTS OF MACKINAC
Walter Havighurst

FORTS OF THE UPPER MISSOURI
Robert G. Athearn

Books by Fairfax Downey

★

History

Indian Wars of the U. S. Army, 1776–1865
Storming of the Gateway; Chattanooga, 1863
Clash of Cavalry: The Battle of Brandy Station, June 9, 1863
The Guns at Gettysburg
Sound of the Guns
Indian-Fighting Army
Disaster Fighters
Our Lusty Forefathers
History of Dogs for Defense
Horses of Destiny
Dogs of Destiny
Cats of Destiny
Mascots
General Crook, Indian Fighter
Famous Horses of the Civil War
Texas and the War With Mexico

Biographies

The Grande Turke: Suleyman the Magnificent
Burton, Arabian Nights Adventurer
Richard Harding Davis: His Day
Portrait of an Era, as Drawn by C. D. Gibson

Anthologies

My Kingdom for a Horse (*comp.*)
Great Dog Stories of All Time (*comp.*)

Historical Novels, Juveniles

War Horse
Dog of War
Jezebel the Jeep
Cavalry Mount
The Seventh's Staghound
Army Mule
Trail of the Iron Horse
A Horse for General Lee
The Shining Filly
Guns for General Washington

Humor and Light Verse

A Comic History of Yale
Father's First Two Years
When We Were Rather Older
Young Enough To Know Better
Laughing Verse (*comp.*)

Louisbourg:

KEY TO A CONTINENT

Fairfax Downey

c.1

PRENTICE-HALL, INC. * Englewood Cliffs, N. J.

Louisbourg: Key to a Continent
by Fairfax Downey

Library of Congress Catalog Card Number: 65-20232

Printed in the United States of America

T 54075

PRENTICE-HALL INTERNATIONAL, INC., *London*
PRENTICE-HALL OF AUSTRALIA, PTY., LTD., *Sydney*
PRENTICE-HALL OF CANADA, LTD., *Toronto*
PRENTICE-HALL OF INDIA (PRIVATE) LTD., *New Delhi*
PRENTICE-HALL OF JAPAN, INC., *Tokyo*

To my friend
GEORGE M. EMMERTON
student of military history, particularly forts;
former sergeant, U. S. Marine Corps,
and present New Hampshire
State trooper.

Preface

For invaluable aid in research and for other assistance on this book, the author gratefully acknowledges his indebtedness to the following.

J. D. Herbert, chief, National Historic Sites Division, Department of Northern Affairs and National Resources, Ottawa; John Lunn, park superintendent, Louisbourg.

L. S. Loomer, managing editor, *The Atlantic Advocate,* Fredericton, New Brunswick; Miss Phyllis R. Blakely, assistant archivist, Nova Scotia Public Archives, Halifax.

Senator Norris Cotton of New Hampshire.

Joseph W. P. Frost, descendant of Sir William Pepperrell, who lives in the Pepperrell Mansion, Kittery Point, Maine.

Leonard W. Larabee, editor, *The Papers of Benjamin Franklin,* Yale University.

Eugene Leliepvre, official artist of the French Army, for uniform details.

George M. Emmerton for a report with color slides on the Louisbourg site.

Miss Jill Adams and Nouailles Degoue for translation of the Du Chambon report.

John Gudmundsen, editor, trade division, Prentice-Hall, for encouraging supervision and collection of illustrations; the late Stewart Holbrook for my nomination to cover Louisbourg in the fort series; my literary agent, Oliver G. Swan of Paul R. Reynolds & Son; my wife, Mildred Adams Downey, for loyal help on this as on all my other books.

Baker Library, Dartmouth College, for its rich resources, including the efficient interlibrary loan service; Sterling Library, Yale University; New Hampshire State Library, Concord.

FAIRFAX DOWNEY
West Springfield
New Hampshire

Contents

LOUISBOURG: KEY TO A CONTINENT

one

Mighty Stronghold

The strongest fortress in America, a walled city without a peer in the New World—so Louisbourg was acclaimed. Its bastions and battlements, surmounted by the lofty spire of its château, seemed to mariners, entering its spacious harbor on remote Cape Breton Island in the North Atlantic, to have been miraculously transplanted from France. Guardian of the approaches to the St. Lawrence River, gateway to the heart of French Canada, Louisbourg also stood sentinel over the immensely valuable cod fisheries of the Banks. Men hailed it as another Gibraltar and as a worthy successor to Dunkirk, the formidable fastness commanding the straits of Dover which France had yielded as part of the treaty price of fortifying Louisbourg.[1] As Dunkirk had been "a pistol held at England's head," so the guns of Louisbourg menaced the lifeline of the New England colonies.

In token of the destiny the fortress was built to fulfill, a medal was proudly struck. *Ludovicoburgum Fundatum et Munitum, M.DCC.XX*—Louisbourg Founded and Fortified, 1720—read its inscription with its obverse bearing the handsome profile of young King Louis XV. Its glitter was reflected and magnified a thousandfold by the golden stream pouring from the coffers of France to realize the event the medal commemorated. The flow of treasure swelled to reach the amount of thirty million livres, equivalent to ten million dollars in modern money. Although that sum was not excessive for so monumental a work, it was still a huge one for the period, and it gave pause even to lavish King Louis when he faced the outlay. It is related that he wryly remarked that he expected to wake some morning and, from a window of the Palace of Versailles, behold Louisbourg's towers rising above the Atlantic horizon.

Like the peasant who never set eyes on Carcassonne, the monarch was compelled to confess that, except in fantasy, *"Je n'ai jamais vu Louisbourg."* While he complained that its streets must have been paved with gold, was not what remained of French Canada worth the cost of salvation? The fortress not only mounted guard over France's share of the rich fisheries and the fur trade of the western marches; it also preserved the surviving prestige and perquisites of a nation once the greatest colonial power in the world. While numbers of her forts and factories in India had been wrested from her by Great Britain, she still held sway over prosperous islands in the West Indies. In North America, the grasp of France had only begun to loosen. It still clung to wide territories south of the English Hudson's Bay Company's Arctic regions to what is now the State of Maine, from the St. Lawrence to the mouth of the Mississippi, and vast interior regions of the continent west of the Alleghenies. On all those possessions a door was closing, swung by England and

French medal struck at foundation of the fortifications of Louisbourg. Design by the engineer and architect Du Vivier.

her colonies. Yet they could not lock it so long as the key, Louisbourg, remained in enemy hands. While that great fortress and Quebec, the inner citadel, stood fast, the glory of France, dimmed but still resplendent, shone across the ocean.

Louisbourg stood, to have and to hold, by virtue of the Treaty of Utrecht of 1713, which followed British victory in the War of the Spanish Succession. "All Nova Scotia, or Acadia, the island of Newfoundland, with the adjacent islands, and the town and fortress of Placentia shall for this time forth belong of right to Great Britain. But the Island of Cape Breton shall hereafter belong of right to the King of France, who shall have right to fortify places there." Such were the treaty's harsh terms, ruinous except for their all but solitary concession. Besides over Cape Breton, France's Isle Royale, sovereignty was granted only over the westward island, Isle St. Jean, later to be renamed Prince Edward Island by the British. Lost was Acadia, although the tragedy of its French settlers, to be sung in Longfellow's *Evangeline*, was still impending. The first fort of that surrendered province, Port Royal on the Bay of Fundy, became England's Annapolis Royal. The Acadian fishing settlement of Canseau provided, as British Canso, a port of rendezvous where a fleet could assemble to invade Louisbourg, only fifty miles to the northeast. Farther south along the Nova Scotian coast lay the excellent harbor where the British city and citadel of Halifax would later spring up.

By France's defeat in a European war it might be said that all had been lost save honor and Cape Breton with the remnant of French Canada it guarded. It was therefore imperative that a mighty fortress arise, a fortress as invincible as man could make it, a stronghold that would dominate the sea-lanes to conquest, for it could not be bypassed. A hostile fleet, sailing north of Cape Breton and skirting the coast of Labrador, might have entered the Gulf of St. Lawrence through the Strait of Belle Isle, but that perilous and circuitous passage was not then used.

Every stone of the walls rising on their strategic site bid the foe defiance. And Great Britain and her flourishing colonies acknowledged the challenge with the declaration, "Capture Louisbourg and you capture Canada."

Louisbourg was built on the shifting sands of European enmities and alliances, washed across the Atlantic on the tides of conflict—the War of the Spanish Succession, the War of the Austrian Succession, and finally the Seven Years' War.

Slowly the sands funneled through the hourglass of history. In America, the grains of France had seethed with those of England ever since the nations made their early seventeenth century settlements. The forerunner of Louisbourg, Port Royal, the little stockaded fort in the Acadian wilderness erected by Sieur de Monts and his colonists in 1605, had been the first French outpost in the New World. From it Samuel de Champlain had launched his daring explorations that led in 1608 to the founding of Quebec, whose destiny was to be closely linked with that of Louisbourg. Neither Port Royal nor Quebec stood long unmolested by the other great colonial power of the North. The former was captured by a Virginia expedition in 1613 and by New Englanders in 1654. Recovered by the French, it was again taken and again returned, finally to become England's Annapolis Royal. Quebec, stormed by the English as early as 1629, was regained and held by France until it became a permanent British trophy in the aftermath of Louisbourg's second siege. Thrice the Province of Acadia changed hands, and its fate also was bound by close ties to that of Louisbourg.

In the turmoil of the bowl mingled the sands of the red man, doomed to ebb but first long to boil bloodily in the French and Indian Wars as adversaries and allies of the contending white men.

The Fortress of Louisbourg, like many a predecessor and successor, was "a house built upon the sands." No more than surface veneer was its grandeur, legacy of the victorious reign of Louis XIV, *le roi soleil,* for whom it was named. Not half the millions spent by his great-grandson Louis XV to render it impregnable ever reached the military chest. "There were too many thievish fingers by the way." [2] The odds in manpower were heavily stacked against it. At the signing of the Treaty of Utrecht in 1713 there were only 25,000 Frenchmen in Canada, with fifteen times that many British colonists in North America. That same ratio would continue as populations increased. Of paramount significance to the security of the island stronghold was the decline of the

French Navy under Louis XV and the rising power of that of Great Britain. "The wooden walls of England" were to prove mightier than the stone ones of Louisbourg.

Yet it was mainly the marvel of Louisbourg that men beheld when the ramparted city took form on Isle Royale. Here, they avowed, was France in America, a town gayer in the hearts of its people than Quebec or Montreal, as gay as it seemed unconquerable. "This is Louisbourg in its enchanted and legendary glory"; "a strong and fabled city the whole world had heard of but few had gazed upon"; "a strange and fearful place of high towers and massive walls." So admiring witnesses proclaimed it.

"Lord, it was like some magic scene as I pictured at Versailles or the Louvre where I had never been except in imagination!" a vistor exclaimed in awe at his first sight. Indeed it impressed all as "such stuff as dreams are made on." Beyond their wonder may have lain forebodings of its fate.

> . . . The baseless fabric of this vision,
> The cloud-capp'd towers, the gorgeous palaces,
> The solemn temples, the great globe itself,
> Yea, all which it inherit, shall dissolve,
> And, like this insubstantial pageant faded,
> Leave not a rack behind.[3]

For, if a second commemorative medal had been struck for the fortress, it might have been thus engraven:

LOUISBOURG

FOUNDED, SETTLED, FORTIFIED, BESEIGED, CAPTURED, RETURNED, RETAKEN, AND DESTROYED—ALL WITHIN THE SPAN OF FORTY-FIVE YEARS.

two

Gage of Battle

Long before the royal standard of France with its golden *fleur-de-lis* on a field of white was unfurled on the ramparts of Louisbourg, another flag figuratively flew at the site—a banner with a strange device. Indeed the mind's eye, if guilty of *lèse-majesté,* could merge the actual with the invisible, transforming the adornments of one into those of the other, turning royal lilies into peculiar heraldic emblems: codfish *d'or.*

For a gilded cod might have stood as a Louisbourg symbol as suitably as the one that came to decorate the Boston State House. As aptly as the Massachusetts promontory, Cape Breton could have been named Cape Cod. Teeming in their myriads, the codfish of all those waters were a magnet for mariners and settlements, a source of wealth, and a gage of battle.

Prows of fisher craft early breasted the northern seas. The Basques, "that primeval people older than history," claimed to have fished the codbanks of the North Atlantic before the caravels of Columbus carved their path far to the south. The daring voyage of John and Sebastian Cabot brought them close to Newfoundland, and they reported on their return to England in 1497 that the sea fairly swarmed with large codfish as well as salmon and sole and seal.

The Cabots [1] swore cod were so abundant that the vast schools sometimes halted the progress of their ships. So unbelievably bountiful did the harvest of the sea prove that there was often no need of hook, line, and bait. It was enough to dip baskets over the side and hoist them up brimful. Or simply trail grapnels, said sailors, and you could haul them in impaling layers of fish.

Fishermen began to throng to the banks soon after the dawn of the sixteenth century: French and Spanish Basques, Portuguese, Normans. By 1512 the hardy Bretons had established a fishing station on the island to one of whose capes, then to the whole, they gave their name. The French and the English outlasted the fishermen of Portugal, which thereupon, instead of a supplier, became an eager market for others' catches, along with sister Catholic countries of Europe, Spain, and Italy and the Moslem Levant.

Codfish Land. So Newfoundland and all the coasts were dubbed by Marc Lescarbot, a member of the French expedition which in 1605 founded the Port Royal Habitation in Acadia, the first European settlement on American shores giving promise of permanency, save only the Spanish towns in the far-distant South. The cod reigned as king of the sea. Masses of tiny plankton were its prey as were caplin and herring. To spawn in the many bays and deep inlets cod came close inshore, and frequently fishermen did not need to fare far but could use open boats. Not only by virtue of numbers was the cod supreme. Properly salted as "dry fish" or pickled in casks of brine as "wet fish," it kept excellently through long voyages to markets and through lengthy storage as a staple. "While many finny fellows have finer tissues and more exquisite flavours, few survive time, endure salt, and serve daily use as well as the Cod."[2] Train oil (codliver oil) found a ready sale in Europe. One of the more enterprising Louisbourg governors tried to promote a by-product of fish glue.

Ample evidence was given by the fisheries that the northern seas were a gold mine rivaling the riches the new Indies poured into the coffers of Spain. As a source of income and a base for government taxation, they far surpassed the risky fur trade. Cargoes of codfish were currency of exchange for brandy, wines, and rum; for molasses, sugar, lime juice, and tobacco; for silks, linen, canvas, hats, and paper; for beef, pork, sheep, apples and onions; for bread and flour; for pitch, tar, and lumber, for all the needs of the colonies and their commerce.

From the outset the cod bred warfare only less prolifically than he spawned his kind. It was he, *casus piscarius belli,* who divided the antagonists. As early as 1524 the English seized a laden French fishing craft. Indian raids were a constant threat. Fishermen, coming ashore for fresh water, to refit, to shoot sea birds for bait, and to dry catches on stages, were savagely attacked. A hasty departure was all that saved the crew of the English ship *Marigold* from massacre when in 1593 it landed on Cape Breton Island in the harbor of future Louisbourg. Bold warriors in canoes sometimes boarded and captured fisher boats and even armed vessels.

Clashes between white men soon developed. The various nationalities, preempting their own harbors and fishing grounds, did not long refrain from trespass. The season was short, from June to late August. There was urgency to fill holds and sail home before the cyclonic storms, the icebergs, and the fogs of the rest of the year barred the fishing fleets. If a better run of cod was to be found in another nation's territory, few hesitated at invasion. As unscrupulously as the Portuguese were pushed out, their successors sought to oust one another. In 1613 Frenchmen descended on a colony of Scots near Louisbourg's site, razed their little fort, and forced the prisoners to build a new and stronger one for the victors.

The English and the French repeatedly expelled each other from coveted stations by force of arms. A French governor bitterly complained of poaching by New Englanders on fishing grounds claimed by France. "It grieves me to the heart," he lamented, "to see *les Bostonnais* enrich themselves in our domain; for the base of the commerce is the fish they catch off our coasts and send to all parts of the world." [3] New England, in turn, scorning French claims, was as hotly resentful of competition.

Piracy was a regular practice along the coasts. Fishing fleets were not always safe even after passage back across the Atlantic. English craft, homeward bound from the banks, were taken at the very entrance to the Channel by Barbary pirates venturing out of the Mediterranean. The North African corsairs "were daring enough to cooperate with the French in attacks upon the ships along the northeast coast and also threatened to raid Newfoundland." [4]

From 1699 to 1713 the French fisheries on the coasts and banks of North America annually engaged from four hundred to eight hundred ships and from sixteen thousand to thirty thousand men.[5] The industry furnished not only cause and sinews for war but navies to wage it, for fisher crews were rightly regarded as "a nursery of seamen." Governor Shirley of Massachusetts would estimate the number of French fishermen on the banks in 1745 at 27,000 and declare that something ought to be done about the menace "as these cost the King nothing in time of peace, and are immediately available for his ships in time of war, and are no less skillful in handling a vessel on dangerous coasts than intrepid in combat."

It was such fishermen, manning much of the French Navy, that enabled it to cope with the combined English and Dutch fleets until the days of France's maritime decline under Louis XV. No less were fishing crews siphoned off for the warships of England and its American colonies. Many fishermen, British and French, would turn from hooking cod to handling sail and guns in sea fights that would sway the fate of Louisbourg.

In the early years there had seemed room enough for all on Cape Breton, that large island shaped like a fist, clenched except for a jutting, minatory forefinger pointing northeast. Bounded on the northwest by the Gulf of St. Lawrence, on the southwest by St. George's Bay and the Strait of Canso, on the northeast and southeast by the Atlantic Ocean, it stretches to a length of 110 miles. At the greatest breadth it is 87 miles wide. Hills rise in the north, tapering down to lower slopes in the south. Lakes and swamps cover one-third of its area; the remainder is timbered by softwoods and hardwoods. Harbors and inlets, rare on the west coast, are generous along the eastern littoral.

St. Anne's was the French fishery's base, Baie des Espagnols that of the Spaniards. The former was blessed with good soil and thick forests, but its bay froze in winter, and it lay an inconvenient distance from fishing grounds. Spanish Bay also froze, and its entrance was too wide to be covered by cannon. England's base, English Harbor or Havre à l'Anglais, was the prize despite its disadvantages of fog, rocky soil, and the fact that its adjacent woods were no better than scrub spruce. It was largely ice-free all winter and close to fine fishing. Counting heavily was a feature which must have been noted by some soldier early on the scene, a soldier with an eye for defenses and vision of the need for them. Ingress to the port with its ample anchorage was narrow, easily to be commanded by cannon. Furthermore, a small island stood sentinel at its mouth. Place a well-manned battery there, and its guns and those on mainland ramparts could blow any hostile fleet seeking to force an entrance out of the water.

Havre à l'Anglais. The change of its nationality and name would cost England lives and treasure when the Treaty of Utrecht granted it and all Cape Breton Island to France, and around the harbor rose the walls of the Fortress of Louisbourg.

By the 1740s the annual catch of French Louisbourg's fishing fleet was running as high as 150,000 quintals—a quintal amounting to about one hundred fish. It brought to the port some 154 trading vessels every year with barter goods.[6] As long as the inhabitants of Louisbourg could catch, salt, and store cod, no siege could starve them out.

Future North American armies would complain no more heartily of pork and beans than did Louisbourg's garrison of its monotonous, sometimes almost exclusive, fish ration. Not only Fridays but all the week might and often did become fast days both for the Catholic French soldiers and the Protestant Swiss mercenaries. Meat was scarce. While trout from the streams of the countryside offered some variety, the usual fare was cod *ad infinitum*. The Chevalier Johnstone, a Scot who had taken service with France and been assigned to Louisbourg, endured with difficulty its standard diet. All winter it consisted "solely of cod-fish and hog's lard, and during the summer, fresh fish, bad rancid butter, and bad oil."[7] Paid as an ensign though commissioned a captain, his annual stipend of 424 livres allowed the purchase of no extra food; indeed, he said, it was too little to cover his lodging in the most miserable garret in Louisbourg. Consequently he arranged a transfer back to France and obtained permission to board his ship, where a better table was set, twelve days before sailing "in order to repair the bad fare which I had suffered during a year."

Perforce "a very ancient and fish-like smell" pervaded the town. Governors' ladies sniffed delicately but vainly at their perfumed pomander balls; there was no suppressing the omnipresent odor of cod, gutted and drying, and the effluvia of steaming train-oil vats. Only the reek of powder smoke would overcome them.

three

Pawns to the Castle

The number of Indians inhabiting the coastal regions and forests of eastern Canada in the seventeenth and eighteenth centuries has been estimated at no more than eight thousand. Seldom did the various tribes act in concert, yet they constituted a constant threat as enemies of the invading white man or allies of his warring nations. Forts along the shores and rivers and in forest clearings—stockades, blockhouses, or the stronger buildings of settlements, heavily shuttered and barricaded—usually held the red man at bay because of his reluctance to attack fortified places. Sometimes the little strongholds, cordoned off, succumbed to starvation or were burned over the heads of defenders by the Indian's artillery, the fire arrow. Some fell by surprise of the unwary or such strategy as sending in squaws, who begged shelter on a winter night and, when householders were asleep, unbarred a door for lurking warriors.

But for the most part the isolated forts remained islands of safety in a red sea. Port Royal, later Annapolis Royal, was several times captured by white men but never by Indians even after its defenses were allowed to fall into such disrepair that "a wandering cow found its ramparts practicable for assault." While generally forts and towns were successfully attacked by Indians only under a white leader, or by white troops with Indians merely as auxiliaries, the power of the tribes was never to be discounted. Even the iron gates of Louisbourg would swing open for sachems come to demand tribute, the *véhicule à la foix* or bribe to buy their loyalty.

North of the St. Lawrence River and to the east, in the present Canadian provinces of Nova Scotia and New Brunswick and on some of the North Atlantic islands, lived the Micmacs, called Souriquois by the French. The Montagnais ranged from Quebec eastward. Maine was the Penobscots' country, while most of New England was the domain of the Abenakis. All those tribes intermingled to some extent, fighting for or sharing hunting grounds. The alliance they early entered into with the French was as firm as that of the Iroquois and Hurons to the south with the English.

Strongest of the tribes loyal to France and to be linked closest with the destiny of Louisbourg were the Micmacs and the Abenakis. Their original hostility as raiders of fishing stations was converted into friendship through enlightened treatment by pioneer French settlers and the extraordinary efforts of Jesuit missionaries, to be described later.

It was in the territory of the Micmacs that New France was founded when the Port Royal Habitation was built on the shores of the Bay of Fundy in 1605. A thriving fur trade was carried on, the Indians exchanging beaver and otter pelts and moose hides for knives, hatchets, kettles, scarves, and beads. The aged chieftain Membertou, who learned to speak fluent French, was an honored guest at winter banquets served in the little fort by Champlain's Order of Good Cheer. Tasty French cooking so appealed to the savages that they questioned priests, "If we ask God only for our daily bread, will we be without moose meat and fish?" Or, "In Heaven will there be pies like those the French bake?" The colorful Roman Catholic faith made far more Indian converts than did the stern and staid precepts of the Puritans. Membertou was christened Henri after the King of France and his favorite squaw Marie after the Queen, while one of their sons bore the name of the Pope.[1]

Numerous unions, some of them legalized by marriage, took place between Frenchmen and Indian women. Ignored were such warnings as Lescarbot's [2] that "the chastisement ought to be very rigorous against them that mingle the Christian blood with the infidels." Indian fathers, he declared, "do serve as panders to their daughters, and they repute it an honour to communicate them to the men of these parts that go thither, to the end to have of their race . . . The savages have no great regard for continence and virginity, for they do not think to do evil in corrupting it, whether by frequentation with the French or otherwise." Fishermen, settlers, and troops, following an age-old custom in foreign lands, in New France bought favors with trinkets or brandy. Rape was seldom resorted to, with the result that *laissez-faire* relations between the two races went undisturbed. In addition to the frequent casual liaisons occurred such markedly influential, formal alliances as the solemnized marriage of the Baron de Saint-Castin, colonel of the famous Carignan Regiment, to the daughter of an Abenaki chief. Their son became like his father a power in the tribe. Many other half-breeds established a status as Frenchmen.[3]

Too little heeded were admonitions to the Crown by the New England colonies, in emphasizing the importance of Cape Breton, that "the French by their unwearied industry, and many artful Methods, gain ground constantly, by making new alliances with the Indian Nations . . . that by intermarrying with the Natives, they have always a great number of Jesuits and Priests with them, and by instructing them that the Saviour of the World was a Frenchman, and murdered by the English,[4] they are excited to commit all manner of Cruelties upon the English as meritorious . . .

"That the Mast Trade is endangered; many persons having been surprised and murdered whilst cutting Masts for the support of the Crown. The whole trade of New England, out of home, is very much awed and dampened, especially by l'Acadie . . .

"That this Country . . . has the best Fishing in the World, on its Coasts, so that the French King may resign up all Newfoundland, and we may not obtain our End, whilst l'Acadie is left their's, which will support French of the Streights notwithstanding."[5]

What if the English sold European goods more cheaply to the Indians than did the French? "This," avowed the same memorandum, "together with furnishing them with Fire Arms, Powder and Ammunition, Tobacco, and Brandy is the only Method I know that the English employ to keep the Savages their Friends." And both means were completely unsuccessful in seducing the northern tribes from their attachment to the French.

Besides assiduously maintaining their friendship with those tribes, Frenchmen persisted in attempts to win away the enemy's Indian allies. "Do you know what is the difference between the King of France and the Englishmen?" Governor Duquesne harangued a council of Iroquois. "Go and look at the forts which the King has set up and you will see that the land beneath his walls is still a hunting ground, he having chosen the spots frequented by you simply to serve your need. The Englishman, on the other hand, is no sooner in possession of the land than the game is forced to quit, the woods are felled, the soil is uncovered, and you can scarcely find the wherewithal to shelter yourselves at night." There was enough truth in his words so that even the Iroquois gave heed, and some were persuaded to turn from outright hostility to neutrality.

French brandy and English rum. They bought the loyalty of warriors and the bodies of their women. Liquor, irresistibly craved by the savages once they tasted it,[6] was more highly prized than the large gold medallions, bearing the likeness of Louis XV, which one governor of Louisbourg hung around the necks of visiting sachems; than tribute money, ransom for captives, and scalp bounties; than quantities of goods from firearms down. Traders, high officials, military commanders, and troops of garrisons and expeditions plied the Indians with drink. Halfhearted government disapproval was ignored. It was in vain that missionaries inveighed against the debauchery of a race and the corruption of chastity "in accordance with the proverb, *In vino Venus.*" Father Le Clercq bewailed that, "Lewdness, adulteries, incests, and several other crimes which decency prevents me from naming, are the usual disorders which are committed through the trade of brandy, of which some traders make use in order to abuse the Indian Women, who yield themselves readily during their drunkenness to all kinds of indecency, although at other times, as we have said, they would be more likely to give a box on the ears than a kiss to whomsoever wished to engage them in evil, if they were in their right minds." [7]

Priests branded forts and trading posts as taverns as regards drunkenness and Sodoms as regards immorality because of the commerce of Frenchmen with the savage women. That the

Fortress of Louisbourg remained comparatively clear on the second count was due neither to its size nor to a state of discipline but to its location. The Micmacs had largely abandoned Cape Breton to the white men for the better hunting and refuge of the mainland forests. Attempts to persuade them to return, in any but small numbers, failed since they rightly suspected that they would be drafted for farming and other labor.

Consequently other garrisons were the envy of the men at Louisbourg. Women of tribes in other vicinities were employed by soldiers to pound corn, cook, cut wood, launder, and make clothing. "But," the missionaries complained, "all those necessities were purely Optional on the part of robust young men who are in good health and have nothing else to do"; in essence these tasks were a cover for universal lewdness, pretexts to lure the women into barracks and cabins. A Jesuit denunciation, written to be conveyed to the King of France, declared: "All the soldiers keep open house in their dwellings for all the women of their acquaintance. From morning to night, they pass entire Days there, one after another—sitting by their fire, and often on their beds engaged in conversations and actions proper to their commerce. This generally ends only at night, because the crowd is too great during the day to allow of their concluding it then, although they frequently arrange among themselves to leave a house empty, so as not to defer the conclusion until night." [8] Marches in changes of station were accompanied by throngs of native camp followers. "They are," avowed a missionary, "all the prostitutes of Montreal, who are alternately brought here and taken back." With the traffic spread its concomitant, venereal disease, which each nation named after another—"French sickness," "Spanish pox," and so on.[9]

Shipments of brandy, wines, and rum from Europe for troops and Indian allies preempted considerable cargo space. Louisbourg in particular would suffer when sorely needed military supplies were crowded out of holds by casks of liquor. A sinew for the French and Indian Wars—as for others—strong drink fueled many of the Indian raids on New England settlements. Scalped bodies in the smoldering ruins and hundreds of captives, men, women, and children herded by warriors to Canada for ransom, fanned flames of burning enmity, as much to the French, who instigated and led not a few of the inroads, as to the savages. It was not strange that New England hatred should finally focus on Louisbourg, because of the part played by its governors and commandants in inspiring some of the depredations. The fortress became a symbol of the ruthlessness of the power of France, with which the British Crown and its colonies were engaged in a death struggle.

In that struggle the red men were pawns, doomed to be swept from the board. Among the players that moved them for better or worse or themselves served as pieces in the game whose prize was Canada, were the French missionaries, notably the black-robed Jesuits.

The Jesuits dared the perils of the New World with the soldiers and settlers of France, as valiantly as with the conquistadores of Spain. Ignatius Loyola, who had founded the brotherhood of monks in 1533 to combat the Reformation and propagate the faith among the heathen, inspired its name by calling it "a little battalion of Jesus." The military term was well chosen, for members of the Society of Jesus were indeed front-line troops of His Most Christian Majesty the King of France, unarmed but displaying discipline, courage, and self-sacrifice rarely matched in professional armies. As means to further its missions, the Order acquired such great political power that it came into conflict with both government and Church and was expelled from one country after another, finally to be suppressed by a pope, though it was later revived.

Yet in the strife for Canada the Jesuits remained key pieces. A lesser yet effective part was played by the brown-robed Franciscans and the gray-clad Recollet friars. In Louisbourg's and other hospitals the Brothers of Charity of St. John and the Sisters of Notre Dame de la Congrégation gave devoted service, the nuns being both nurses and schoolteachers. Most intensely burned the zeal of the Black Robes. By virtue of the closer ties between State and Church in France than those between the English Crown and the Puritans, French missionaries were far more successful than their English counterparts in making converts and allies of the northern Indians. They strove mightily though vainly to wean even the hostile Iroquois and Hurons from British allegiance. Without the missionaries France would have lost its hold on Canada years earlier than it did.

Tonsured, cowled, and sandaled, their coarse robes bound at the waist by a cord from which hung a crucifix, the Jesuits ventured fearlessly among the tribes. "*In hoc signo vinces*," they echoed Constantine's words, and conquer they did by their selfless ministrations, their unquenchable fervor, and their willingness to endure anything for the faith. Their *Relations*, those reports to superiors at home, were published and became "best sellers" throughout France, as they well deserved to be for the stirring tales of adventure they were.

Such was the account of the heroic martyrdom of Father Isaac Jogues, who, after recovering from frightful tortures inflicted by the Iroquois, returned to face them again until his agonies were ended by a tomahawk sunk in his brain.[10] Martyrdom was embraced for the glory of God whether it granted a quick and merciful death or one that came lingeringly and excruciatingly to a victim whose hair and fingernails had been pulled out, his neck hung about with red-hot hatchets and his body bound by belts of burning pitch, nose, lips, and tongue severed, and eyes burned from their sockets. "Good soldiers," wrote Father Paul Le Jeune, "are not weakened but inspired by their wounds and the sight of their own blood."

The toil of the missionaries to redeem the souls of the savages and protect them from evils brought by the white man was noble in purpose. "On the whole," Parkman estimates, "the labors of the missionaries tended greatly to the benefit of the Indians. Reclaimed, as the Jesuits tried to reclaim them, from the wandering life, settled in peaceful industry, and reduced to a passive and childlike obedience, they would have gained more than enough to compensate them for the loss of their ferocious and miserable independence. At least, they would have escaped annihilation." [11]

It was, however, the militant priests, zealots seldom hesitating at any means that seemed justified by their ends, who chiefly figure in the course of events with which this narrative deals. Such were Father Sebastian Râle or Rasles and Abbé Jean Louis Le Loutre.

Râle was denounced by the English as "no man of God but the

devil's disciple," guilty of fiercely inciting the Abenakis to attack New England settlements. The English hunted him down and shot and scalped him without compunction. None was more fanatical than Le Loutre, missionary to the Micmacs, in using the savages as a scourge to lash heretics from the land. From 1744 onward he preached a crusade to both Indian converts and Acadians, demanding that as their holy duty they drive out or destroy the English. While accused of buying scalps, it is of record that he once saved 37 English captives, who were taken as prisoners to Halifax when the Abbé refused to pay for their hair. If ransom was given, it may have amounted to more than a scalp bounty, though the latter sometimes ran as high as three hundred dollars for a man's scalp, sharply decreasing for a woman's or a child's scalp.

French officers and priests encouraged or led Indian attacks on English trading and fishing vessels. "The success of the Indians against the fishermen of New England was probably the chief reason for the contempt for the military skill of the British colonists, expressed up to 1745, by the Louisbourg people." [12] With the determination of New Englanders to force that contempt down the throats of the French and to end its cause went furious resolve to avenge killings and burnings at so many of their settlements—to halt forever the heart-rending loss by so many families of captives taken north by the Indians, some to return ransomed, some to escape, but more never to be seen by relatives again after they were sold in Canada as indentured servants and married there and became French. Wrote the Abbé Marault, "If one should trace out all the English families brought into Canada by the Abenakis, one would be astonished by the number of persons who are today indebted for the blessing of being Catholic and the advantage of being Canadians." [13] It was a viewpoint which Protestant New England could scarcely be expected to share.

For New England troops and especially their chaplains who sailed to the first siege of Louisbourg, the campaign became in part a religious war. What made it so was less the Protestant distaste for popery than the results of the labors of the Black Robes, the Jesuits of New France.

So on the North American chessboard the red pawns and the black bishops were moved, and with them white pawns, the Acadians.

They were such stuff as empire is made of, those sturdy peasants who had early emigrated from La Rochelle and Brittany to New France. The King and his ministers held them of far less account than the explorers and soldiers who paved the path of conquest and the rich revenues of the fisheries and fur trade that sustained it. The Acadians were farmers, wanting no part in warfare, asking only to be let alone to till the soil in which they sank their own roots so deeply that long and determined efforts would be required to wrench them out. Crops and cattle of their thriving farms were, as elsewhere and always, foundations on which nations are built.

There was peace with the Indians. From first to last it was the British who were the acknowledged enemy of the Acadians, whose loyalty to France was alternately fervent and passive.

Treaties traded the Acadians and their lands back and forth between France and England until that of Utrecht in 1713, signal for the erection of the Fortress of Louisbourg, finally made all Acadia British territory under the new name of Nova Scotia. Migrate to French soil or become British subjects was the choice offered the Acadians, still fewer than two thousand but flourishing and increasing. While most chose surface acceptance of the latter alternative, taking a qualified oath of allegiance that exempted them from bearing arms, they remained as French as ever. On whether a number would migrate hinged a matter of high import to Louisbourg.

The fortress about to rise on Isle Royale (Cape Breton Island) and guard the gateway to the remnants of French Canada would need more than walls, guns, and garrison. A flow of provisions from France and the West Indies could be relied upon as long as the Navy kept the sea-lanes open. If they were cut by an enemy, Louisbourg would have to sustain itself. To a considerable extent the fisheries would accomplish that, and foresightedly several hundred settlers, mostly fishermen, were brought from ceded Nova Scotia in 1713. The first Governor, Philippe Pastour de Costebelle, also made strenuous endeavors to induce as many

Nova Scotia Public Archives

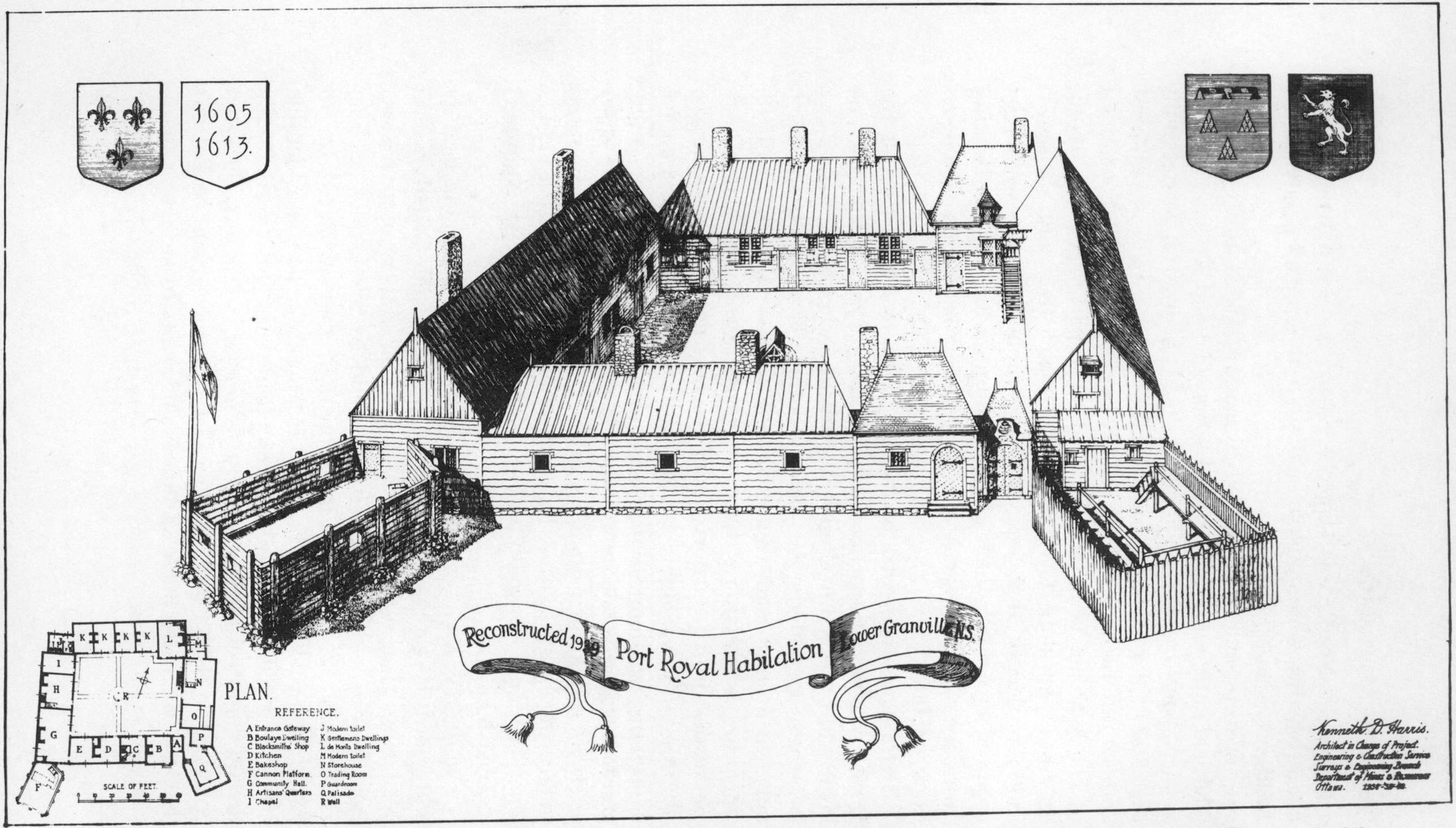

1605
1613.

Reconstructed 1939 Port Royal Habitation Lower Granville N.S.

PLAN.

REFERENCE.

A Entrance Gateway
B Boulaye Dwelling
C Blacksmiths' Shop
D Kitchen
E Bakeshop
F Cannon Platform
G Community Hall
H Artisans' Quarters
I Chapel
J Modern toilet
K Gentlemens Dwellings
L de Monts Dwelling
M Modern toilet
N Storehouse
O Trading Room
P Guardroom
Q Palisade
R Well

SCALE OF FEET.

Kenneth D. Harris.
Architect in Charge of Project.
Engineering & Construction Service
Surveys & Engineering Branch
Department of Mines & Resources
Ottawa.

Reconstruction of the Champlain Habitation, Acadia, which became the French fort of Port Royal. It was eventually captured by the British and renamed Annapolis Royal, Nova Scotia.

more Acadians as possible to move from the mainland and settle around the fortress site. (For a list of governors see Appendix A.)

Such hardworking farmers could be expected to cultivate shore and inland fields of Isle Royale as successfully as they had those of their homes around the Bay of Fundy and fill the granaries of Louisbourg. In the event of a siege, some of them, bringing what produce and cattle they could, would have to take refuge behind the ramparts as had the peasantry dwelling around medieval castles. But who would dare besiege Louisbourg, given the great strength planned for it? De Costebelle offered ample shipping and made lavish promises to all Acadians who would move to Cape Breton. Instead of the mass migration he hoped for, he persuaded only a few and they were men of little substance and shiftless. In his failure lay potentials for disaster.

De Costebelle left promises unkept to the Acadians he recruited, which strengthened their brethren's resolution to stay home. There the British authorities, aware of the French purpose in attempting to attract the Acadians to Louisbourg, for some time maintained a tolerant, hands-off policy. The Acadians, despite their stubborn nationalism, might eventually have been absorbed.

As already noted, Abbé Le Loutre, called "the evil genius of Acadia,"[14] stood in the way. His machinations inexorably trapped a simple people, always priest-ruled. He menaced them with the Indians he controlled and warned them of the vengeance of the King of France on traitors. In fiery sermons he preached that they must defend their farms and fisheries or lose them to covetous New Englanders, nor did he hesitate to threaten the disobedient with divine retribution and even with excommunication.

In 1744 Le Loutre commanded an assault by three hundred Micmacs on the British fort at Annapolis Royal and forced the Acadians to stand aside, thus compromising their neutrality. During the first siege of Louisbourg, Le Loutre took his red men on the warpath to march to its relief. After the captured Fortress's restoration to France, the Abbé returned to fan the flames again. Attacks on British forts were delivered by French troops, French-armed Indians, and Acadians, by then more firmly converted into fifth columnists. Though the attacks were repulsed, the doom of the Acadians was sealed.

There followed in 1755 the expulsion and exile of the Acadians from their homes, poignantly related in Longfellow's *Evangeline*. Six thousand men, women, and children were deported in groups, widely scattered, forced to abandon their lands and most of their household goods, clinging to little more than their memories. "Louisbourg is not forgotten, nor Beau Séjour, nor Port Royal" was their lament as the poet would put it.

Georgia, Louisiana, Massachusetts, France, and other Canadian provinces received the exiles. While some returned to Nova Scotia and were accepted as citizens, most of the white pawns, like the red ones, had been swept forever from the board when the kings, queens, bishops, and knights moved, and checkmate was called with the capture of the castle that was Louisbourg.

four

Building of a Fortress

Shades of the builders of the battlements of Constantinople and many other walled cities and strongholds, on to the frustrate ghost of Sébastien Le Prestre Vauban, the once celebrated French military engineer, haunted Louisbourg from the moment earth was turned for its foundations.

Had not the knell of castles been sounded in 1453 when Sultan Mohammed II of the Ottoman Turks assailed the citadel of the last of the Byzantine Caesars and his monster cannon opened breaches for the stormers? Ever since, forts had succumbed to artillery. Some fell after only brief resistance. For others the glint of sunlight on bronze barrels emplaced to command them was enough to send white flags soaring up staffs. There were some that withstood long sieges before they surrendered, and others that held out successfully by counterbattery of the besiegers' guns.

Yet ultimate doom was written across the ramparts of one and all, though men persisted in building them for lack of better defenses on through the eighteenth century and well into the twentieth until the inglorious debacle of the Maginot Line and the breaching of the Siegfried Line.

Vauban was the great apostle of fortification's heyday. The beautifully designed forts he erected for Louis XIV made him a Marshal of France, but by the time of the War of the Spanish Succession they were being taken and retaken, their impregnability only a legend. Vauban died disillusioned in 1707. "Place besieged means place taken," he had at last acknowledged.

Nevertheless, no heed was paid to his maxim by the French military engineers Verville and Verrier, who planned and built Louisbourg when such a mighty North American fortress was recognized as an imperative to the defense of the remnant of French Canada.

Its gray stone walls were to be strong enough to defy artillery, whether the guns of warships or land cannon, if any could be brought ashore through the tossing waves that broke over rock-strewn beaches and then, incredibly, dragged through surrounding marshes. Let the dead past bury the fallen forts of the Old World. This splendid one of the New surely would not share their fate. Strength lay in its very remoteness, as with other colonial fastnesses distant from bases of attack. The sea was Louisbourg's moat, as the wilderness was the natural abatis of sister strongholds. Along with necessary supplies, artillery potent enough to reduce them—preferably pieces as heavy as 13-inch mortars and 38-pounders—would have to be transported by waterways or over roads hewn through forests. "It was almost axiomatic that once this was accomplished the fort would have to surrender. An analysis of all the various French and British expeditions against frontier forts during the colonial period shows that this rule held, without exception, and in the cases where artillery did not arrive or was not employed the fort was successfully defended." [1] But Louisbourg, standing secure for the reasons named, might confidently challenge such guns as could be brought against it.

The work of fortifying it was slow in starting. Meanwhile 180 settlers, mostly fishermen, had been transferred from Newfoundland, which had been ceded to Britain by the terms of the Treaty of Utrecht. At Havre à l'Anglais, renamed Louisbourg when Cape Breton Island become Isle Royale, they were joined by the few hundred uprooted Acadian farmers.

For those *habitants* the first winter was a cruelly bitter one. They shivered in log huts roofed with brush, were plagued by scurvy, and nearly starved as their supplies dwindled. Before the snows vanished, all their horses had died, and they had been compelled to kill all but two of their horned cattle for food. Only 22 of the Acadians could be persuaded to stay and face a second winter. There would be a dearth of cultivated fields and herds and flocks to sustain Louisbourg in peace and war.

Engineers arrived to survey the site and draw plans after Vauban's "First System" for the Fortress, whose walls would encircle 57 acres. For lack of labor, tools, and materials it remained a stronghold on paper until the summer of 1720 when actual work began, and it was soon learned that construction must be performed by soldiers, as no other working force could be obtained. Troops did the building, as in the case of almost all North American forts, and no garrison ever stood more fatigue details than did that at Louisbourg.

Heavy-laden vessels brought Caen and other stone and bricks from France; much hold space was later saved when brick clay was found on the island and some stone quarried and coal mined there. Despite large use of beach stones, considerable building material along with supplies had to be imported. Lumber and flour came from New England—fourteen shiploads from Boston in one year. Produce came from Acadia. Coffee, sugar, and rum from the West Indies. Cargo after cargo of French wines and brandy. Only in codfish were Louisbourg resources more than sufficient, and that staple's export helped lower the heavy balance of trade against her, though it never approached par.

Solid masonry, 10 to 12 inches thick and 30 feet high, was specified for the walls of the main fortifications, including the seven redoubts. What if the stone blocks were joined by cement made from poor lime and salt water, unfit to long withstand the heavy frosts? What if some of the best stone was diverted to the construction of the Château St. Louis with its quarters for the Governor? At least the walls gave the appearance of solidity. And they were far more imposing than the earthworks which supplemented them at points, earthworks which, withstanding time and climate and the cannonballs they absorbed, outlasted the masonry.

That the walls were dwarfed in height by those of the castles of yore proved that military architects had learned a lesson from the might of cannon and gunpowder. They had been "forced to exchange the trowel for the spade, digging in for protection instead of building upward to create targets." [2] Louisbourg's land-side defenses took classic form: On the ground level a parapet to protect troops and ordnance declined in a stone-embedded face and escarp to a ditch; on the further side of the ditch rose the stoned counterscarp, topped by a covered way, to be manned as was the parapet. Above that platform an earthwork called the glacis sloped gently downward to the ground over which an assault could be delivered, cleared ground to be swept by plunging fire from the rampart. Seaward walls and those of the several batteries were not unbroken expanses but jutted out here and there in angles, forming bastions and curtains. It was the salient angles that gave Vauban's forts their star shape. Guns in their embrasures could rake with deadly flanking fire attack waves that reached the ditches and attempted escalades.

The thrill the builder knows must have lifted the hearts of both Verville and his successor Verrier, as they watched ramparts and buildings take form from the drawings on their boards, plans true to the tradition of their great preceptor.

Outer guardians of the harbor, the Grand or Royal Battery rose on the northeastern shore and across from it the water-circled Island Battery. Warships, striving to force an entrance, would have to run the gantlet of their fire. Any that succeeded would then have to engage French ships of the line and frigates with ample room for maneuver in the spacious harbor. Such defenders would be covered by guns of the shore redoubts, the Dauphin and Maurepas Bastions, with those of the Princess Bastion to the south around Rochefort Point. Land approaches were protected by the King's and Queen's Bastions. Those fortifications were pierced by embrasures for 148 cannon, though not more than 90 were ever actually mounted.[3] Temporary emplacements for a few more guns were dug along the shores of Gabarus Bay, southwest of Louisbourg, a likely place for an enemy landing. Those were to be armed in time of danger. Meanwhile, like other embrasures, they gaped empty for lack of ordnance.

Across from the Island Battery at the harbor entrance a lighthouse was erected on the northeast peninsula. Beacon Light replaced the wood fires lit to guide mariners. Its illumination, first from a coal oven, then fueled by oil, was visible for six leagues and drastically reduced the toll of disastrous wrecks on Cape Breton such as that of a French warship in 1725 in which all aboard were lost.[4]

In the manner of castles Louisbourg was given its inner keep, its donjon. This was the Château St. Louis or Citadel, a massive stone building at the rear of the King's Bastion serving as a residence for the Governor and a barracks for the garrison. "The lines of defense which ran parallel to the harbor and to the sea were of lighter construction—a wall of masonry with banquette; but the short north-eastern face of the fortress was of the more massive and elaborate type. The north-east corner of the town had no wall or defensive works for a space of about two hundred yards; but it was protected from attack by a large pond, which extended along its front. A somewhat similar gap existed on the sea face, between the Princess' and Brouillan bastions, a palisade and ditch being the sole defenses; but in front, shoals, rocky islands, and a continuous heavy surf formed an effectual barrier against hostile attack from this quarter." [5]

Strong walls, frowning guns, casemates, and covered ways as shelter from bombardment: surely here stood a mighty fortress secure against attack, a stronghold that was the wonder of the New World. What if Dunkirk, "that pistol held at England's head," had been yielded and even Gibraltar had once succumbed to siege? Could Louisbourg's impregnability be doubted?

But the confidence and pride of achievement of the military engineers who designed the fortifications could not go untroubled by qualms. Verville, examining the shores adjacent to the town, shores reported to be inaccessible, found that at five points he could land from a boat without wetting his shoes, yet official insistence demanded concentration on the Fortress walls. Weakest link of the fort chain was the Grand Battery. Its walls were low. The terrain on which it was built hampered its seaward field of fire. Guns positioned on the high ground behind could command it. Cut off from the main works, it could not easily be reinforced. Once in enemy hands, the Battery could bombard the town and the defenders would be caught between two fires. The peninsula where the lighthouse stood remained undefended. Long-range cannonading from there could reach the Island Battery and Louisbourg itself. On the land side low hills, scarcely half a mile away, offered vantage ground for guns which could bombard the town.

Flaws and faults, duly noted, were intended to be eliminated, granted the necessary money, men, and materials. But the urgent representations of various governors, increasing as war clouds gathered, fell on deaf ears. King Louis began to shut off the golden stream of livres, which had come to appall even him. More revenue was imperative for the defense of the realm of France itself and its Old World colonies, though they too were dwindling. Let Louisbourg depend upon the strength he already had given it, upon the still formidable French Navy, upon its own natural resources. Even if a hostile fleet were to rule the seas, the fogs and the reefs and the guns of the shore batteries would bar it from the harbor. Should an expedition manage a landing through the surging surf, surrounding swamps could be counted on to bog down its artillery.

Louisbourg itself, no less than its forbidding fortifications, aroused the awe of traders and other visitors. Here stood a city of France sprung up on the Canadian frontier. Nowhere in all the British colonies were any buildings more imposing than Louisbourg's château, its hospital, and other principal mansions of stone.

Foreigners, mouths agape in wonder, trod the narrow cobbled or graveled streets. They stared up at the ramparts, high perched on a curtain wall between the Dauphin Bastion and the King's Bastion. Where it opened on the town side stood the stately Château St. Louis of four stories, its roof slated, its only entrance a drawbridge which brought the Middle Ages back to life. A New Englander thus described it: "The entrance is by a large gate over which is a drawbridge over a small ditch . . . in passing which on the left hand the door opens into a King's Chapell, on the right hand into a dungeon, one of which has a greater resemblance of Hell than the other of Heaven."

The Château contained the Governor's state apartments and living quarters along with another chapel, which served as a parish church, while half of the building was occupied by barracks. Abutting it was the Place d'Armes, devoted to drills, parades, and other ceremonies. Streets whose names were redolent

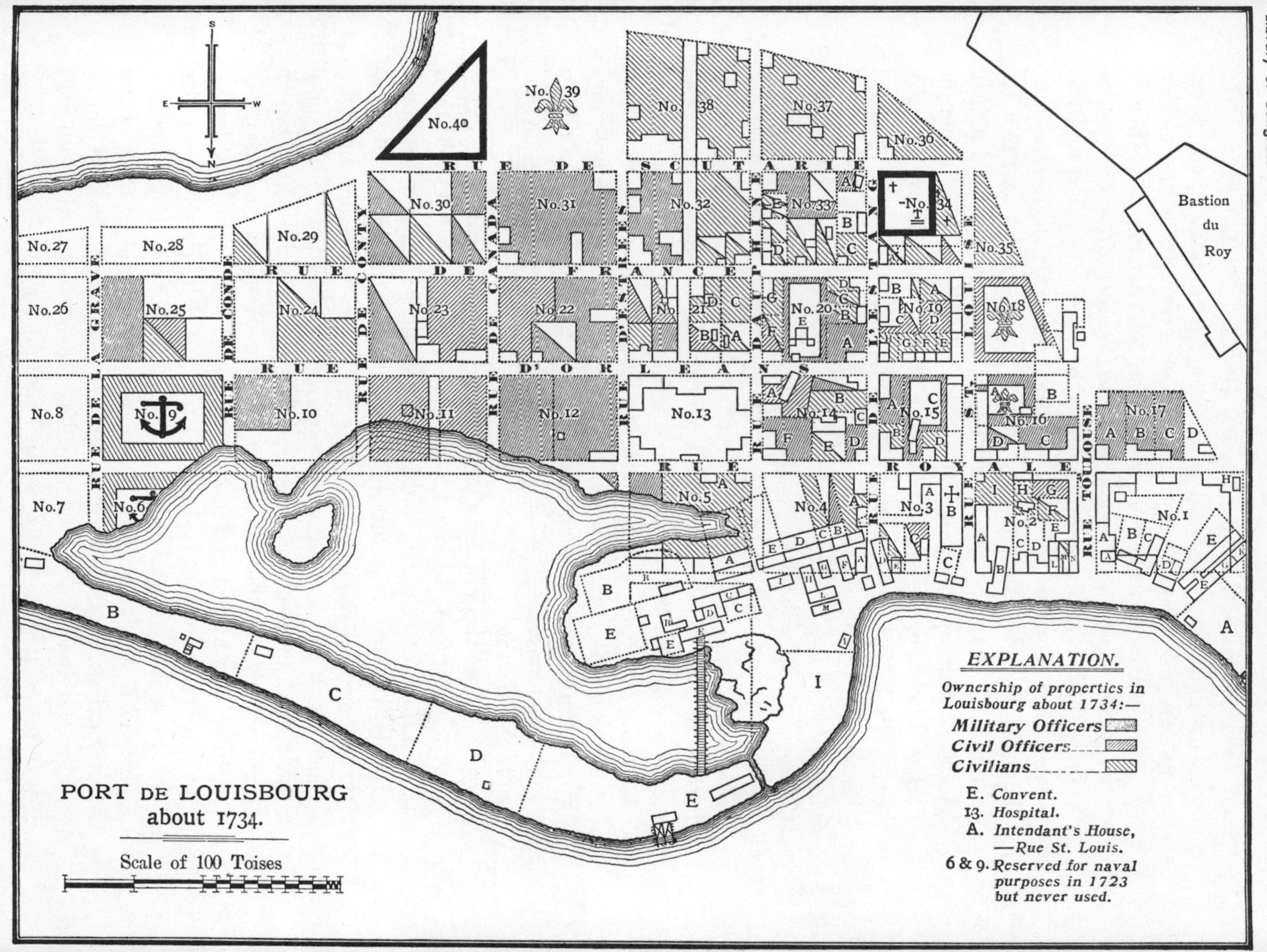
PORT DE LOUISBOURG
about 1734.
Scale of 100 Toises
EXPLANATION.
Ownership of properties in Louisbourg about 1734:—
Military Officers
Civil Officers
Civilians
E. Convent.
13. Hospital.
A. Intendant's House, —Rue St. Louis.
6 & 9. Reserved for naval purposes in 1723 but never used.
Bastion du Roy
RUE DE SCUTARIE
RUE DE FRANCE
RUE D'ORLEANS
RUE ROYALE
RUE DE LA GRAVE
RUE DE CONDE
RUE DE CONTY
RUE DE CANADA
RUE D'ESTREES
RUE DAUPHINE
RUE DE L'ESTANG
RUE ST. LOUIS
RUE TOULOUSE
No.40
No.39
No.38
No.37
No.36
No.35
No.34
No.33
No.32
No.31
No.30
No.29
No.28
No.27
No.26
No.25
No.24
No.23
No.22
No.21
No.20
No.19
No.18
No.17
No.16
No.15
No.14
No.13
No.12
No.11
No.10
No.9
No.8
No.7
No.6
No.5
No.4
No.3
No.2
No.1
S
E
W
N

of France—rues Toulouse, Royale, Orléans, St. Louis, and the rest—divided the town into neat squares. Flanking them stood stone or wooden buildings, some enclosing courtyards and garden pools: the *Magazin des Vivres,* the King's Provisions Storehouse; the Council Chamber; the house of the Commissaire-Ordonnateur (the Intendant), equivalent to a combined comptroller, quartermaster, and commissary general; the Logement des Ingenieurs, home of Verville, and stables, a small arms arsenal and one for artillery on a street to be rechristened Gun Lane by the English. Smaller buildings included the surgeon's house and numerous other residences, a jail, a bakery, markets, and shops. The inn was called La Grange. Le Billiard was the name of a gaming house and bistro, which was supplemented by grog shops and *bordelles* where soldiers dispelled the monotony of garrison life. Homes of officials, higher-ranking officers, and merchants enriched by the cod trade descended in scale to dwellings for fishermen. Many were of well-dressed stone throughout or of stone on the ground floor and timber above, their slate roofs sharply pitched. Windows were small and doors stout and close-fitted against the winter cold. No house was more than two stories high by fiat of Verrier, who believed that taller buildings would impede the free circulation of air in summer when all the ventilation possible was needed against the pervading stench of split cod drying.

Edifices to the greater glory of God embellished Louisbourg, nor could Protestant beholders from New England withhold their admiration though they muttered of popery. Besides the inner chapels, the religious installations included the monastery and chapel of the Recollets and the convent of the Sisters of Notre Dame de la Congrégation, nuns who helped staff the hospital and taught in a school for girls. That two-story hospital, which required a whole block, was run by the Brothers of Charity of St. John. The largest and most impressive building in Louisbourg, save for the Château St. Louis, it was a 112-bed institution, plus private rooms. It was complete with apothecary shop, a guardroom, the prior's chamber overlooking a terrace sloping down into gardens, its own chapel, refectory, kitchens, bakery, brewhouse, laundry, storerooms, morgue, and latrines. Other adjuncts were a sheep pen, hencoop, and slaughterhouse.

The sick of Louisbourg, soldiers, sailors, townsfolk, and indigents, "received care scarcely matched in the largest cities of North America."

As the eyes of visitors were filled by the spectacle of the dream city, so were their ears regaled with deep tones issuing from its belfries. Every day the bells of the church, hospital, and convent tolled, great bells cast in France and shipped to Louisbourg as the gift of King Louis. Duly blessed and christened, they bore the names of "St. Louis," "St. Antoine Marie," and "St. Jean." Their sound soared above the roar of the surf and the bustle of the streets. Lesser bells summoned to masses, to musters for proclamation of orders, to meals, to drill and work. Imperious yet nostalgic, on that remote island their chimes plucked answering chords from the heartstrings of the homesick. For some they struck a note of pride in their mission to maintain this splendid stronghold, France's last northern outpost in the New World. For they carried the same message brought to Lescarbot when more than a century earlier that pioneer *voyageur* had hearkened to the little bell above the gateway of Port Royal Habitation in the Acadian wilderness and written:

> *Faut-il abandonner les beautez de ce lieu,*
> *Et dire au Port Royal un éternel adieu?*
> *Serons-nous donc toujours accusez d'inconstance*
> *En l'establissement d'une Nouvelle-France?*
>
> Must we our lives from this most lovely spot dissever
> And bid Port Royal a farewell forever?
> Shall it be always charged to us perchance
> That naught but fickle fancy bred New France? [6]

No one in Louisbourg realized in 1735, when all the bells had been installed, that they were also ringing a knell, that of the Fortress. In a short course of years the beat of their clappers would be drowned by the boom of cannon, and they would become trophies of victors.

"St. Louis," booty of the first siege, was transported to a Portsmouth, New Hampshire, church, in whose tower it hung till it crashed to the ground in a fire. Cracked, it was recast by Paul Revere and served on until it again split from constant ringing and was again recast and inscribed:

Vox ego sum vitae.
Voco vos orate venite.

I am the voice of life.
I call you to come to prayer.[7]

"St. Antoine Marie" and "St. Jean" both were prizes of the second siege. The former rang for a Lutheran congregation in Nova Scotia; the latter first served as school bell, then in a church.

A vivid picture of Louisbourg at a later date is drawn by F. Van Wyck Mason in his novel, *The Young Titan*. As a ship approaches the harbor, Baron Trevendal, an emissary of the French Court, sights the undergunned Island Battery, the Fortress's outer guardian, then scrutinizes the fortification beyond. The ship's captain identifies it.

" 'That, Monsieur le Baron, is the Royal, sometimes called the Grand—battery. As you will observe, it dominates the harbor entrance, and at a range which would mean annihilation of an enemy attempting to fight his way in. Can you deny that here, in this Ultima Thule, lies one of Vauban's great masterpieces? Can you wonder that Louisbourg is called the "Dunkirk of North America"?' "

Later the Baron inspects the ramparts with an officer of Swiss mercenaries. "Without seeming to, he learned that the fortress stone walls were never less than ten feet thick and thirty feet high. The outer faces of various bastions and salients, said Cailly, were much thicker and protected by a fosse, or dry moat, thirty feet in width and fifteen in depth. Beyond the counterscarp a series of glacis extended like giant teeth gnawing into open country on its landward side. On the fortress's other three sides they neared the water's edge.

" 'Excellent,' murmured the visitor. 'Such glacis afford clear fields of fire for your guns. Musketry from the firesteps can annihilate besiegers attempting to attack across them. And how many guns does the fortress mount?'

" 'The walls,' the Swiss explained as they strode along with snow squeaking under their boots, 'have been pierced for one hundred and forty-eight guns. But'—Lieutenant Cailly broke off to blow a blunt red nose between his fingers—'so far not more than seventy-seven cannon have been emplaced. M. Forant's predecessors have importuned the Minister of Marine—who administers this colony, but not Canada—in vain.' "

Importunities were largely futile. Increasingly, pleas were denied or ignored. There were no more guns, no more men to be spared for Louisbourg. Louis XV was hard pressed to muster sufficient ordnance and soldiers for his Continental wars. Token of his shortage of troops were the companies of Swiss mercenaries hired to piece out the Louisbourg garrison. Though their pay was not a considerable item, it added to the millions of livres lavished on the fortress, and there was no end to further demands —more supplies, more warships, to keep the sea-lanes open and fend off British and New England encroachments on French fishing grounds.

All these demands M. de Maurepas, the Minister of Marine under whose department came Louisbourg along with all French colonies, exerted his best endeavors to fulfill, but the concern of Louis for the remote fastness that guarded the gateway to Canada diminished yearly. How much more might the Minister have accomplished had he later paid court to Madame de Pompadour, the King's all-powerful mistress, instead of lampooning her with scurrilous verses. The interest of the lady, who could sway the award of a marshal's baton, remained uncaptured for the Fortress overseas. It might have been politic, *comme il faut* or not, for Maurepas to change the name of one of the redoubts from his own and call it Bastion Pompadour. One who seeks causes for the final downfall of Louisbourg cannot disregard the classic French maxim: *Cherchez la femme.*

Yet Louisbourg, for all its deficiencies, had indeed developed from the first makeshift defenses, thrown up to repel pirates, into a formidable stronghold. With it grew its garrison and its population, increasing from 951 souls in 1726 to 1,463 in 1737, and to 4,000 in 1758. In its soldiers and civilians lay the potentialities —and weaknesses—its bastions and batteries possessed.

five

Within the Walls

A French garrison town, Louisbourg, but with a marked and unhappy difference: The majority of its garrison and other inhabitants were confined for long years by its walls. Some never ventured far beyond its gates. Uninviting, no place for a *fête champêtre,* was the surrounding countryside of broad, moss-covered marshes and bleak slopes dotted with stumps of spruce and fir, the timber cut farther and farther back in the unending need for firewood. There was a welcome change for those who trudged as far as the outlying farms. Still all who dwelt on Isle Royale were prisoners of the sea, their only escape by ship. Louisbourg was almost as isolated in peace as by blockade during its two famous sieges.

Home, far-off France, lay over the horizon, vainly longed for by those who would never again see

> *. . . Versailles,*
> *Paris et San Denis,*
> *Les tours de Notre-Dame,*
> *Et le clocher de mon pays.*

Only the fortunate would once more enjoy such beloved sights: retiring governors glad to be recalled and rid of the frustrations of office; other officials with enough influence at Court for preferment to better berths; well-to-do families with the means to end pangs of homesickness by returning or at least sending their children back for education; officers whose periods of foreign service had expired. For troops there was seldom rotation, relief, and a new assignment. Replacements were hard to obtain. And what good were brief furloughs for Louisbourg soldiers, who unlike comrades in France or elsewhere in Canada, had no place to go?

The seasons passed in processional, and life in the Fortress took its cue from them. Louisbourg's heyday was summer, gorgeous weeks when France might momentarily be forgotten. In the eloquent words of one familiar with the scene in our own century, "On fine days the moor is a sheet of glowing russet and gold, the rocks are so noble a background for the most pellucid of seas, the clouds which hang in the overarching blue are so monumental in shape, the line of the coast which dies down to the eastern horizon is so picturesque in outline, that they, seen through an air sparkling, limpid, exhilarating to the highest degree, make of Louisbourg a delight which must have applied to the people of the past, as it does to the visitor today." [1]

It was then that the fishermen put to sea, and the town took on new animation as they returned with their catches. Trading vessels from the West Indies and the New England colonies and cargo ships from France made port. Like the unwrapping of a Christmas package was the opening of their holds and the unloading of their contents at the docks. Here were not only sorely needed supplies but luxuries as well. Because the latter fetched high prices, there were more of them than was justified by Louisbourg's chronic shortage of essentials. Officials and officers, scanning manifests to see if cannon, muskets, and powder were listed, were no less interested in the number of casks of brandy and wine aboard.[2] The eagerness of building contractors for lumber and tools was more than matched by that of their wives for dress goods, cosmetics, and household furnishings.

Most welcome was the arrival of ships of the French Navy, saluting and saluted by the guns of the Island Battery, as they swept into the spacious harbor. The flaming gunports gave assurance that Louisbourg's safety was still regarded. These towering ships of the line and frigates were its outer defense, its link with home. While they lay moored, their armaments augmented the Fortress's defenses. They brought orders, all manner of news, and gossip of the Court. Their officers and crews came ashore and swaggered through the streets with rolling gait. There was gaiety in the Governor's salon and still more in the taverns and bistros, toasts and rollicking choruses. When the ships departed, sailors cast back pitying glances at the receding walls of Louisbourg, walls cooping up the soldiers with whom they had caroused. Voyages, however distant, would end long before the tours of duty of those poor devils were up.

With the ships departed the summer of Louisbourg's content. "There are weeks in autumn when a dull earth meets a leaden sea, in winter when the ground is white, the sea sombre. In spring the sea is white and glistening with drift ice, the land dreary in dead vegetation. In early summer sea and land are dank in fog, and at any time occur gales of wind which are always blasting and often destructive."[3] Mists and high-flung salt spray dulled the beacon of the lighthouse; the roar of breakers muffled the bells; and the ships came no more.

Life in Louisbourg can perhaps best be pictured through a recreation of a number of its people, actual or typical of those who dwelt in the fortress. Let, for example, Isaac Louis Forant, captain in the French Navy and Louisbourg's Governor for a period, cross the stage.[4]

THE GOVERNOR

Shivering, he bent over his desk in the Citadel, its chill, little dispelled by crackling logs in the fireplace, reviving the ache of an old wound in his back. As persistent as the penetrating damp was his regret that he had accepted this remote post. It was the key to the approaches to the St. Lawrence River, avenue to New France, this fortress he ruled, but he had far rather, as a *capitaine de vaisseau,* still be treading the quarterback of his man-o'-war, the *Jason.*

Peste, what a climate! Give him the West Indies station with the fleet or even a winter cruise off the coast of the Low Countries of which the Flemish tapestries, hung in his chamber, reminded him. At sea a sailor took icy blasts as they came. They seemed to penetrate the walls of this dank stone fortress to freeze a man's marrow. Colder than the Governor looked his secretary and his Negro slave Néron, brought from Martinique. The poor black kept moaning, *"Ay de mi, ay de mi."*

Upon this Fortress depended the fate of French Canada. That had been dinned into Forant's ears when he had allowed himself, *malheureusement,* to be dragooned into taking command of Louisbourg. Wherefore, then, were they failing to give him adequate means to defend it—the additional cannon and powder he constantly but vainly demanded—more and better troops than his eight free companies of marines and one hundred Swiss mercenaries, scarce enough for ordinary duty, let alone war service. And at times they stood on the verge of mutiny, *ces salauds.* Aboard ship Capitaine Forant would have had their like dangling from a yardarm. It might be well to set such an example here, though he could ill spare a single man. In order to drill his artillerymen in angles of fire, the Governor had to resort to placing wooden cannon in the all too many empty embrasures.[5]

Vessels of his proud Navy sailed hither less frequently. As an old sailor he knew how vital they were to the safety of the Fortress. Surely Monsieur de Maurepas, Minister of Marine, was as well aware, but too often his hands were tied by court intrigues. More frequently it was English frigates that were sighted impudently cruising off Cape Breton, along with craft of *les Bostonnais,* preempting French fishing waters—craft apt to turn into pirates or privateers, given any occasion or slightest pretext.

Lose Louisbourg and one lost Quebec, Montreal, and all that remained to France of Canada. So the Governor was repeatedly reminded by dispatches in the masses of documents that poured in with every ship from France. At least there was no dearth of paper in Louisbourg. Reams blanketed his desk as the winter snows filled the fosses of the Fortress.

The Governor's gusty sigh ended in a hacking cough that flecked with spots of blood the lace-edged handkerchief he held to his mouth. He turned again to the heap of dispatches before him. There was truth, *sans aucun doute,* in those warnings uttered in the King's name. Lose Louisbourg and ——. Then, *nom de Dieu,* let him be given the means to hold it!

A MERCHANT'S WIFE

Here my man has done well. Many a day our shop is thronged both by the *haut monde* and by lesser folk. Even the Indians—and would there were more of them despite their wild-beast odor—sometimes come to barter their furs for trinkets. By winter's end our shelves are bare of cloths of Carcassonne and linens, wines of Provence, sugar and tobacco from the West Indies, and goods of the *Bostonnais*. When the ships of summer come in with wherewithal to replenish them again, my husband outbargains the shrewdest traders.

Hélas, that he must make most of his profit from the stinking cod of our fisheries. Though we do not keep them in the shop but in storehouses, their reek so fills the town that one is almost stifled by it. Beside it, the smell of the rich and lofty piles of manure in the courtyards of farms at home was sweet aroma. Little wonder ladies of the town buy all the perfumes and scented powders we can stock. Yet I can endure the stench, for my husband has turned the fish into golden livres. I was wise in wedding him though I, of the *petite noblesse*, married beneath me.

Our commerce has earned us enough to send our daughter to school in France and none too soon. Young officers without a sou to their names were beginning to flirt with our pretty Renée. *Ma foi*, what a dowry they would have demanded! With what we can give her, she may well look higher.

How may a woman amuse herself in this wretched town? There are few establishments such as ours, which makes for our greater profit but robs life of one of its pleasures, the joy of shopping. Only two dressmakers are to be found, and they with far more work than they can manage. Of our few *coiffeuses* there is none with the skill even faintly to imitate the mode we hear Madame de Pompadour affects. Fortunately, we have a dancing master, newly arrived from France. If some of our ladies scarcely dare smile when they attend one of the rare balls or state dinners, it is because they have failed to learn, as did I from an Acadian girl, to chew spruce gum to keep the teeth white. To banish ennui our ladies sit for hours at cards, and some solace themselves too well with wine, like a neighbor of mine. At dinner last night she grew so gay that she declared she saw eight candles instead of the one that burned on the table.

Yet in this lonely place women of all degrees are greatly needed. Thus has written one of our Jesuit fathers: "For my part I shall always believe that in any settlement whatsoever, nothing will be accomplished without the presence of women. Without them life is sad, sickness comes, and we die uncared for. Therefore I despise those woman-haters who have wished them all sorts of evil, which I hope will overtake that lunatic in particular, who has been placed among the number of the Seven Sages, who said that woman is a necessary evil, since there is no blessing in the world to be compared to her. Therefore God gave her as a companion to man, to aid and comfort him. And the Wise Man says:—'Woe to him that is alone, for when he falleth, he hath none to lift him up. And if two lie together, they shall warm one another.' If there are some worthless women, we must remember that men are not faultless."

Bien sûr, well spoken, *mon père*.

THE INTENDANT

It was said of François Bigot, the Commissaire-Ordonnateur, right hand of the Governor of Louisbourg, that he thrust his big hairy nose into everything—particularly into anything that might prove profitable. Yet superiors did not question so astute, able, and powerful an official, nor did inferiors dare. Too many of the latter were involved in lining their own pockets.

Contractors continued to take their cuts, as they had from the beginning, on materials for the building of the fortress or its repair. Officers exacted high percentages on the sale of liquor in canteens for troops.[6] Well aware of it, the Intendant looked the other way. Was it not an all but universal practice in France? Surely then it was amply justified by the hardships of Louisbourg, with pay and salaries so miserably low. Could a man be expected to forgo *quelque chose pour boire?*

When supply ships landed their cargoes at the wharves of Louisbourg, somehow only a portion of the goods—woolens, costly draperies, fine wines, and liquors—reached the King's Store

House. The rest, unlisted, vanished into the holds of Yankee trading vessels whose skippers were extremely cooperative for all their Puritan cant. Part was sold in Boston and the rest shipped back to Louisbourg. There a deficiency in stores would be suddenly noted by M. Bigot. As Minister of Supply it was his duty to remedy it. Here, providentially, appeared needed items to be had at bargain prices, at least bargains for the Intendant and conniving officials who simply paid the skippers' carrying charges and then resold the King's goods to the King's Store House. So clever an arrangement deserved the handsome profit of 300 percent it earned.

M. Bigot might have greatly increased his gains had he included arms and munitions in his transactions. But he was sensible of his responsibility to France and his high reputation as an administrator. Measure for measure and all in good time. Foresight was natural in one who could well expect some day to be promoted to the Intendant's post in Quebec with its considerably richer gleanings.

A FRENCH LIEUTENANT

Here no glory is to be won unless the English attack. They threaten but do not dare come against our walls. Here glory, bright when my forebears fought in Flanders, tarnishes to a dim legend. Soldiers raise a chorus in the bistros, few knowing whereof they sing:

Malbrouck s'en va-t-en guerre,
Mironton, mironton, mirontaire.
Malbrouck s'en va-t-en guerre.
Ne sait quand reviendra.[7]

"Marlborough's off to war, and nobody knows when he'll be back," *hein?* Well, he did return and beat us, but still we French gained honor on those fields. Could we achieve it in defense of Louisbourg with the miserable troops given us? From France they send us the scourings of the army. Men under regulation height—*chenapans,* scamps who fill the guardhouse or feign illness so they may take their ease in the hospital.[8] Such must I command, I who wear the white uniform with black facings which is the proud badge of the Regiment St. Onge.

This fortress is a house divided. There is friction between the *gens de l'épee* and the *gens de la plume,* between us of the sword and pen-pushing officialdom. Our own corps is split into three quarreling factions: the ancients who have long served here, those newly from France, and those from other garrisons in Canada. It is little to be wondered at that there are quarrels and sometimes duels over preferments, fancied slights, gambling, and women.

Servir le roi, servir les dames,
Voila l'esprit du régiment.
Et r'li, et r'lan.

So runs an old army song of the gallant days of *le roi soleil. Mais, comment servir les dames à Louisbourg?* Parents pack their marriageable daughters off to school in France. More than flirt with a citizen's wife, even a fisherman's, and one risks a knife in the back. There remain the *bordelles.* True, they are plentiful enough, but the only choice one, "The Paphos," kept by a Creole from Martinique, is barred to mere lieutenants. There the girls are reserved for high-ranking officers and bigwig officials. For us are only lesser establishments where the women are ragged, worn-out, bony hags.

Hunting and fishing at times, now and then a ball or a dinner—these for moments brighten monotonous months. Then there are the dress parades when the garrison turns out to deliver a *feu de joie* of musketry and artillery to celebrate the news of the birth of another child to the King and Queen. Happily there have been ten such gala occasions. A man of prowess, our King Louis. It is said that on his wedding night he gave proof of his love seven times. None of us when we were lusty young cadets at St. Cyr could have done better.

Always, at least, there is brandy and wine, and when they give out, *le sapinette*—spruce beer—*faute de mieux.* How are we of the profession of arms, with no chance to practice it, to be blamed if many a night we sit in the bistros, lift our cups, and sing?

Chevaliers de la table ronde,
Goûtons voir si le vin est bon.

Knights of Round Table Order,
Taste and see if the wine is good.

If here in Louisbourg I perish of ennui rather than in battle, let later verses of the old *chanson* be my requiem.

Si je meurs je veux qu'on m'enterre
Dans la cave auprès du bon vin . . .
Les deux pieds contre le muraille
Et la tête sous le robinet.

If I die, prithee have me planted
In a cellar near the good wine.
Both my feet up against the stone wall,
And my head underneath the tap.[9]

Mort sur le champ du buveur, n'est-ce pas?

A FRENCH SOLDIER

Jacques Leblanc still bitterly bemoaned the day in his Normandy village when he had met the recruiting sergeant. "Don a uniform like mine," the sergeant urged. "Fight the King's battles, win your booty, and go home and take your pick of the girls clustering around you." Jacques protested that he was too short for a soldier. "*Fait rien,*" declared the sergeant. "Wearing the tall, mitred cap of a grenadier, you will tower in the ranks." Another bottle of wine, and the farm lad made his mark on a paper. He sobered up in the hold of a ship, crammed with a company of marines en route to Louisbourg.

Battle, booty, and girls—*merde!* Nothing but drill and endless work on the fortifications, with miserly pay twice a year and that often in arrears. They had issued him a coat, sleeved vest, breeches, hat, three shirts, a pair of gaiters, two pairs of shoes with spare soles, two pairs of socks, and a black stock. When he needed new clothing, or was told he did, he was forced to buy it from officers, and it had been stripped from the bodies of men who had died in hospital. His haversack contained knife, fork, and spoon, a wooden comb, awl, and needles. Soon he found that, lacking a greatcoat, he must wrap one or two of his three blankets around him when he mounted guard on the ramparts in freezing weather, musket clutched in numbed fingers.[10] Some privates who knew how to curry favor had never stood guard in a dozen years. Hence Jacques's name came up more often on the duty roster.

In the sour stench of the barracks Jacques shared a bunk with a comrade, a bunk lined with hay changed only once a year and infested with vermin. No wonder he and others preferred to sleep in the open during summer.

At mass he heard the Abbé Maillard thunder that the garrison had made a den of infamy of Louisbourg—that the canteens, maintained by officers, were schools of Satan where the Church was derided and the drunken talk was indecent and blasphemous. Did the Abbé, then, expect a soldier of France to drink water? If for no other reason a man had need of wine to wash down the eternal ration of codfish. Most of the time it was eat salt fish or starve. Even a hare, brought in by the Indians, cost five livres yet was worth the money for a rare taste of meat. If paying for wine at the prices charged left him penniless, he might find off-duty work with a civilian, or furtively sell some of his equipment.

The rasping voice of a sergeant, turning out the guard, reminded Jacques of that scoundrel of a recruiter who had got him into this fix. Muttering curses as he grabbed his musket, he stumbled out into the cold.

A NUN

The hospital is the pride of us, *les filles de Nôtre Dame de la Congrégation.* Here as nurses we fulfill our vows. Ah, *les pauvres malades,* how grateful they are for our care! With the surgeons, chaplains, and monks we tend those who suffer from injuries, scurvy, the flux, the dread smallpox, and from a sickness modesty forbids me to name. Nowhere else in these distant lands, so we hear, are the ill given such comfort. They are loath to leave the hospital when they are cured, especially the soldiers to return to their cheerless barracks and hard lot.

Hélas, that some brethren of the orders serving the hospital with us look too long on the wine when it is red. They scant their duties, and we sisters must perform them for them.[11] I recall a mocking song I used to hear before my novitiate, a song of monks given to wine-bibbing and worse.[12] But such thoughts should not cross my mind. *Mea maxima culpa.* I must make confession, be admonished, and be given penance.

Besides the hospital, our joy is teaching in the school for girls. How good it is to help bring them up in the way they should go, *ces jeunes filles de France*. Among them are children born out of wedlock, not numerous considering the circumstances of this fortress. They are given our tender care and that of people of position who act as their godfathers and godmothers.

Here, far from France, we sometimes know longing for home. Yet the years pass swiftly in devotion to our task. May we never fail to give our hearts to it all our lives! *Ave Maria, gratia plena. Dominus tecum. Ora pro nobis.*

A SWISS SERGEANT

Generations of soldiers lie behind us. For centuries our young men, carrying the flags of the cantons, have marched out of our little, mountain-girt country to fight on countless battlefields of Europe. For hire we served the Italian states, France, Prussia. It did not matter which. We chose the highest bidder. And we bought them victory with our blood until the French artillery broke our pike phalanxes, till then invincible, at Marignano.

Yet still they have need of our fighting men when they cannot muster enough of their own. So now two companies of our Karrer Regiment take French pay in this God-forsaken fortress across the sea. Though we are the smaller complement of the garrison, we are its backbone. Few of the French troops are worthy to be called comrades-in-arms of us who wear the red and blue of the Karrer.

A poor bargain the cantons made for us. Pay is low and always late. There is no chance to prove our mettle in combat, no town to pillage. Rumors that the English colonies will attack Louisbourg, or that we are to forestall them by a raid on their coast, seem groundless.

Not a man of the Karrer but would gladly quit this nest of papists and sail home. Here they hate us Protestants and slight and maltreat us all they dare. But they hold us and will not let our contract be broken. We must serve our term, intolerably long.

Nevertheless there is one avenue of escape from this dreary existence, a way some of us Swiss have taken: marriage, which the French army calls *un ménage monté.* Officers frown on it, declaring that a bachelor makes the best soldier. Bah! Who cares? A married sergeant may have a household of his own with one to warm his bed and he is permitted to keep a profitable tavern. There is a Canadian woman I know, a fisherman's widow of substance who still owns and operates her late husband's ship. No question but she is willing. I have but to twirl my mustache, and her eyes grow fond.

Yet if I am to marry, I must turn Catholic.

Well and good then. So be it. When I was a boy, I remember my teacher telling of a Protestant duke—was it not Henry of Navarre?—who changed his religion to establish himself as King of France. "Paris," said he, "is worth a mass."

No less so is a better life in Louisbourg.

six

The Three Spectres

Over Louisbourg in the year 1744 hovered the three dread spectres of famine, mutiny, and war. From the first two it almost perished. The doom of the Fortress by the third was to be withheld until the year following.

Louis le Prévost, Seigneur du Quesnel de Chagny Pourteville had been named Governor of Isle Royale in 1740. Court gossip from France ran that his only qualifications for the office were noble birth and a Navy career and that he had accepted the appointment solely because his affairs were in disorder and close to ruin. He stumped about on a peg leg replacing a limb lost in battle—there was no question of his courage—but he was arrogant and overbearing, a martinet who from the first had undermined the authority of the officers of the garrison. Often befuddled by drink, he knew no decency nor restraint when in his cups, so townsfolk declared.[1] Even worse, Du Quesnel, charged with the responsibility for the security and well-being of France's key stronghold in North America, was guilty of appalling improvidence.

Failure to stock sufficiently the *Magazin des Vivres*—the King's Provisions Storehouse—reduced Louisbourg to shorter rations than usual at the end of the winter of 1743-1744. It was urgent that the fishing fleet put to sea as soon as the ice broke. Fishermen demanded supplies from military stores to sustain them through voyages. When the Governor denied them, the fishermen refused to sail. Du Quesnel's rantings accomplished nothing, and he took no effective measures to cope with a situation that was already an emergency. By May the people were forced to subsist largely on shellfish. Starvation approached so close that the authorities planned to ship all civilians back to France at the earliest opportunity. Military men realized how drastic such a measure would prove. Abandonment of the Fortress by all save its garrison would compel its defense to be conducted without militia or noncombatants to back up the inadequate troops. Yet no other choice seemed possible.

At the last moment Louisbourg was saved by the arrival of provisions from Quebec. As still more supplies and arms came in, Du Quesnel was inspired to launch an enterprise against New England on his own responsibility, to deliver a *coup de main* that would redeem his damaged reputation and mark him as a strategist of high order.

Hostilities, the War of the Austrian Succession, in which France opposed England and Austria, had broken out and were about to spread to the colonies across the Atlantic as "King George's War." Louisbourg was informed of the declaration of war through a merchant vessel on May 3, a month before dispatches reached New England. Governor du Quesnel, in the belief his news was prior, prepared to strike the enemy unawares. He assured himself that he could count on the support of French warships in American waters; and the prestige of France's Navy, which had just inflicted a heavy defeat on England at Toulon, was high.

With unusual promptitude the Governor organized an expedition against Canso, the Acadian fishing port that had been surrendered to England with the rest of Nova Scotia. Once famine had been staved off, a force was embarked on schooners and fishing boats. Its leader, Captain Dupont du Vivier, commanded 22 officers, 80 French marines, 37 Swiss, and 218 sailors. The last were volunteers, assigned to man the ship of war *Caribou,* built in Quebec and now fitting out at the King's Dock, Louisbourg.

The fishing station at Canso was situated on a strait of that name which separates Nova Scotia from Cape Breton Island. Its only defense was a flimsy little fort, garrisoned by about one hundred men, and a British guard sloop anchored at the harbor's entrance. Gray and ugly cabins and shacks clustered around the blockhouses and straggled down to the wharves and drying racks for codfish. The town stood in a wide clearing, the timber, cut far back, testifying to nearly a century's gathering of wood for buildings and fires.

Du Vivier's force pounced on its quarry, unwarned and utterly unsuspecting. The French sloops had only to swing broadside on and run out their guns. Down its staff slid the fort's flag in acknowledgment that resistance was hopeless, and the guard sloop as swiftly lowered its colors. Canso and all the small craft that tried to flee were easy prey. The fort and town were put to the torch. None of the garrison dared attempt to escape through the cordon of Indians, French allies, lurking in the woods. Soldiers and townspeople were crammed into holds, along with the booty, a considerable supply of dried cod, which would be welcome at still hungry Louisbourg, and the flotilla set sail.

That was the time to exploit success by a descent on a second English fort, Annapolis Royal, the old Port Royal of France. Du Quesnel ordered it, but no cooperation from the Navy was received. Chiefly due to that lack but also because Du Vivier was superseded by the inefficient Captain Pierre De Gannes and because the Annapolis fort was stronger than Canso, the second raid was abortive.

Canso had been destroyed, but its harbor was still available as a base for attack on Louisbourg. And its prisoners and booty sowed the seeds of far more trouble than gain. The prisoners, held at Louisbourg for some months before release and shipment to Boston, were not kept in strict confinement. They took careful note of the fortifications, armament, and morale of the garrison, and their reports proved to be of great value in planning the assault of the forthcoming spring. As dangerous a mistake was made in the disposition of the captured codfish. The troops vainly protested that the Governor had promised it to them. Instead its appropriation by officers was permitted at a low price and on long credit for them to sell for their private benefit. When the bitter knowledge of that outrageous piece of chicanery reached the soldiers, it, more than any other factor, brought the second spectre swooping down on Louisbourg.[2]

Tramp of boots, half muffled by the snow, thudded on the cobbles of Louisbourg's Place d'Armes at dawn on December 27, 1744. The crunching steadily increased in volume, and above it rose the muttering of angry men. Faces pressed against frosted panes of windows of the surrounding houses. No small detachment for relief of the guard could cause such commotion—only troops in force.

They were forming ranks now under arms. Dull light gleamed fitfully on the fixed bayonets of heavy muskets, as sergeants barked commands. Watchers began to be able to make out the uniforms—hats bordered in white, red coats with blue facings crossed by leather slings for swords and cartridge boxes. It was the Swiss of the Karrer Regiment, the two companies in garrison. Perhaps they were mustering to meet an enemy attack, unlikely though one was at this season of stormy seas and deep snows. But no cannonading was heard from the Island Battery or the land redoubts, and no tocsin clanged in the belfries.

Du Chambon was now Acting Governor, Du Quesnel having died in October. He was roused by his valet and loud knocks on the door. An excited officer burst in to report that no assembly had been ordered, nor had any shots been heard from the landside sentry posts. In that case the garrison would be turning out to repulse a surprise attack, one the *Bostonnais* might be staging in retaliation for Canso. They might manage it with a snowshoe brigade, such as the French and Indians used when they had winter-raided New England settlements. High drifts could build a broad natural causeway to the walls; once they had swiftly piled up so deep that sentries had to be dug out of their boxes. But no whooping onrush of the enemy came bursting into Louisbourg. This dawn muster in the Place d'Armes had some other cause, and it bore a look as ominous as an attack. It might be mutiny.

Du Chambon was incredulous. How dare troops forsake their duty when a state of war existed, or at any time for that matter? The outbreak, if such it was, was the more unexpected since it was so soon after Christmas, with the feast of St. Stephen to be celebrated that very morning.

Down on the parade ground the clamor swelled steadily.

White uniforms with blue facings were seen mingling with the red of the Swiss. The companies of French marines, forming the bulk of the garrison, had joined the mercenaries. Recruited with enlistment standards lowered for service in the colonies, possessing little of the discipline of regular marines, they had been easily incited.

Streets resounded with roll and rataplan, as the marines with fixed bayonets forced twenty drummers to beat to arms. There could be no doubt now. Mutiny was afoot. Du Chambon, raging, commanded all officers to quell it and bid the troops return at once to quarters on pain of death.

It was too late for the Governor to reflect, even if the thought had entered his stubborn mind, that this outbreak might have been forestalled. He had demanded more cannon, other arms, and powder but like his predecessor had done nothing to dispel the long-mounting grievances of the soldiery that would use them. Their pay was six months in arrears, and they had not received the extra stipend promised for work on the fortifications. Miserable conditions persisted: poor and scant rations, damp, lice-ridden barracks, no recreation except for the brandy hovels —and drink limited there even for those who could afford it. Small wonder little or no morale remained. The only action most of the garrison ever had seen was the raid on Canso.

As much was true of most of the officers. They were blades rusted in scabbards after long, dull years at Louisbourg. Commands passed from grandfather to father and to son, few being able to manage transfer to more active service. They smarted under the destruction of their authority over the soldiers that had been the common lot under Du Quesnel. Governor du Chambon, as incompetent if not as overbearing, treated his officers little better. Yet they gave him loyalty that day, along with the French sergeants and the small company of artillerymen who refused to join the mutiny.

Officers, shouting orders and threats, converged on the Citadel. A few succeeded in entering it and were cooped up as prisoners. Others, swords in hand, vainly sought to shoulder their way past mutinous guards. Leveled muskets, cocked hammers, and bayonet points at their stomachs halted them. Prudently they recoiled before the glaring soldiery. Had any of them risked death for glory, there would have been bloodshed, and the mutiny might have flared into massacre.

Terror-stricken townsfolk cowered in their homes, as mutineers flooded through the streets. The Swiss, flaunting the watchword on their banner, *Fidelité et Honore Terra et Mari,* broke into shops. They swept goods from the shelves, flinging down a few sous, far below marked-up prices, in payment. Again it was touch and go. Any resistance, and the whole town would have been plundered.

Inhabitants quailed before the bayonets of the mercenaries, as had the foe before the pikes of Swiss phalanxes, triumphant on many a battlefield of the past.

Walls threw back the strident echoes of the rolling drums. While they beat, no orders could be heard, no persuasion exerted. A major rushed forward, arms upraised for silence. For a tense instant he was at the point of being shot down. Instead soldiers pushed through the line of drummer boys, picked up the officer and lugged him away. The major, a brave man, ran back and this time succeeded in stilling the drums.

Then the mutineers were induced to return to the parade ground, form ranks, and state their grievances. The Governor, shaking in his boots, listened to their demands. More firewood, more food, they shouted. The bread, what there was of it, was good enough, but the messes were devoid of bacon and butter, and the rare issues of beans were moldy. Better provisions were reserved for officials, officers, and townsfolk, the soldiers complained. What rankled worst was their being cheated of the Canso codfish.

The fuming, frustrated Governor dumped the handling of the mutiny into the lap of Bigot, whose conscience could by no means have been clear. Soldiers forced the Intendant to disgorge their back pay and promise that officers would cease manipulating payrolls to their own advantage. Also clothing, which had been withheld from recruits, was handed out.[3]

Partly conciliated and promised pardons, but still deeply distrustful, the mutineers maintained control through the rest of winter and on into spring. Louisbourg continued in a state of near anarchy. Shops were rifled if merchants refused to donate food. Officers dared give no orders, and threat of punishment was held in abeyance. Even if it had been possible to subdue and try the Swiss by court-martial the authorities could inflict no executions, since they must account through the King to the Swiss government for the lives of those hired soldiers except as expended in battle—and then a stipulated sum for each casualty must be paid.

Du Chambon was afraid even to send out calls for help lest the mutineers learn of them and ransack the town. Finally, when weather permitted, he dispatched a secret appeal by two merchant vessels. Their sailing papers, to allay the suspicions of the troops, showed that they were bound for the West Indies instead of for their actual destination, France.

News of the mutiny reached New England before it did France, through the release of the Canso prisoners. Along with their report on the undependability of the garrison of Louisbourg, they brought valuable information about its defenses. Their word carried conviction through the colonies that the moment to seize the mighty French fortress was at hand.

As prevalent as that growing assurance was the apprehension spreading through Louisbourg. A townsman, writing after the siege, voiced it: "Troops with so little discipline were scarcely able to inspire us with confidence; we therefore did not think it well to make any sorties, fearing that such men might range themselves on the side of the enemy . . . In justice to them, indeed, it ought to be said that they did their duty well throughout the siege; but who knows whether they would have still done this if an opportunity had offered to escape [only a few took such opportunities] from the punishment of a crime which is rarely pardoned? I confess I thought it only natural to distrust them."[4]

The aftermath of the mutiny may here properly be related ahead of preceding events.

Interchange of communications, reports, and instructions between the Louisbourg authorities and the Ministry in France extended for more than a year.[5] Meanwhile the first siege, shortly to be recounted, had run its course. Although the garrison had fought well, its behavior was deemed not to have erased the black stigma of mutiny. The troops involved in it, transported to France following the surrender of the fortress, were ordered to stand trial.

King Louis, while requiring that clemency be shown because of bravery in Louisbourg's defense, insisted on a thorough investigation for the good of the service. Had Swiss sergeant leaders of the mutiny been instigated by the English? How much of the blame lay on the officers?

Treachery could not be pinned on the Swiss, but various officers, more interested in canteen and other profits than in maintaining discipline, were reprimanded. That the present and past governors had failed to keep them to their duty and support those making an effort to do so was ignored.

The upshot of the investigation was a royal order to punish ringleaders of the mutiny. Several of those so charged had escaped by deserting during the siege. A number of others were condemned by court-martial and hanged.

Dealing with the convicted Swiss was a more difficult matter. Strong representations by France through Switzerland to the colonel of the Karrer Regiment finally resulted in the execution of a sergeant and a corporal, with lesser punishments for other ranks. Reluctant though the Swiss were to sacrifice salable soldiers, they were forced to take action in order to maintain the reliability and value of their troops for hire.

Throughout New England and south into New York, the wildly daring concept of an assault on Louisbourg began to take vague form in the minds of men. It had long lain dormant. Every French-led Indian raid on the settlements—the scalped dead in the charred ruins of homes, the strings of captives herded to French Canada—had stirred it toward awakening. Louisbourg stood as the symbol of the power of France under which those outrages had been perpetrated.

New England fishermen, if they returned with poor catches, cursed the French fleets they accused of poaching on their preserves, although the charge could be hurled back at them. They ignored the fact that their mother country by force of arms had taken Newfoundland and most of the banks fisheries from France. It irked them to share what remained.

Was it not high time the depredations of French privateers

on New England commerce were ended? While retaliations by the more numerous privateers of the English colonies were considerably more effective, let that be ascribed to the fortunes of war in conflicts commenced by the King of France to extend his rule in Europe and America.

True, trade with Louisbourg was remunerative, but it was only a drop in a bucket to prospective profits if the fortress—and with it the rest of French Canada—were to lie in English hands.

Such were the American undercurrents in a struggle for empire between the two great nations, currents that would swell into a flood and sweep a new nation into being.

Slowly the dream of taking Louisbourg emerged from the fantastic into the possible. An overt act, the French seizure and burning of Canso, had quickened it. Reports from the released Canso prisoners, supplementing those from crews of trading vessels, lent the dream vividness. What if the Fortress were acclaimed the Gibraltar and Dunkirk of America? The rock-borne stronghold at the mouth of the Mediterranean had once fallen to siege, and Dunkirk as well, with King Louis finally forced by the English to demolish the latter's defenses. Might not Louisbourg's reputed invincibility then be only a legend?

If any unpuritanical New Englander was aware of an old proverb, to be later quoted by an American author, he might have voiced it then:

"The walls of an impregnable fortress, like the virtue of women, have their weak points of attack." [6]

seven

Demand for Destruction

William Vaughan of Damariscotta, Maine, a Harvard graduate and a fisheries and lumber baron, was an impetuous man, as gusty and driving as the gales into whose teeth he dared to launch his fleet. The Louisbourg-mounted raid and burning of the fishing port of Canso, surely the precursor of more to come, aroused his ready wrath. He poured angry words into the willing ears of William Shirley, Governor of Massachusetts and Maine, its subprovince. It was, he said, high time (as high as the Vaughan dudgeon) to deal with the menacing fortress on Cape Breton Island.

Shirley, a former London barrister who had emigrated to Boston in 1731 and had climbed the rungs of office to become, ten years later, an able Royal Governor, possessed a temperament more ambitious than judicial. Vaughan's startling proposal for a sudden, unsuspected counterattack in vengeance for Canso strongly appealed. Capture of Louisbourg would write the name of Shirley large in history. Failure might . . . but the Governor entertained no defeatist notions.

First he had to obtain the consent of the General Court of Massachusetts for the enterprise. Until that body granted its sanction for an expedition to destroy Louisbourg, he was prepared to importune it as persistently as had Cato the Roman Senate with his *Carthago delenda est!*

Called into session, the General Court was sworn to secrecy, essential for a surprise assault. The Governor thereupon rocked members in their seats with his plan for the reduction of the redoubtable stronghold. Shirley was no forerunner of Patrick Henry in eloquence, but he made a good case for his proposal, mentioning intelligence received on Louisbourg's situation and stressing the commercial angle. Without ado he let them have it:

"Gentlemen of the General Court, either we must take Louisbourg or see our trade annihilated. If you are of my mind, we will take it. I have reason to know that the garrison is unsubordinate. There is good ground for believing that the commandant is afraid of his own men, that the works are out of repair, and the stores are running low. I need not dwell further on what is known to you all. Now with four thousand such soldiers as this and the neighboring provinces can furnish, aided by a naval force similarly equipped, the place must surely fall into our hands. I have, moreover, strong hopes of aid from his Majesty's ships now in our waters. But the great thing is to throw our forces on Louisbourg before the enemy can hear of our design. Secrecy and celerity are therefore a first imperative. Consider well, gentlemen, that such an opportunity is not likely to occur again. What say you? Is Louisbourg to be ours or not?"

While the idea was not novel—it had recently been urged upon the British Ministry, with the full support of the colonies promised—the suggestion that it be undertaken mainly by Massachusetts, though with the possible backing of other provinces, was utterly astounding. The cost would be enormous, and the treasury was empty. Few experienced officers and trained troops were available, and their knowledge of siegecraft extended no further than storming a blockhouse. The Court's vote after several days of consideration was unanimously adverse.

Two odd occurrences with seriocomic elements intervened to overturn the decision. Before the taking of the vote a Puritan member of the Court, uncertain of his course, had wrestled in prayer beseeching divine guidance. He prayed so vocally and vociferously that he broadcast the secret. Eavesdroppers spread the startling news, and it ran like wildfire through the province. A merchant and militiaman, James Gibson, who was a Shirley partisan, promptly circulated a petition in favor of the scheme among all the trading establishments he could reach. Signatures snowballed it into a bulky scroll; almost to a man merchants were keen to suppress competition in seaborne commerce provided or protected by Louisbourg. Before the petition was finished the Court had rejected the original proposal, but the potent pleas of business compelled reconsideration.

This time the vote was close. The war party argued that the moment for action was at hand. Let the golden opportunity slip, and Louisbourg would be reinforced. It would be long before such a chance presented itself again, and meanwhile the colonies would suffer the consequences of forbearance. Pointedly the opposition asked what would be used for money and where an adequate army and fleet could be found. Shirley, counting heads, feared he could hope for no better than a nullifying tie vote.

Then the second accident happened. A member of the opposition, hurrying to the House, slipped on the icy street and fell asprawl. Bystanders stopped grinning at the mishap when they found he had fractured a leg and they carried him home. His absence broke the expected tie, and the ayes had it by a single vote.

Yet there was general agreement that Massachusetts could not manage the enterprise alone. Shirley wrote to enlist the support of brother governors as far south as Pennsylvania. Vaughan rode hard on an embassy to Benning Wentworth of New Hampshire, who was told that Shirley had neatly, if deviously, solved the problem of financing the war. Although the King had forbade the printing of any more paper money, nothing had been said about bills of credit, which now had been duly issued to the amount of fifty thousand pounds. New Hampshire could adopt the same device to raise and equip 500 men, and Massachusetts would ease her burden by paying and rationing 150 of them. Governor Wentworth accepted and enlisted his province in the cause. Connecticut responded to the call with enthusiasm. Only Rhode Island was lukewarm, embittered by an old grudge—Massachusetts' ill-treatment of her founding father, Roger Williams—and by a current boundary dispute. However, that province contributed an armed sloop and crew. New York promised cannon and money but not soldiers, while other colonies to the south held aloof except for New Jersey and Pennsylvania who forwarded funds. Their skepticism was expressed by Benjamin Franklin, who wrote from Philadelphia to his brother in Boston:

"Fortified towns are hard nuts to crack, and your teeth are

not accustomed to it. Taking strong places is a particular trade, which you have taken up without serving an apprenticeship to it. Armies and veterans need skillful engineers to direct them in their attack. Have you any? But some seem to think that forts are as easy taken as snuff." [See Appendix D.]

The sage's warning dampened not at all the ardor of the citizens of his birthplace for the crusade, as the expedition against Louisbourg, haunt and hold of popery, was regarded by Protestant New England—a crusade that must surely commend itself to heaven. Church and meetinghouse resounded to fervent prayer. Long and vehement sermons were preached by ministers, many of whom were eager to demonstrate their zeal by service at the front. So far as chaplains were concerned, the army could pick and choose.

Foremost to offer himself and soon made senior chaplain was the Reverend Samuel Moody of York, Maine, a tough, fiery seventy-year-old, famed for his "lungs of brass and nerves of hammered iron." He never hesitated to chastise unruly parishioners with his cane. Anyone who attempted to leave a meeting when offended by his strictures was halted by a shout, "Come back, you graceless sinner, come back." None was safe to revel undisturbed in the alehouse of a Saturday night. The parson would collar tosspots, drag them out, and send them home admonished. Militiamen in Boston taprooms drew the same treatment from Chaplain Moody. While his thundering threats of hellfire and damnation from the pulpit were relished, not so were the lengthy prayers and two-hour sermons in which they were voiced while the congregation stood and shivered in the unheated meetinghouse's biting cold. But Parson Moody was one to inspire fighting men about to face the heat of combat, and they trooped after him with admiring grins when the irascible old zealot embarked for Louisbourg armed with his Bible and an axe, intended, as he announced, to hew down the altars of the papists and smash their idols to smithereens.

To the all-important post of Commander in Chief Shirley appointed William Pepperrell, a merchant and lumberman from Kittery, Maine, widely known and respected. First the candidacy of Governor Wentworth, patently disqualified by inexperience, gout, and other factors, had been disposed of diplomatically.

Pepperrell was not without military experience. He had served in the Maine militia, rising from capitain to colonel, yet his service by no means qualified him for the high command he assumed and which he would fulfill far beyond expectations. It was because he was widely liked and admired that he was chosen. A broadside, now preserved in the Massachusetts Historical Society's manuscript collection of Louisbourg papers, correctly stated it, while taking a dig at his second in command, Samuel Waldo.

> You was made G-n-r-l being a popular man
> most likely to raise soldiers soonest.
> The Expedition was calculated to establish Sh-rl-y
> and to make his creature W - - - o Governor of Cape
> Breton which is to be a place of Refuge for him
> from his creditors.
> He is to go home from thence immediately if the Place
> be taken.
> Beware of Snakes in the Grass and mark their hissing.
> We are, Sir: Your Servants - - -
>
> The Birds of the Air.
>
> P.S. Word to the Wise is enough.

Pepperrell's best qualities, as Parkman points out,[1] were good sense and good will. A career in politics and trade had given him the ability to get on with men, an essential talent since he would be commanding volunteers and cooperating, if hopes were realized, with the British Navy. Overcoming religious scruples against war, and reluctance to leave his family, the Kittery squire accepted the proffered command. Events proved that Shirley had chosen far better than he could have known.

Fervor sped preparations extraordinarily. A flotilla of warships and transports was quickly assembled from the provinces' little navies, privateers, and trading and fishing vessels. "For a naval commander Shirley chose Captain Edward Tyng, who had signalized himself in the past summer by capturing a French privateer of greater strength than his own. Shirley authorized him to buy for the province the best ship he could find, equip her for fighting, and take command of her. Tyng soon found a brig to his mind, on the stocks nearly ready for launching. She was rapidly fitted for her new destination, converted into a frigate, mounted with 24 guns, and named the *Massachusetts*. The rest of the naval force consisted of the ship *Caesar*, of 20 guns, a vessel called the *Shirley*, commanded by Captain Rous, and also carrying 20 guns; another of the kind called snow, carrying 16 guns; one sloop of 12 guns, and two of 8 guns each; the *Boston Packet*, of 16 guns; two sloops from Connecticut of 16 guns each; a privateer hired in Rhode Island, of 20 guns; the government sloop *Tartar* of the same colony, carrying 14 carriage guns and 12 swivels; and finally the sloop of 14 guns which formed the navy of New Hampshire." [2]

Optimism had not blinded the Govenor to the grave danger of an encounter with the enemy at sea before his fleet could reach and assemble in Canso's harbor and sail on to Cape Breton. Two French warships were said to be cruising offcoast, with more surely to be expected in spring. Even one heavily gunned ship of the line could blow the colonial squadron out of the water and then hold the transports at her mercy. The Governor rushed off fast-sailing dispatch vessels with an appeal for protection and cooperation to both the British Admiralty and to Commodore Sir Peter Warren, on station with three ships of war at Antigua in the West Indies. Warren, while eager for patriotic and personal reasons to comply, had received no orders from the Admiralty to support the venture and so felt compelled to decline.

It was bad news, so alarming that Shirley dared disclose it only to Pepperrell and two other key officers. Nevertheless it was agreed that the die was cast. The expedition would set sail regardless and take its chances on evading the Frenchmen.

The march on Louisbourg, like all expeditions in history, can be said to have begun when the first soldier took arms and set foot on the path to war. Those pioneers are seldom recognized, their names lost in the clamor of events and the tread of the ranks.

Among that unknown company may have been a member of the 4th Massachusetts Regiment whose anonymous diary survives.[3] When he joined up, he held no doubt of the right of the cause he meant to serve.

> The News of our Government's Raising an army, (Together with the Help of the other Neighboring Governments) in order to the Reduction of Cape Breton. (Viz) Louisbourg, which was Like to prove Detremental if not Destroying to our Country. So affected the minds of many. (together with the Expectation of Seeing Great things, etc.)—As to incline many, yea, Very Many to Venture themselves and Enlist into the Service. Among whom, I was one, which was the, 14th of March, 1745.
>
> And having the Consent of my friends, (and asking their prayers), which was A great Comfort to me. (Even all the Time of my being Asent.) I set out for Boston, Tuesday March 19th. Wee was well Entertained Upon the road, and arrived, the fryday following On Saturday wee all Appeared before Coll. Pollard, to be View'd. Both our Persons And arms, Those that found their own, and Those that had none, were ordered to Mr. Wheelwright's (Commissary General) to get Equipt. That being Done, wee Receiv'd our Blankets At the Sametime, and Return'd to our Lodging.

Patriots and adventurers, the footloose and ne'er-do-wells, flocked to the colors, their mother country's as well as a specially devised Louisbourg flag confidently depicting an armed and helmeted Britannia already enthroned on a Cape Breton rock; its background displaying a full-rigged warship, perhaps a hopeful token that the British Navy might arrive after all. "Out of New England's population of less than 700,000 whites—men, women, and children—an army was going to be raised. Enrollments for it commenced in earnest and, on the first of February, recruiting parties set out. Some struggled along crude, snow-banked roads, others snowshoed along lonely trails or sailed the stormy and bitterly cold sea. Some parties were accompanied by a fifer and drummer." [4]

Harvard students, resembling so many boys getting out of school, enthusiastically quit classes and signed up. Not a few were divinity students, as eager to crusade as the chaplains. A leader's name, Pepperrell's especially, drew many a recruit. Scores who made their mark on the recruiters' rolls and tossed off the bonus of a tankard of Barbados rum, were uncertain who the enemy was. Whether it was the Spaniards or the "damned, popish mounseers" did not matter. It was enough that they were escaping a humdrum existence for a good, rousing fight and plenty of loot in prospect. Few mobilizations have been as speedily accomplished as this seven-week mustering of 4,270 men, equipped after a fashion, provisioned, and with the shipping necessity for transport. Massachusetts and Maine supplied the large majority contingent of 3,300, Connecticut 516, and New Hampshire 454. Rhode Island still abstained except for naval aid; three companies, sent later, did not arrive until the siege was over.

Cannon to counter the fire of the French batteries and breach the massive walls of the Gibraltar of the West comprised only eight 22-pounders, ten 18s, twelve 9s, and four mortars from 12- to 9-inch. A large proportion of the ammunition consisted of 42-pounder cannonballs, almost twice too large to fit the bores of the expedition's heaviest ordnance. Those, however, were provided for the heavy guns reported by the Canso prisoners to be mounted on Louisbourg's ramparts. It would be necessary only to storm the batteries, load their captured 42s with imported balls supplementing the rounds on hand, then blaze away and demolish remaining defenses. Such sublime assurance went undiminished by the caustic remark of a doubting Thomas that it was "like selling the skin of a bear before catching him."

Experienced artillerymen were as few as the guns were scant and light. Fortunately some twenty stepped forward from the Ancient and Honorable Artillery Company of Boston, scion of England's own. Founded in 1638 as "scholars of great gunnes," the Company was the oldest military organization in America.[5] Colonel Joseph Dwight and Lieutenant Colonel Richard Gridley, assembling artificers to maintain the cannon, could also count on gunsmiths like Major Seth Pomeroy of one of the infantry regiments. Gun crews would have to be trained in action. Artillery resources were augmented by the 216 guns of the warships. Though most of them were too light for siege work, some might be landed and serve as fieldpieces.

Such was the expedition mustered against the might of Louisbourg, an undertaking which a sarcastic Bostoner declared had a lawyer for a contriver, a merchant for a general, and farmers, fishermen, and mechanics for soldiers. *Nil desperandum Christo duce* was proclaimed its motto, inspired by the recent religious revival called "The Great Awakening." It did not matter that even the revivalist who contributed the motto disparaged the project as "not very promising." Never despairing, New Englanders turned from fighting the devil and prepared to fight the French—which to their minds was much the same thing.

At the docks, cannon stripped from New England and New York harbor defenses (from the latter came the ten 18-pounders) were hoisted aboard. Slings of roundshot and casks of salt meat and hard bread were lowered into holds, along with kegs of water and rum. Particular care was taken of the latter. It would be cold and wet around Louisbourg, and a man would need to warm his blood with a pannikin of the Good Creature of God.

Cargo stowed, troops went aboard and crammed themselves with their arms and equipment [6] into 'tween-deck space reeking of codfish, no aroma to soothe queasy stomachs if the seas turned rough.

On March 24, 1745, the fleet of warships and the ninety transports they convoyed set sail, cheered from the thronged wharves and tendered Godspeed in prayers, benedictions, and bumpers of rum punch.

They sailed before what the Massachusetts diarist called a "Pleasant Gale," but he soon revised the adjective. "This day," he wrote, "our Vessel was A Very Hospital, wee were all Sick, in a Greater or Less Degree. Wee Sail'd a good pace all Day, Towards Night, the Wind Began to rise, it also Grew foggy and Something Rainy. So That wee Could not be Upon Deck, as the Night before—But was Shut down in the hold; and a Long, Dark and Tedious night wee had, Such a one I Never See before; wee was also Much Crouded, even So as to Lay, one on Another. Sick etc. My Friends, you can Scarsely think What Distress we were in.—

"*Thursday 28* Our distress Encreas'd, inasmuch as our Sickness not only Continued, but the weather Grew, Thicker and more Stormy. And our Captain Upon whom (under God) was our dependence Began to Drink too hard. As the storm Encreas'd, (As is too frequently the Manner of Seamen) so that he was Altogether Uncapeable to manage the Vessel, Neither was he able to go down in to the Cabin, but Lay Great part of the Last

Night Upon the Quarter Deck: the Mate also was Something Disguised with Liquor: So that our Dependence was—Upon An Old fisherman: to Stear her, which he Could well do: altho he knew nothing of Navigation . . . But we was so Sick and concern'd etc., that being taken Seem'd No great Matter. As we then Said one to another Going to France is no great matter." [7]

The stormy, foggy weather served to hide the fleet from interception by whatever French warships might be at sea and increased the expedition's prospect of surprising Louisbourg, so the commanders believed. They were unaware that they had been double-crossed in spite of having taken the precaution of jailing several Frenchmen and putting an embargo on shipping. One of the prisoners had earlier arranged to slip out two flour-laden ships with news of the coming assault. The ships sailed before the embargo was clamped on, with, it is said, the connivance of a prominent Boston merchant who reckoned profit above patriotism.[8] Louisbourg would be doubly forearmed, being forewarned.

eight

Fortunes of War

Fortune, the blind goddess, spins a wheel, grasps a rudder, and rolls a ball, unsteady symbol of her fickleness. Also she carries a cornucopia from which she distributes gifts. In amazing profusion she conferred them on the wildly audacious New England expedition against Louisbourg. Who can say she gave blindly since—*Fortuna favet fortibus*—she favors the bold? She spun the steering wheels and guided the rudders of the fleet that dared the still wintery Atlantic gales, bringing it safe to port without the loss of a single vessel. Throughout the campaign her ball more often rolled the way of the force assaulting the Fortress.

It had been a grave risk to launch the undertaking as early as March, the anonymous *Habitant de Louisbourg* wrote,

> a month usually extremely dangerous in a climate which seems to confound the seasons, for the spring, everywhere else so pleasant, here is frightful. The English, however, appeared to have enlisted Heaven in their interests. So long as the expedition lasted they enjoyed the most beautiful weather in the world, and this greatly favored an enterprise against which were heavy odds that it would fail on account of the season. Contrary to what is usual there were no storms [in the Cape Breton vicinity]. Even the winds, so unrestrained in those dreadful seas in the months of March, April, and May, were to them always favourable; the fogs were so thick and frequent in these months that ships are in danger of running upon the land without seeing it, disappeared earlier than usual, and gave place to a clear and serene

sky; in a word, the enemy had always beautiful weather, as fine as they could desire.[1]

As lucky as the weather was a timely decision made in London. The British Admiralty, having concluded that the Newfoundland fisheries were menaced by the French Navy, which Louisbourg served as a base, rushed orders to Commodore Warren in the West Indies to sail at once and support the New England expedition "for the annoyance of the enemy, and his Majesty's service in North America." Warren, who had reluctantly refused Shirley's request only three days earlier, gladly complied, once he had authorization. He would be maintaining not only Britannia's rule over the waves but also her New World possessions, of which the dowry of New York-born Lady Warren constituted a not inconsiderable share: large tracts of land in the Mohawk Valley. It was said of Commodore Warren, "Where Sir Peter's treasure was, there was his heart also." [2] He made all sail northward with his flagship the *Superbe,* of sixty guns; the *Launceton* and the *Mermaid,* of forty guns each; two small armed vessels, and ten merchantmen. The frigate *Eltham,* forty guns, later joined. En route Warren met a Marblehead schooner and was informed that the Provincial fleet was bound for Canso. Warren sent word to Massachusetts and, taking the schooner's master aboard as pilot, shaped his course direct for the assembly port.

There the American flotilla lay at anchor, storm-battered but safe and sound. It had not been idle since arrival. Some of the warships had already scouted Louisbourg, found its harbor still filled with ice blocks, and reported that the attack must be delayed a little longer. They returned not only with that intelligence but also with captured French vessels whose cargoes of rum, molasses, and other supplies were as welcome to the colonials as they would have been to Louisbourg. Still other warships swooped down on a French frigate of 36 guns, bearing dispatches for the Governor of the fortress. Only after a thirty-hour running fight did she manage to escape; then she cruised about for some days, made a vain attempt to intercept a Boston convoy, and returned ingloriously to France.

The ice in Louisbourg's harbor had seemed a dire misfortune

since it postponed an attack which could not now partake of surprise; even if the scout ships had not been sighted from the Fortress, surely the cannonading at sea must have been heard. But essentially the delay was another stroke of good luck. It allowed the Provincial troops, encamped at Canso, three weeks of much-needed drill. Many of them being Indian fighters and hunters, they knew how to handle muskets, but of discipline and command they were utterly ignorant except for a smattering picked up by the militiamen. Now as much training as was possible in a short time was pounded into them.

Drillmasters like Major Seth Pomeroy ground them through the military mill. A born soldier, the forty-five-year-old Massachusetts gunsmith would serve again, ten years after Louisbourg, in the battle of Lake George. "Again, twenty years later still, when Northampton was astir with rumors of war from Boston, he borrowed a neighbor's horse, rode a hundred miles, reached Cambridge on the morning of the battle of Bunker Hill, left his borrowed horse out of the way of harm, walked over Charlestown Neck, then swept by the fire of the ships-of-war, and reached the scene of action as the British were forming for the attack. When Israel Putnam, his comrade in the last war, saw from the rebel breastwork the old man striding, gun in hand, up the hill, he shouted, 'By God, Pomeroy, you here! A cannon-shot would waken you from your grave!' "[3] A year later the veteran, who had declined a brigadier generalcy from Congress and retired to his farm, took up arms once more and marched to join Washington's imperiled army in New Jersey. En route the grand old soldier died of fever.

At Canso, Pomeroy, other officers, and the sergeants struggled with the awkward squads which made up most of this army of green recruits, a few hundred in some sort of uniform, the rest wearing the clothes in which they had enlisted. A weird assortment of firearms slanted over the shoulders of companies vainly trying to march in step. The daily racket of drilling and target practice in the clearings around the new blockhouse rose to a height on Sundays when, the sacred vying with profane, stentorian exhortations of the chaplains mingled with the bellowings of the drillmasters. As Pomeroy wrote in his journal,[4] "several sorts of Busnesses was a-Going on: Sum a-Exercising, Sum a-Hearing of the Preaching." The clamor was augmented by "a Very Large Band: Thirty Six Drummers, which was Ordered to Beat at once, which they did for a considerable time, altho I knew no reason for it. There was also many Fiddlers, Trumpetters, etc." [5] As is always the way with army musicians performing or practicing, they were hard to shut off, and an unwilling auditor was moved to complain in his journal. "After the Exercise was Over there was a Vast Deal More Drumming and Trumpiting than was needful Which I Trust Displeased a great many, while other Tollarated it."

Slowly but noticeably some semblance of order was achieved, for the men were eager to learn. When General Pepperrell ordered a review, troops were pushed and shoved into a formation the manuals termed "battalia" and called to attention. The flag soared up the staff of the blockhouse. All its eight guns, grudgingly spared powder by the artillery commanders, who knew how sorely it would be needed before Louisbourg, boomed a salute. Batteries of the cruisers in the harbor seconded them. Soldiers, too deeply impressed to mind military decorum, craned their necks to count the long, serried ranks—more men in one place than most of them had ever seen, except maybe some of the Bostonians. Mason's novel, *The Young Titan,* re-creates the scene.

" 'Say, Luke,' muttered Abner Tuckerman in the ranks, 'you ever figger there were so many of us?'

" 'No. This here's quite an array. We're a bigger army, I reckon, than the one Joshua led agin Jericho.'

" 'Quiet, you dunderheads!' hissed a corporal. 'You'll tote plenty firewood for this.'

"About the only people who didn't witness the flag-raising were the sick. They lay, wan and hollow-eyed, upon pine bough couches beneath a couple of old mainsails rigged between convenient trees. What tents were available were too small or too rotten." [6]

The drums rolled; the fiddles, sawed mightily, shrilled, and the trumpets blared so loudly that only distance could have saved the walls of Louisbourg from tumbling down like those of Jericho.

But even that uproar was dwarfed when Warren's fleet hove

in view off Canso on April 23. Only the most sanguine could, after outright refusal, have expected those powerful warships, grandly flying the Cross of St. George at their peaks. Likely not many fully realized what the presence of His Majesty's men-o'-war meant. They could stave off the French Navy, prevent its sinking the Provincial cruisers and transports, and save the expedition from being marooned on Cape Breton with its only retreat across the island to Canso—if it could find boats to ferry it across the Strait.

Well, the army had gone ahead, but it was a comfort to have the Royal Navy standing by. Now Louisbourg seemed as good as taken. So thought a citizen of Boston who wrote an optimistic letter to a soldier friend at the front.

> I hope this will find you at Louisbourg with a bowl of Punch, a Pipe, and a Pack of Cards, and whatever else you desire. (I had forgot to mention a Pretty French Madammoselle.) Your Friend Luke has lost several Beaver Hatts already concerning the Expedition. He is so very zealous about it that he has turned poor Boutier out of his house for saying he believed you wouldn't take the place. Damn his Blood, says Luke, let him be an Englishman or a Frenchman and not pretend to be an Englishman when he is a Frenchman in His Heart. If Drinking to your Success would take Cape Britton you must be in possession of it now, for it's a Standing Toast.

Warren, after a conference with Pepperrell, sailed on to blockade Louisbourg. The Canso troops cheered him off magnanimously. They were glad to have the British Navy along, but the job of storming the Fortress would be up to the army.

Assuredly cheers and thanksgiving were in order, not to mention a bow by the unregenerate to the pagan divinity Fortuna.

The goddess had still other gifts to bestow from her cornucopia.

No appearance in strength by the French Navy, which might have proved Louisbourg's salvation, would be made. France's Minister of Marine, the usually astute Maurepas, was doubtful that the Fortress was seriously threatened and so delayed sending vital naval aid.

High also on the list of fortune's gifts to the enemy was the gross incompetence of Governor du Chambon in whose hands rested the safety of Louisbourg. Blame for leaving such a man in command of the stronghold guarding the gateway to French Canada ran up the chain of authority to the King. Louis XV and his ministers, preoccupied with a Continental war, gave little heed to Louisbourg on which—so they may have reasoned—so much money had been spent that it ought to be able to fend for itself. The inefficiency of Du Chambon, like that of his predecessor, Du Quesnel, must have been apparent,[7] but it was long ignored, just as their pleas for reinforcements and more cannon and munitions were ignored; those urgent but vain requests which were, nevertheless, to their credit.

Even before the mutiny it was plain that Du Chambon was a fiasco, his follies abetted by subordinates who shared the responsibility for them. The account is long and damaging: his raid on Canso, a brief flash of a man of action, was not pressed through to the capture of Annapolis Royal; he permitted profiteering by his officers on the codfish loot, thus triggering the mutiny; he released the Canso prisoners after they had had the run of the Fortress, which was equivalent to handing back so many well-informed spies to the enemy.

Sooner or later the French attack on Nova Scotia would provoke retaliation. The Governor kept his mind closed to that probability. Due partly to the mutiny and partly to inertia work on the fortifications, particularly a much-needed strengthening of the defenses of the Grand Battery, was not demanded. Among the higher officials, only the shrewd Bigot was much disturbed, and he prompted in vain. "Du Chambon seems to have been incapable of foresight" and "in doubt of what was going on, or perhaps was in that frame of mind which tries not to see the indications of a crisis to which he felt himself unequal." [8] The warning brought by the flour ships sneaked out of Boston, had fallen on deaf ears.

Even the actual presence of warships in the offing proved no more than disquieting; perhaps they were the promised succor from home, although it was strange they did not sail into the harbor if such they were. Reported activity around Canso might be only the English fortifying the ruined port. The Governor did send three scouts to investigate. They captured four prisoners, then were themselves overpowered; one scout, an Indian, escaped and made a little-heeded report.[9]

The running fight between the French frigate and the Provincial cruisers left little doubt that something was afoot, and the question was clinched by the arrival of a vessel from the West Indies, which had beaten off an enemy attack, and by the taking of three New England coasters. At last the Governor, jolted into action, sent a dispatch ship to France. The alarming news belatedly shattered the complacency of Maurepas.

The mutinous garrison which had been promised pardon had returned to duty, but Du Chambon was slow in calling up the militia. Some men from the outlying countryside were unable to reach Louisbourg once the siege closed it in.

There was still another instance of "the unlit lamp and the ungirt loin," one so flagrant that it seems incredible.

The Governor General of Canada had ordered Lieutenant Colonel Michel du Bourzt Marin to march from Quebec with a strong detachment and attack Annapolis Royal or proceed to the aid of Louisbourg. Marin, a competent officer with a knowledge of artillery, left on January 15, 1745, and in spite of hard winter travel was deep in Acadia and ready to fulfill either mission. He so notified Du Chambon in March, his messenger bearing a request for powder and provisions. That the Governor spared some of the former from his inadequate supply might have been justified if at the same time he had called on Marin to march to Louisbourg's aid. Instead the offer of reinforcement was declined as unneeded. Marin (one can imagine the Gallic shrug of his shoulders) turned and proceeded to attack Annapolis, as it transpired, vainly.

"It is necessity that makes men reflect," the *Habitant* lamented. "In the month of May we began to be anxious about the mistake we had made; then, without thinking that with the enemy extending all along the coast and masters of the surrounding country it was impossible for M. Marin to penetrate to the place, two messengers were sent, beseeching him to succor us. Both had the good fortune to pass out, but they were obliged to make so wide a circuit that they took nearly a month to reach him. The Canadian officer, learning from them the extremity in which we found ourselves, collected some Indians to strengthen his detachment, being resolved to help us if he should reach us. After a fight in crossing the strait, he had the chagrin to learn that he had arrived too late, and that Louisbourg had surrendered. The brave fellow had only time to throw himself into the woods with his five or six hundred men, to get back to Acadia."

One more event—was it a bit of empty folly or a gesture of bravado?—crowned the series of neglects and failures that were portents of the doom of a mighty fortress. On the very night the entire hostile fleet hove to off Isle Royale and prepared to land troops on the shores of Gabarus Bay, a ball was held in the Governor's Palace.[10]

> There was a sound of revelry by night . . .
> On with the dance; let joy be unconfined;
> No sleep till morn, when Youth and Pleasure meet
> To chase the glowing Hours with flying feet.[11]

Louisbourg's ball like the one described above in Byron's verse —the gala affair in Brussels on the eve of the Battle of Waterloo —may well have suffered the same kind of interruption:

> But Hark!—that heavy sound breaks in once more,
> As if the clouds its echo would repeat;
> And nearer, clearer, deadlier than before!
> Arm! Arm! it is—it is—the cannon's opening roar!

The booming guns of Warren's warships and the Provincial cruisers shattered the stillness of dawn. Those of the Island Battery, thundering in reply, woke the tocsin bells of the town to wild clanging and gay officers from their post-ball naps. Three miles south of the harbor entrance, where Gabarus Bay spread sheltering arms, the New England transports sailed in as close to shore as they dared and lowered whaleboats and dories for the landing force.

nine

By the Mouths of Cannon

Behind the parapets of the Island Battery, guardian of the harbor's entrance, drummers of the artillery, *Les Bombardiers de la Marine,* stood ready to beat firing signals. Boyish faces—the lads could scarcely have been twelve years old—looked pale under mitred blue caps. Metal plaques fronting the caps bore the regimental motto: *Alter Post Fulmina Terror,* words about to come alive in the frightfulness of lightning bolts loosed by the guns.

Sleeves of the drummers' skirted coats, blue like their caps, were decorated with stripes in the link design of the royal livery, testifying service to the King. Only collars and inner linings were artillery scarlet like the coats of the cannoneers, since colors were reversed for musicians.[1] Small hands trembled a little when they poised sticks over the heads of drums whose cases were painted scarlet and ornamented in yellow with a flaming bomb, insignia of their arm of the service, and with the same legend that adorned the caps. But the boys steadily rattled out the signals for loading, beats that would cut through the din of combat better than shouted orders.

A scabbarded sword clanked, as Captain Louis d'Aillebout made the rounds of the battery he commanded. He fully realized how formidable and vital was this isolated post athwart the harbor mouth. If the hostile fleet yonder attempted to force a passage to his right, despite the dangerous shoals, he could blast it out of the water. As for the entrance usually used, the deep-water channel to his left no more than a scant half-mile wide, the rashest enemy dare not try to pierce it while the Island Battery remained in action. Any vessel which by some chance got through must face the guns of the Grand Battery across the harbor.

D'Aillebout stared across the channel to where the lighthouse rose on the point of the harbor's eastern arm opposite him. If the English planted a battery there, it might give trouble—might cover a crossing to storm the island fort. But to cope with such an unlikely event the Captain had placed four guns behind fascines, with swivels in reserve, to defend the only landing place.

The thirty guns on the ramparts stood manned by 75 regular artillerymen and 150 militiamen. Section commanders, *cadets-gentilhommes,* with powderhorns to lay trains to vents swung across their shoulders, doffed their tricornes and reported ready as the Captain strode by. Around the iron 24s and the mortars hovered crews with powder ladles, rammer and sponge staffs, and worms, gigantic corkscrews for drawing out wads clogging a bore. At hand were shells, roundshot, and powder kegs brought up from the amply supply in the stone magazine. The regular artillerymen were too few, although their numbers had increased from the detachment of the corps organized in 1743 to defend Louisbourg; the Citadel complement was then only one captain, one lieutenant, one ensign, two *cadets-gentilhommes,* two sergeants, three corporals, forty-one cannoneers, and two drummer boys. But these scarlet-clad men were an elite group, not involved in the mutiny. In the present emergency, crews had been filled out with militiamen, hastily trained by the regulars to handle the simpler duties such as ammunition passing.

Lay the guns, sounded the drum signals. Cannoneers flung themselves on the bronze pieces, some of the large ones handsomely embossed with the arms of the Duke of Maine whose son was Grand Master of Artillery for Louis XV. Muzzles peering out of embrasures swung right or left as cannoneers heaved on trail handspikes, obeying gunners' motions. The latter adjusted the handled, triangular blocks of wood called quoins under breeches to raise or lower a piece's elevation while, estimating ranges, they sighted along barrels at the approaching targets, the British warships. Let them come on. The Island Battery and its cannon bid them the defiance of a watchword to be voiced in a future war: *On ne passe pas!*

It found no echo in the Grand or Royal Battery which, although on the mainland, was isolated like the Island Battery, being an outlying work more than one mile from the town. Considering its importance as both a seaward and a landward defense, the existence of two dangerous defects, seems impossible to excuse. Now, in time of greatest need, a stretch of the Battery's landside fortifications was open to attack, having been leveled preparatory to repair. The second flaw dated back to the Battery's original siting. Like French Fort Carillon (Ticonderoga) on Lake Champlain, it was commanded by higher ground.[2]

Failure to restore the dismantled ramparts could be ascribed to the mutiny, but Governor du Chambon could not avoid the charge that when faced by insubordinate troops he had not drafted other labor to push repairs at all costs after repeated warnings of invasion. Nor could Engineer Verrier, still at Louisbourg, adequately excuse the vulnerability of the Battery on its chosen site, although he might have argued that even if an enemy succeeded in landing artillery, it was next to impossible for cannon to be brought through intervening marshes to the higher commanding ground. True, the heights could have been defended by redoubts and entrenchments, but that would have demanded more money and more men, and neither had been forthcoming.

So Captain Chassin de Thierry of the Grand Battery gloomily glanced from ready-made breaches toward the Provincial fleet, anchoring in Gabarus Bay to put a landing force ashore, and duly reported his post untenable. Just as disconsolately, crews patted the barrels of the twenty-two big 42-pounders and the two long 18s they were destined never to man against the enemy. For a council of war was about to order the Grand Battery abandoned. Blow it up, De Thierry strongly advised, lest it become a menace in the foe's hands. No, protested Verrier reluctant to see his work demolished, and his feelings were deferred to by the rest. Spiking the guns haphazardly, the garrison withdrew.[3] As Parkman observes, "The hasty abandonment of this important post was not Duchambon's only blunder, but it was the worst of them all."

Yet on the walls of Louisbourg itself, as at the Island Battery, the cannon stood ready, though many embrasures yawned empty. No ordnance to fill them could arrive from France now, and it was too late to repair any of the 33 damaged pieces on hand that might have been made serviceable. No one thought of fishing up a number of guns from ships wrecked in the channel, guns that could be spotted through clear water. That was a bright idea that would occur later to the enemy.

N'importe, Louisbourg's ninety cannon (less those of the Grand Battery) would serve to repulse the heretics. And might not warships of the French Navy, sailing to the rescue, loom over the horizon at any moment? They would deal with the English frigates whose guns meanwhile would prove impotent against those of the Fortress they dared not too closely approach. As for the cannon stowed in the holds of the transports of the *Bostonnais*—reputed to be only a small number—they would be reckoned with in the doubtful possibility that they could be landed through the heavy, rock-studded surf.

Governor du Chambon prepared a spirited reply to the customary summons to surrender that could be expected from the besiegers. His answer, he declaimed, would be given "by the mouths of cannon."

So indeed it would, and answer and contradiction would stage one of history's notable artillery engagements.

Cannonading shattered the calm of the bright morning of April 30, 1745. Warren's frigates hurled broadsides at the Island Battery, whose guns flamed in reply. In Louisbourg alarm bells clanged, belatedly calling in such militia as had not yet reported. Provincial cruisers in Gabarus Bay, warping as close inshore as safety permitted, lobbed ranging shots for fire to cover the imminent landing.

Crews of transports lowered whaleboats for soldiers crowding the decks and readied the Canso-built flatboats that would follow, ferrying guns, munitions, and provisions ashore. A crack amphibious operation was under way, one that well merits comparison to those of two centuries later. Expert seamanship by privateersmen and fishermen and the bravery of green troops would bring it off.

General Pepperrell directed it skillfully. He sent the first boats dashing toward Flat Point in a feint that drew French defenders to that quarter to meet them. Then signal flags fluttered from a yardarm of the command ship, and the leading boats veered away and rowed at top speed for Fresh Water Cove, two miles farther up the Bay, the rest of the flotilla following. The Frenchmen turned and raced to face the new threat, but the shore arc gave them the longer route. Before they could traverse it, the leading boats had thrust into the shallows, and New Englanders, muskets and powderhorns held high, had waded ashore yelping at the iciness of the water, had swarmed up the beach, and taken cover behind rocks and sand dunes.

Louis Morpain, Port Captain of Louisbourg, and young Mesillac du Chambon, the Governor's son, were leading the sortie of eighty men of the garrison who had joined the mere forty already on guard along the shore where the landing was anticipated. Once more on the scroll of the Fortress's fate was written the damning indictment: too little and too late.[4] Repulse of a landing was crucial. It would have justified stripping the garrison of most of its troops for a mobile defense supported by light guns and swivels which could have raked and sunk many of the heavily laden boats. Had the landing failed, Louisbourg would still have stood impregnable.

Foremost in the ranks of the white-coated French emerging from the woods was a tall officer in a black coat. Retired Colonel Poupet de la Boulardie, once of the Regiment of Richelieu, had returned to the wars, having rowed in an open boat from his outlying estate to answer the call of duty. As his sword waved the attack forward, a musket ball dropped him. He struggled up, led on, was hit again. Surely admiration gleamed in the eyes of the rough backwoodsmen who tool him prisoner. In the old soldier *la gloire* still shone at Louisbourg. Morpain, also wounded, was rescued under fire by his faithful Negro slave. The French, leaving sixteen or seventeen dead and wounded from the deadly fire of Indian fighters and deerhunters, beat a retreat to the Fortress.

The Provincials, at the cost of a few wounded, had secured the landing, and before nightfall of the next day two thousand men had been put ashore.

Triumphantly the landing force celebrated. Rum kegs were broached, and there was "Singing and Great Rejoicing." A Boston volunteer recorded that he had seen nothing like it except a Harvard Commencement. But the night—and many thereafter—was sobering and comfortless for men still without blankets or any shelter. Later some sailcloth tents would be rigged and sod huts built, but most of the force slept wet and cold in the open, an ordeal tolerable for the frontiersmen but tough on the townsmen. The sick list began to mount steadily. Even the French, staring from the Louisbourg ramparts toward the encampments of the Provincials where drenched, chilled men were huddling around smoky fires, would feel momentary pity and speak of the enemy as *"les misérables."*

But hardships could not dim the magnificence of the fact that they were ashore on Cape Breton with Louisbourg looming yonder, ripe for the taking. They raided outlying farms still occupied by *habitants* in stubborn disbelief that an invasion was possible. Loot included some hoards of gold coins and cows, sheep, and pigs to slaughter for meat to supplement scanty rations. On view were even examples of that "Pretty French Madammoselle" whom a Boston correspondent had wished for his friend at the front, for a diarist testified to beholding "four Hansom Ladeys" among the farm women. However, no instances of rape in the countryside or later in the captured town are recorded. Discipline and decency seem to have exercised restraints unknown in many an European siege.

Soon after the landing a scouting party pushed inland and made a wide circuit to the rear of Louisbourg and beyond until it came within sight of the Grand or Royal Battery. It was far from a reconnaissance in force since it comprised only thirteen soldiers, but it was vigorously led by Colonel William Vaughan, he who can be said to have sparked the expedition by fiery arguments to Governor Shirley. It was time now to make his words good with deeds, and the Colonel proceeded to perform.

Before him rose several large storehouses, separated by some distance from the Battery but well within range of its guns. Vaughan and his party swooped on them and set them afire. Full of naval supplies—pitch, tar, cordage, and wood—they blazed up in dense black smoke and burned to the ground. Elated at having deprived the enemy of such valuable stores, the scouts retired and got ready to cut and run before a French sortie.

The Battery was strangely silent. There was a lifeless look to it; no smoke from the chimneys, a soldier pointed out. But even the impetuous Vaughan was not going to be drawn into a trap with a rush to storm a fort of that size with thirteen men. He beckoned an expendable one of them, a Cape Cod Indian, gave him two lusty swigs from his silver flash of brandy and told him to take a look inside. The Indian slithered through the brush like a snake and up and over a low-leveled stretch of rampart. He vanished, reappeared, stood up and waved them forward.

Muskets cocked—it might still be a trap—the colonials crawled through embrasures, squeezed past the big spiked 42s, and entered the deserted stronghold. Aside from themselves, the only living things in the fort were a forlorn woman, left behind in the haste of departure, and a puppy. Vaughan called over eighteen-year-old William Tufts of Massachusetts, borrowed his bright red coat, and had it hoisted up the bare flagstaff.

Smoke and the extemporized flag told Louisbourg that the Grand Battery lay in enemy hands. Although nothing else could have been expected, the French, taking tardy second thought, decided to retrieve some of the fort's munitions and spike its guns more thoroughly. Four boatloads of troops raced toward the Grand Battery, a good deal stronger force than its few captors could handle.

Colonel Vaughan had already dispatched a courier to Pepperrell with a report: "May it please your Honour to be informed that by the grace of God and the courage of 13 men, I entered the Royal Battery about 9 o'clock, and am waiting for reinforcement and a flag." Willie Tufts' coat would still do for a flag, but the need for aid was urgent. Meanwhile the little party took position on the beach and regardless of cannonading from Louisbourg and the Island Battery began to pepper the approaching barges with musket balls. Their valiant defense, aided by "shorts" from the batteries that bothered the troops in boats more than the Colonials, staved off the French attempt until the arrival of reinforcements forced its hasty withdrawal in complete repulse.

"The English occupation of the Grand Battery," Parkman declares, "may be called the decisive event of the siege. There seems to be no doubt that the French could have averted the disaster long enough to make it of little help to the invaders. The water-front of the battery was impregnable." In spite of the partial demolition of the land-front, it was still protected by a loopholed wall of masonry, with a ditch ten feet deep and twelve feet wide, and also a covered way and glacis. Swivels still mounted in the rear wall towers could have long and bloodily wrecked attacks. Estimated one of the Provincial generals, "Two hundred men might hold the battery against five thousand without cannon." No cannon had yet been landed nor was it certain they could be.

Major Seth Pomeroy and other gunsmiths, quickly summoned to the Grand Battery, competently drilled out the spiked vents of the 28 42-pounders. By next morning the first of them were in action against the town. They "damaged the houses and made the women cry," a defender wrote, while the *Habitant* bewailed that "The enemy saluted us with our own cannon, and made a terrific fire, smashing everything within range."

There was no lack of ammunition in the magazines for the 42s. If a shortage developed, there was still more of the proper caliber in the holds of the Provincial transports, those balls, fitting none of their own ordnance, which had been stowed in ineffable confidence that they would be used in captured guns.

But Louisbourg's main fortifications, not to mention the Island Battery, remained "a hard nut to crack." The expedition's cannon were not ashore to crack it—if they could be brought into position. How tremendous was that "if," in view of the unsuspected and almost insuperable obstacles in the way, was still to be discovered.

The infantry landing was easy going compared to bringing the artillery ashore. Out on the bay the sun, glittering on metal barrels being hoisted from holds by block and tackle secured to main yardarms, signaled the beginning of a tremendous feat.

> Flatboats were launched from the transports, tossing at anchor. Down into those clumsy craft were lowered cannon, ammuni-

> tion, and stores. Rowers plunged sweeps into waves that dashed over gunwales, threatening swamping, and pulled with all their might. The flatboats, too big and heavily laden to clear rocky barriers offshore and be beached, had to be held in the shallows by force of oar and arm, while soldiers swung overside and waded waistdeep through icy surf, unloading them. Tide and backwash wrenched at them as they struggled ashore, powder casks lifted high on head and shoulders. They risked the rocks to bring the cannon barges closer in and, for every gun landed, lost a boat, pounded to pulpwood. Drenched, exhausted men slept shelterless through cold, foggy nights and each morning limped stiffly back to their task until it was finished.[5]

The mighty effort took a toll in drownings, bodies crushed between plunging flatboats, and limbs broken when straining men slipped on icy rocks. That price, along with the pneumonia and rheumatism that would strike not a few of the soaked and weary toilers, was grimly but willingly paid. Yankee shrewdness, aside from orders, convinced them that the job had to be done. One look at the battlements of Louisbourg had made it plain that only those cannon they were landing would open a way into the Fortress. A surprise assault, harped on by leaders back in Boston —that was so much poppycock. Scouts who had ventured within range of the ramparts had been promptly shelled. What would happen to an attack, unpreceded by a long and powerful bombardment, was unmistakable. It would be wiped out before scaling ladders could be placed against the walls.

Some of the Latinists in the army may have learnedly spouted the quotation that artillery was *ultima ratio regnum*—the last argument of kings. Well, it was the first one for soldiers of the line confronted by the Fortress of Louisbourg.

So with toil and tribulation the weighty bronze and iron pieces with their ammunition and equipment were brought ashore. At long last the 34 guns and mortars stood ranked on their wheeled carriages or platforms along the beach. Men who had accomplished the great feat surveyed them proudly. It did not matter that few knew how to load, lay, and fire a cannon. They would learn. Though some of them would die in the learning, that, too, was a price worth paying. It was these battering pieces which at range of a mile—or better closer—could burst open the gates of Louisbourg.

But the road (or rather the distance, for there was no road) to the ramparts and the flanking Grand Battery was a long, forbidding three miles.

With worried frowns General Pepperrell, the artillery commanders, and others with an eye for the lay of the land scanned the intervening woods and rocky slopes. Beyond them, according to reconnaissance reports, stretched a wide expanse of treeless, treacherous marshes to be passed before gaining Green Hill, the high ground where batteries must be sited. Engineer Verrier's confidence that such barriers insured Louisbourg from attack from the southwest might well be justified.

Nil desperandum Christo duce, declared the expedition's motto, as Chief Chaplain Moody may have reminded his companions while he hefted his axe for the destruction of papist idols. General Pepperrell issued terse orders. Build a road. Get the guns moving.

There were no gun teams; some farm horses might have been found but too few for practical use. As often before and afterwards in artillery annals the recourse was man-draft.

Scores of brawny hands laid hold on long anchor cables attached to gun carriages, and heaved away. Even the soft sand beyond the firm stretch of the beach line slowed them little. Rocks retarded them somewhat lest wheels be broken, but on they rolled at a good pace toward the slopes. Up ahead, axemen and sawyers were busy felling trees and cutting brush. They corduroyed road and bridged gulleys with logs. Over them panting men from Massachusetts, Maine, Connecticut, and New Hampshire dragged the bumping guns upward and onward. Shovelers filled in gravel for a hairpin turn route up a steep rise that skilled engineers could envy.

The shades of artillerymen of yore, who had hoisted and heaved their guns over the Alps, may have watched from Valhalla condescendingly. This was not bad for men without the help of horses, oxen, or windlasses, but after all those were mere foothills they were mounting. But the obstacle that lay ahead presented a challenge worthy of wagon soldiers of any era.

Call it marsh, swamp, or bog—what you will—it was a miry

barrier, a mud-sucking trap. Pioneers, scouting it, sank through its deceptive moss covering to their waists. They waded around in it, cursing bitterly at the freezing slime. The end of the road—so some declared it—only half a mile from the firm ground of Green Hill, but it might as well have been a hundred. Other explorers, persisting, found a channel where the muck was not more than three feet deep. Promptly they proceeded to stake it out and report to Pepperrell and his staff.

Lieutenant Colonel Gridley of the artillery, scowling at the prospect of never bringing his guns into action, shook his head. What if that pathway did offer solid bottom? There were still three feet of mud on top of it. Try to pull wheeled gun carriages through that! They'd be stuck there until hell and the swamp froze over. Then maybe you could chop 'em out.

Sometimes the man and the hour meet fortuitously. This was such a time, and the man was Lieutenant Colonel Nathaniel Meserve of the New Hampshire Regiment, militiaman in his spare time, shipbuilder by trade, and farmer. He may have had to repeat the laconic suggestion he made to the General, because of the rising racket of the Louisbourg guns which had opened fire on the Colonials, forcing many to take cover.

Meserve's word was "stone-boats."

Familiar to all who tilled the rocky fields of New England were the flat sledges, ox- or horse-drawn, on which boulders and stones were loaded when ground was being cleared for crops or pasture, encumbrances that then became New England landmarks—stone walls. Build them long, 16 by 5 feet, said Meserve, and they'd hold the guns and buoy them up on the swamp mud so they could be hauled across.

Lumbermen and handy carpenters built the stone-boats under Meserve's supervision. Other workers rigged and tied breast- and head-straps to the anchor cables, man-harnesses that the artillery called "bricoles." By the time they were ready the hail of shells from the French batteries forced them to wait till nightfall; thereafter all the passage demanded cover of darkness or fog to escape cannonading.

One hundred men harnessed themselves to the long lines, plunged into the swamp and tugged with all their might. A hundred more were needed before the first stone-boat with its burden began to slide across the gripping ooze. A halt to scrape a mass of mud from the sledge's front edge, more heaving—a sudden lurch forward, and rearmost men were overrum by the stone-boat which submerged them and broke legs. Volunteers replaced them, as did relays the exhausted. Gluey slime wrenched off boots or moccasins, then stockings. Barefoot men hauled on. Following loads met increasingly tougher going through the churned-up channel.

"Praise God from whom all blessings flow." Somebody had raised the Doxology. Incongruous though it must have seemed under the circumstances, voices all along the rope lines took it up, heaving in time to the words of the sonorous old hymn. As if by its grace, the stone-boats forged forward. "Onlookers joined in, made the whole marsh resound. Chaplains joined palms and exhorted the men to toil harder. They raised transfigured faces and invoked the Lord's blessing on these toilers in His cause." [6]

Corporals and sergeants pitched in and took their turns on the ropes. So did officers of all grades, ignoring rank's privileges. Even Pepperrell waded into the quagmire that blackened his scarlet coat and lent a hand. Soldiers cheered the amateur general who instinctively knew more about morale than aloof veteran commanders ever learned.

Gun by gun they won through. Incredibly, in the space of four days and nights, that prodigious feat was accomplished.

Up on Green Hill the first redoubt of stone-faced earth, with embrasures for six guns, had been constructed at a one-mile range to the King's Bastion. Its battery was quickly installed while Governor du Chambon and his officers, utterly dumbfounded, watched from the ramparts. A spurt of smoke, a booming report, and an arching cannonball plunged through the roof of a barracks behind the bastion.

That first shot was the crack of doom for Louisbourg.

ten

Battery and Counterbattery

In the chapel of the captured Grand Battery, an expedition chaplain preached a jubilant sermon on the text, "Enter into His gates with thanksgiving, and into His courts with praise." His congregation readily transposed the gates and courts from heavenly ones to Louisbourg's and resolved to enter into them with cannonading.

Four batteries had been planted on Green Hill in a wide semicircle, all well protected by earthworks and fascines. Their guns were 22s and 18s, supplemented by ten of the small mortars called coehorns after the Dutch baron who invented them. Major Pomeroy spoke and wrote of them as "cowhorns," and his version would persist through the long career of the little bronze tubes in American wars.[1] Lobbing their shells in high arc fire over the battlements of Louisbourg, they played their part along with the big, flat trajectory pieces that battered the walls.

A fifth battery was added when several 42s were spared from the Grand Battery. They were brought by the same route as their predecessors, but the passage of those ponderous guns through the quagmire demanded teams of three hundred men. Damage done by their fire was worth the tremendous effort, though the amount of powder they "devoured" caused anxiety as the supply diminished.

Their iron fists knocked clangorously at the gates of Louisbourg. Gradually the batteries were moved forward, closing the range, which was originally a little more than a mile. Gunners carefully concentrated fire on the most strategic points such as the West

Gate and the Dauphin Bastion. Ball and bomb struck with terrific impact as the range shortened, eventually to as close as 250 yards. "The walls were continually being smashed from without and patched up from within. The streets were ploughed from end to end. Many houses were laid in ruins; only one remained intact when the siege was over. The non-combatants, who now exceeded the garrison effectives, were half buried in the smothering casemates underground; and though the fighting men had light, air, and food enough, and though they were losing very few in killed and wounded, they too began to feel that Louisbourg must fall if it was not soon relieved from outside." [2]

Yet to withstand siege was the destiny for which the great Fortress had been stoutly built. Despite gaps opened in the masonry, there were still no breaches practical for assault. Storming them would exact too high a cost. It was as counterbattery to the French guns that the Yankee shooting was most effective, as well as in wrecking the morale of the populace.

Cannon of the defenders continued to thunder in retaliation. Their shells disemboweled or blew off legs of men here and there, but they wrought comparatively little destruction on the thin line of the spaced and protected batteries of the Provincials. Even after those were advanced to within musket range, fire from the parapets picked off only such gunners as rashly exposed themselves. But the spirit of most of the French troops did not seem to flag. Peering through the embrasures, they shouted taunts and raised wine cups in derisive toasts. Women, they called out, could repulse this assault. And yet they failed to take the bold action that could have saved Louisbourg: a sudden sortie in force that might have overrun the enemy batteries, spiked their cannon, and blown up their ammunition. Only once did the French try a sortie, a half-hearted one easily thrown back. General Pepperrell kept in readiness a strong force for just such a contingency.

Little hindered, Yankee crews worked their guns with a will. Their few artillery officers strove mightily to enforce proper procedure and precautions on amateur matrosses, convinced that the science of gunnery consisted of pouring powder—the more the better—down the muzzle, ramming a ball (or better two) on top of it and touching her off. Instructors were greatly aided by three or four master gunners, lent by Commodore Warren from the fleet, and by some from the privateers. An unexpected reinforcement was talented Chaplain Coffin, who turned out to be a born artillerist besides being a thunderer from the pulpit and a drum-beater so skillful that he was known as "the drum ecclesiastick."

"Charge your piece," the officers bellowed and saw to it that only the correct amount of powder was ladled in and tamped with a wad. "Regard your shot," and balls were inspected to be sure they were free of clinging grit. "Put home your shot gently" —violent ramming might set off the charge and blow the rammerstaff and its wielder from the muzzle. Stand clear of recoil and fire. Guns roared and bucked back, their flying quoins dodged. Squat mortars rocked on their beds.

"Search your piece," came the next order. Matrosses peered down murky barrels as soon as they were clear of smoke, looking for burning powder particles or smoldering wads that must be drawn out with the worm. Rammerstaffs were reversed, and their wetted sponge ends swabbed and cooled bores. Load again, serving the vent. On that touchhole, near the breech where the powder train for firing was laid, a matross pressed a thumb, protected by a leather shield from hot metal. Otherwise an inrush of air from loading might kindle a lingering spark and cause a premature explosion with the result already described. If that cannoneer neglected to stop the vent, the rammerstaff man was privileged to rap him smartly on the noggin to recall him to his duty.

"It is silly to run danger without reason," the manual advised. Furthermore, it could be fatal, as the tyros discovered. Records of the siege are too often punctuated by such diary entries as: "I am Inform'd that we have Lost five men at our batteries This day. One was Kill'd by the breaking of a Cannon Being Carried by a Large Piece of it (about 400 Weight) About Eight rods and then fell and Ground him to Pieces." [3] "The thirteenth two of them [mortars] burst, owing to their not being sound . . . The damage received at this Battery [one of those on Green Hill] was breaking the Trunion of one of the Coehorns and bursting another; six men wounded of whom one died, by the bursting of two 22:lb Cannon . . . The 25th of May the thirteen Inch Mortar was burst and a Bombardier wounded, occasioned by some flaw in the Shell which broke in the Mortar." [4] One of the big 42s and members of its crew suffered the same fate. Seven men were killed when two barrels of powder were ignited.

Experienced artillerymen were spread too thin to prevent repeated accidents. They warned in vain against deliberate overcharging and carelessness. Crews, delighting in watching the soaring parabolas and detonation of "bums" as the diarists described them, crammed in more powder and shot to make the next round an even more magnificent display. Copious draughts of rum sometimes fired enthusiasm even higher, and General Pepperrell complained, "We are in great want of good gunners that have a disposition to be sober in daytime." The dreadful explosion of a piece and slaughter by rending metal served as a lesson to survivors of its crew but not to rash matrosses in the next battery. No artilleryman of Protestant New England would have implored the intercession of Saint Barbara, patron of gunners, against such disasters. It was left to the Roman Catholics of Louisbourg to pray to the martyred maiden, whose medallion they wore, to avert sudden death from thundering lightning, divine or man-made.[5] Nor were their petitions always answered, for several French pieces also burst, killing members of their crews.[6] Militiamen, drafted to serve the guns, were as ignorant as their counterparts beyond the walls.

Yet the New England novices maintained a hot and telling cannonade, the guns seldom silent except when they had to be "refreshed"—allowed to cool. Intendant Bigot paid rueful tribute to the destructive fire on the fortress. "The enemy established their batteries to such effect that they soon destroyed the greater part of the town, broke the right flank of the King's Bastion, ruined the Dauphin Battery with its spur, and made a breach at the Port Dauphine, the neighboring wall, and the sort of redan adjacent." Governor du Chambon with dismay saw the guns on the right flank of the King's Bastion silenced by enemy bombardment, their embrasures shattered to such an extent that they could not be manned. No sooner had repairs been made than the battlements were again dismantled. The wall of the quay was so riddled that it no longer offered shelter. Civilian morale sank lower and lower as people fled from cannonballs with burning fuses rolling through the streets. Only in the stifling casemates was there any safety. Three gentlemen who ventured to sit down to dinner in the home of one of them were blown to bits by a shell that plunged through the roof.

Cannonading by the French batteries diminished as pieces were knocked out and from the need to conserve ammunition. Colonial artillerymen noticed that an increasing number of enemy shells were "duds"; examined, they were found to be filled with what seemed to be bran or sawdust.

The invaders' powder supply was also running dangerously low. At the Grand Battery, rate of fire had to be reduced from one salvo every fifteen minutes to one per hour. Urgent appeals for more powder had been dispatched to Boston. Unless it arrived soon, the guns would go out of action. Free of bombardment, Louisbourg could maintain its defiance until the waning season brought the salvation of storms before which the expedition would have to beat an inglorious retreat.

Fortuna or providence once more smiled on the undertaking which skeptics had declared a mad scheme.

Bellied topsails jutted over the horizon on May 20, 1745. The wind wafted the sound of distant gunfire. A Colonial privateer, one sail riddled and drooping, crowded on all the rest of her canvas an raced back toward Cape Breton in flight before the newcomer. The British warship *Mermaid*, dashing forward in challenge, quickly came about and, stern guns blazing, joined the privateer's retreat. It was not for a forty-gun frigate to dare engage a ship of the line, the towering three-decker yonder flying the white flag of France, its golden *fleur-de-lis* gleaming in the sunlight.

Help for beleaguered Louisbourg had at last arrived from France—the *Vigilant*, 64 guns, Captain Alexandre Boisdescourt, Marquis de la Maisonfort, commanding. She carried a reinforcement of three hundred soldiers and a precious cargo for Louisbourg—one thousand barrels of powder, twenty bronze cannon, and four months' provisions. Because the Ministry believed that the harbor was not yet blockaded, or, if it were, that *Vigilant* could fight her way through, she had been allowed to sail alone. She might have made port had not her captain succumbed to the temptation to accept the impudent *Mermaid*'s challenge to follow and sink her. Craftily the frigate led her pursuer toward the rest of the British fleet.

From the *Superbe,* Commodore Warren signaled *Launceton, Eltham,* and the Provincial cruisers to clear for action. Here was opportunity to redeem the oversight which had allowed an enemy sloop to slip past his blockade into the harbor [7]—to redeem it a hundredfold—and success was imperative. It was as true then as when Nelson would signal it at Trafalgar that England expected every man to do his duty. In the Royal Navy punishment for dereliction of duty was equally rigorous for all ratings and ranks from seaman to admiral, whether or not the charge was completely sustained. Admiral Thomas Mathews had been dismissed from the service in 1744 for allowing a Spanish fleet to escape. In 1757 Admiral John Byng would be condemned by a court-martial and executed by a firing squad on the accusation that he had failed to do his utmost in battle against the French.

Unquestionably Peter Warren, doughty fighter that he was, did his utmost. Under a favoring breeze his frigates and the cruisers closed in, raking the *Vigilant* from both quarters and fore and aft. Captain Maisonfort fought his ship valiantly. Laden heavily with supplies, she lay so low in the water that her third gun tier could not be used, but broadsides blazed from the upper tiers and inflicted considerable damage until concentrated fire from the enemy brought down her foremast with a grinding crash. Only then, unworkable and with sixty of her crew killed or wounded, were her colors lowered in surrender.

The shattered vessel was towed triumphantly into Gabarus Bay and anchored. Provincial prize crews were put aboard to repair her. Another warship was added to the fleet ready to face any further attempt by the French Navy to relieve Louisbourg. None would be made. The *Vigilant* was continental France's last gesture—again too little and too late—to save her New World fortress from its impending fate.[8]

It was not salvation for Louisbourg but destruction the *Vigilant* had brought. Keg after keg of powder was hoisted from her hold and lowered into clustering barges. Now Warren could spare the precious stuff for which Pepperrell had been begging. Gladly manned sweeps drove the barges to shore, and their cargo was hurried to the waiting artillery. Faster and more furiously the batteries bombarded Louisbourg.

Another of the frequent councils of war was held by Warren and Pepperrell following the capture of the *Vigilant*. It was a tribute to both commanders that they got on well. A toplofty member of the Senior Service might well have adopted an arrogant attitude toward a Provincial militiaman, who in turn could have damned him heartily and asked whose men were bearing the brunt of the siege and taking the losses. Instead, consideration and cooperation prevailed.

Warren was worried and told Pepperrell so emphatically. The *Vigilant* might have been the forerunner of a strong French squadron, and naval aid from Quebec might also be on the way. Even if the long spell of fair weather continued, the British fleet would have difficulty maintaining a tight blockade. The season was wearing on. Nothing could be answered for in stormy seas, and the prospect of riding them was no more appealing to the frigates than wintering in siege lines before Louisbourg would be to the troops. Press the storming of the fortress, Warren urged, or the enterprise must be abandoned.

Deferentially and calmly, the General ticked off his own difficulties.

Increasing sickness had reduced his army to 2,100 effectives. Many men were shoeless and all were ragged.

It had been necessary to send out more patrols of the interior. Hostile Indians had been appearing in greater force and had scalped some of the scouts. They might well be the vanguard of the band of the Frenchman Marin, reported to have raised his siege of Annapolis and to be marching to the rescue of Louisbourg.

While the new supply of powder would permit intensive bombardment, there was no greater certainty that breaches wide enough for assault would be opened. Only every tenth soldier had a bayonet. Scaling ladders brought from Boston were ten feet too short to reach the top of the ramparts.

Unsurprisingly, the council adjourned with the resolution: "Advised, that inasmuch as there appears a great Dissatisfaction in many of the officers and Soldiers at the designed attack of the Town by Storm this Night, the said attack is deferred for the present."

That could not solve the expedition's dilemma. If the town's fortifications were still deemed impregnable, an all-out assault must be made in another quarter and it must not fail.

eleven

Assault on an Island

The powerful Island Battery stood inviolate athwart the harbor entrance on its rocky perch, 150 yards long and about a third as wide. Naval gunfire had silenced none of the thirty heavy cannon peering out of its embrasures. The magazine, hewn deep in stone, still held sufficient powder and shot for them and a number of smaller pieces, including four of medium size emplaced by Captain d'Aillebout behind fascines to guard the only landing place against invasion across the channel from Lighthouse Point. Here, in Louisbourg's last outpost since the capture of the Grand Battery, lay the key that could unlock a door to the great Fortress itself.

So insisted Commodore Warren, admitting that the Royal Navy had been unable to pound the Island Battery into submission. Give him access to the spacious harbor with its ample maneuvering space, he declared, and the fleet would bombard the full length of the town's sea defenses. Louisbourg, then caught between two fires—his broadsides and the salvos of the Provincial batteries on the land side—could not long resist. And he added that while the Island Battery held open the harbor gate there was always the chance that French warships might slip in as the *Vigilant* might well have done.

Troops had to storm the Island Battery. Clearly it was the task of the army, which had summarily declined to assault the mainland fortifications. General Pepperrell agreed to make the attempt.

Fiery Colonel Vaughan was eager to lead the enterprise and

add a second trophy to his seizure of the Grand Battery. He commenced to assemble an assault force, whaleboats, hand grenades, pistols, and scaling ladders. Four hundred men stepped forward. But as volunteers they ruggedly asserted their independence and refused Vaughan as their commander, nor would they accept Colonel John Bradstreet, a veteran who had served as a British officer. They demanded the right to elect their own officers, a custom that would persist into the American Civil War and would too often, coupling popularity and inefficiency, contribute to disasters like the one that was about to take place.

On May 26, storm troops for the perilous mission mustered at the Grand Battery. Noisy, disorderly, and some riotously tipsy, they aroused grave misgivings. General Samuel Waldo remarked to Pepperrell, "I doubt whether straggling fellows, three, four, or seven out of a company, ought to go on such service." But neither general asserted his authority and interfered.

The attack, which had to be made under cover of a dark night, was delayed by several evenings of bright moonlight and northern lights. The night of the 26th was ideally black, though the wind was rising, and the flotilla of heavily laden boats, paddles instead of oars being used for greater quietness, shoved off a few hours before twelve o'clock. One hundred fifty men from Colonel Gorham's regiment, already on Lighthouse Point, were to join the storming force.[1]

The volunteers made the Point but had to drag their boats three miles overland to reach the launching place opposite the island's only feasible landing point. There they kept their rendezvous with their reinforcements. Rum flasks gurgled, as weary men refreshed themselves and imbibed "Dutch courage." Gorham rushed around, fiercely demanding silence. His efforts and the roar of heavy surf muffled the noise of loading boats and the crossing of the channel. No sign of alarm was apparent on the ramparts looming faintly ahead through the darkness. One hundred fifty men from the vanguard landed undetected in the narrow cove. No pickets were posted, and the fascine guns were unmanned. The stormers ran forward and planted twelve scaling ladders against the walls. The Island Battery was about to be taken by surprise.

Then a soldier with a bellyful of rum raised three loud, hearty, and triumphant cheers. *"L'ennemy en debarquant commença à crier* hourrah *par trois fois,"* as Du Chambon's official report would put it.[2] Those drunken shouts proved a disastrous betrayal of an undertaking on the verge of success. A few more minutes, and the Provincials, swarming up the ladders, would have been at the throats of crews asleep around their guns. Panic would surely have spread through the garrison, shocked by the sudden apparition of the foe within the defenses, and surrender would have swiftly followed. Now a ruinous debacle was at hand.

The flash of an alerted sentry's musket stabbed the night. Others echoed it with a crackling fusillade. Steel struck tinder, and flaming, oil-soaked linstocks swooped down on the powder trains of loaded cannon. Swivels poured murderous charges of mangling langrage down into assailants massed below. Larger pieces chimed in with thundering detonations. Gunfire raked packed boats crowding in to land. Shrieks and howls of agony pierced the racket of cannonade and musketry.

Caught in the open, brave men stood and fought it out for two and a half hours with defenders behind parapets. Some made supremely valiant but vain attempts to scale the ladders toward bayonets poised above. Daylight, stressing the hopelessness of the assault, saw survivors streaming back to the boats. There were enough not shattered or sunk for about half the force to escape. One hundred eighty-nine were killed in battle, drowned, or made prisoners. Numbers of the wounded were brought off.

Louisbourg jubilantly celebrated its greatest coup of the siege. Surely so long as the Island Battery held out there was hope, with succor from France in prospect. Indeed such promise of relief had arrived by a small vessel that had slipped into the harbor with word of a strong squadron sailing from Brest to the rescue.

As for the Provincial army, it was plunged into the depths of despair by the disaster at the Island Battery. The bloody repulse of the surprise assault, so close to success when a sot ruined it, sickened the most stouthearted. The toll of the dead increased as badly wounded men, brought back in the boats, succumbed. Not a few of those who survived surgery were through with the war, as attested by heaps of amputated arms and legs. Sight of them and of scenes in the crude field hospitals sapped the resolution of beholders. "The wounded lay ranged in double rows on piles of loose straw. Some moaned steadily, others, to stifle their agony, chewed leather straps or blocks of soft pine."[3] All along the front artillerymen slackened fire, the New Englanders from lack of spirit, the French to conserve powder.

Signs of friction between Warren and the conciliatory Pepperrell began to appear. In Boston, Governor Shirley, scanning reports, was ready to override his General and turn full command over to the British Commodore. The latter, made aware of the way the wind was blowing, took advantage of it by evolving a plan that would in fact assure him complete leadership. His fleet, he told Pepperrell, was prepared to take 1,600 troops aboard, run the gantlet of the Island Battery, sail into the harbor, and reduce Louisbourg with an all-out amphibious operation.

Pepperrell offered six hundred men. Courteously but firmly he refused more, since he had only 2,100 fit for duty. On second thought, Warren abandoned his plan, realizing that even if he succeeded in forcing an entrance, his ships might be bottled up by the unsilenced Island Battery and, exposed to fire from the ramparts of the main fortress, be sunk one by one with no chance of escape. An inland raid by the enemy now convinced him that Pepperrell was wise in his opposition to great impairment of his remaining strength. A Colonial scouting party of twenty was waylaid by twice that number of Indians under French leadership. Most of the English were shot down or made prisoner. Those who had surrendered on promise of quarter were slaughtered in cold blood or fiendishly tortured to death.

Warren was thus prompted to supplant his half-baked scheme with a clever stratagem. To prove how well the British treated their captives, in contrast to the French, he persuaded his prisoner, Captain Maisonfort of the *Vigilant*, to write the following letter to the Governor of Louisbourg.

"It is well that you should be informed that the Captains and officers of this squadron treat us, not as their prisoner, but as their good friends, and take particular pains that my officers and crew should want for nothing; therefore it seems just to me to treat them in like manner, and to punish those who do otherwise and offer any insult to the prisoners that may fall into your hands."

Du Chambon replied that Indians were responsible for the recent outrage and that he would take care to curb them in the future. But the letter had achieved still more. The officer who delivered it was fluent in French but pretended to have no knowledge of the language. Consequently the Governor's staff spoke freely before him. They had not known that the captured ship was the *Vigilant,* on which great reliance had been placed, and they openly expressed their deep discouragement. Thus the British envoy was able to report that Louisbourg's morale had been considerably affected.

However, the gain was offset by the threat of a new danger of hitherto unsuspected imminence. Troops on Lighthouse Point captured an Acadian schooner, driven ashore in an attempt to reach Louisbourg. Her crew escaped but aboard was found a dispatch to Governor du Chambon from Lieutenant Colonel Marin. That frontier soldier from Quebec stated that he had turned aside from his siege of Annapolis Royal and was marching on the Gut of Canso with 1,300 men, his own and a strong contingent of Indian allies. Let the Governor at once forward as many small craft as possible to ferry him over the Strait, and he would thrust across Cape Breton Island to the relief of the Fortress.

Consternation reigned in Pepperrell's headquarters. Here was a formidable army under a tough commander poised to take the depleted Colonials' siege lines in the rear. Though the intercepted dispatch assured that no boats would be sent from Louisbourg, Marin could manage the crossing with canoes and whaleboats. He might well be able to take by surprise or elude a Provincial warship, that was guarding a transport full of prisoners of war in Canso harbor, or that vessel might already have sailed for Boston, clearing the way for him. Of little account was the two-company garrison of invalids in the blockhouse. Any sally by it would be overwhelmed by greatly superior numbers.

Under Pepperrell's urgent orders a cruiser and a Rhode Island brig made all sail for Canso. Luckily they found the warship still there, along with two small brigs. The five vessels, taking the garrison aboard, scoured the strait for the enemy and found him at the Passe du Fronsac, his crossing already begun. A swarm of canoes and boats dotted the waters; more were being launched by men emerging from the forest.

Lack of wind and an adverse tide hampered the attempts of the warships to close in. Two of them collided, their rigging fouling, but finally cleared. Slowly the fleet bore down, and broadsides flamed. As the range closed, swivels raked the small craft with blasts of langrage. Whaleboats replied with their own swivels and musketry. For a time the fight raged hotly, but the result could not long remain in doubt. Flotsam of French and Indian bodies and debris covered the bloody water of the channel.

The garrison convalescents and sailors landed. Reinforced by bands of friendly Indians, they drove forward in attack, fire of ships' guns paving the way, on the enemy who had not embarked. Privateers and brigs warped in close to shore and redoubled their bombardment. Marin, who had no artillery with him, could not reply, but his veterans held staunchly until at last they broke, and fugitives, harried by pursuit, scattered through the wilderness.

It had been a near thing, that last attempt to relieve Louisbourg. A few hours more, and the crossing would have been completed, and Marin's force loose on Cape Breton Island. Pepperrell's army, still dwindling from sickness, would have faced it gallantly. Erection of palisades along rear lines had been commenced. Yet a sortie from Louisbourg—and who can doubt a strong one would have been made on such an opportunity—would have gripped the Provincials in pincers. The British Navy could have furnished no help other than landing parties. That day at the Gut of Canso had indeed seen the fate of the expedition trembling in the balance.

But the Fortress of Louisbourg still stood unstormed, and so would stand as long as the Island Battery defended its harbor entrance.

Once more the guns were called on. Having wrought considerable havoc on the town ramparts, their fire, concentrated on the limited area of the Island Battery, could be expected to be devastating. The problem was to land and emplace them on Lighthouse Point, and, in ratio, it posed as severe difficulties as

Photo courtesy the National Maritime Museum, Greenwich

Sir Peter Warren, commander of the British fleet at Louisbourg, 1745. Portrait by Thomas Hudson.

Photo courtesy National Portrait Gallery, London

William Pitt the Elder, Earl of Chatham, Prime Minister of Great Britain when Louisbourg was captured for the second time. Portrait by William Houre.

Lord Jeffrey Amherst, commander of the British Army at Louisbourg, 1758. From a mezzotint by Sir Joshua Reynolds in the Public Archives of Canada.

Photo courtesy the National Portrait Gallery, London

Edward Boscawen, Admiral of the British fleet at Louisbourg in 1758. Studio of Sir Joshua Reynolds.

Public Archives of Canada

Maj. Gen. James Wolfe who, as a brigadier, led the assault on Louisbourg in 1758. Engraving from a portrait by H. Smyth.

Model of the Fortress of Louisbourg, by Miss Katharine McLennan, Honorary Curator of the Louisbourg Museum, where the model is displayed.

Courtesy Louisbourg Museum

courtesy Public Archives of Canada

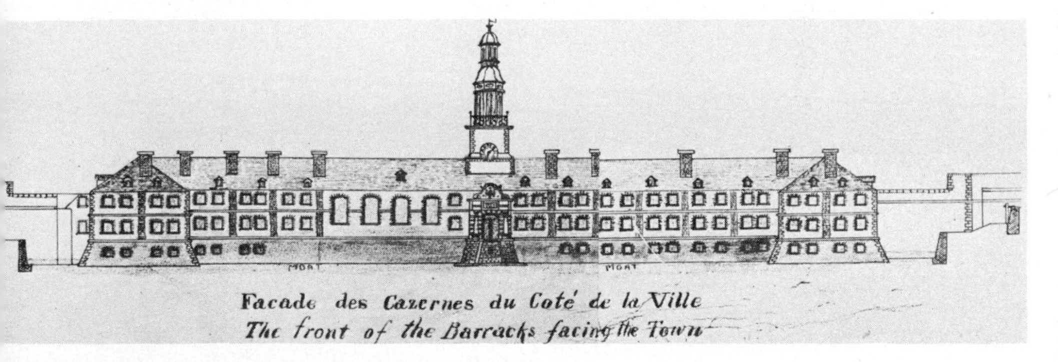

Barracks, chapel and Governor's residence in the King's Bastion. From an undated plan in the *Bibliothèque Nationale,* Paris.

Photo courtesy Library of Congress

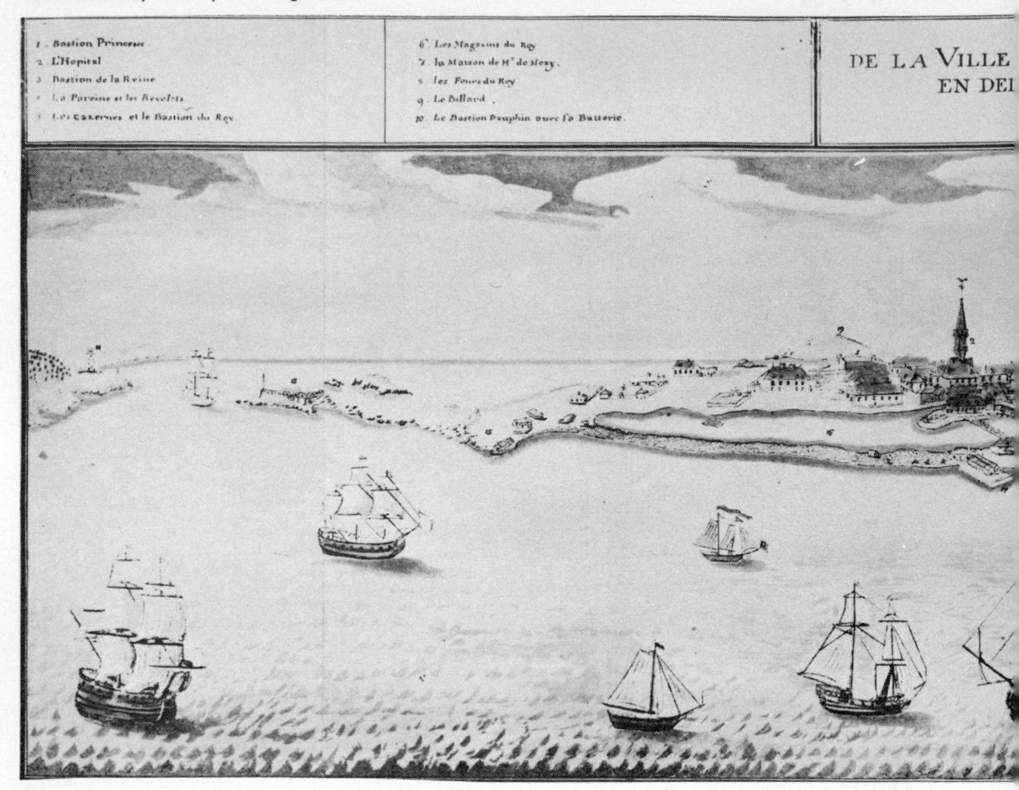

View of Louisbourg from the harbor, by Verrier.

Courtesy New York Historical Society, New York City

Flag carried by the New Englanders at the first siege of Louisbourg.

Photo courtesy *Librarie Hachette*

Louis XV, King of France. Pastel by Quentin de La Tour, in the Louvre.

Photo courtesy Alinari

Madame de Pompadour, mistress of Louis XV. Portrait by François Hubert Drouais, in the *Musée Condé*

Photo courtesy the Essex Institute, Salem, Mass.

Lt. Gen. Sir William Pepperrell, commander of the

An imaginative contemporary German print of the siege, July 26, 1758.

Engraving courtesy National Maritime Museum, Greenwich

The cutting out of the *Prudent* and *Bienfaisant* at Louisbourg, July 26, 1758.

Courtesy Library of Congress

British coins commemorating the capture of Louisbourg.

Photo courtesy Public Archives of Canada

Remains of casemates inside the King's Bastion in which women and children were sheltered during the siege of 1758.

ourtesy the Mabel Brady Garvan Collection, Yale University Art Gallery

The original legend reads: "A View of the Landing the New England Forces in y^e^ Expedition against Cape Breton, 1745. When after a Siege of 40 days the Town and Fortress of LOUISBOURG and the important Territories thereto belonging were recover'd to the British Empire. The brave & Active Commodore Warren, since made Knight of the Bath & Vice Admiral of ye While commanded the British Squadron in this glorious Expedition. The Hon. Willm Pepperell Esq. (since Knighted) went a Voluntier & Commanded the New England Men who bravely offer'd their service and went as private Soldiers in this hazardous but very glorious Enterprize." Engraved by Brooks after Stevens.

From an engraving in the Public Archives of Canada

View of Louisbourg taken near the light house while the city was besieged in 1758. Drawn on the spot by Captain Ince.

The legend on this British print of 1755 reads: "1 Britannia attending to the complaints of her injur'd. Americans receives them into her protection. 2 Neptune & Mars unite in their defence. 3 The British Lion keeping his dominions under his paw, safe from invaders. 4 The British Arms eclipsing those of France. 5 A British Sailor pointing to the eclipse, & leering at a French Politician trapt by his own Schemes. 6 An English Saylor encouraged by a Soldier, Squeezes the Gallic Cock by the throat, & makes him disgorge the French usurpations in America. 7 A French Political Schemer beholds the operation with grief and Confusion. 8 The English Rose erect, the French Lilly drooping. 9 A Gang of brave Saylors exulting at the Starving French coopt up. 10 The French overset at the fall of Niagara. 11 Cromwells device. 12 A Monument due to real Merit."

Photo courtesy Library of Congress

Sea and land operations during the siege, July 1758.

the feat accomplished in dragging them across the mainland marshes.

Lieutenant Colonel Gridley took charge. Second in command of the artillery train, he was also an engineer. (His panoramic drawing of Louisbourg is first-rate military art.) That able officer was then in full vigor; 27 years later at Bunker Hill he would not acquit himself as well. Gridley oversaw the transport of guns and the expedition's heaviest mortars to the Point. Panting, sweating men hoisted them up a steep cliff and hauled them a mile and a quarter to prepared positions.

A windfall, or rather a seafall, strongly reinforced the available cannon. "A keen-eyed artilleryman, peering down into the waters at low tide, spotted the dark bulk of ten heavy pieces, half buried in the sand. Sliding overboard when a ship was careened for barnacle scraping, the guns had lain there for ten years. All the French governors had known their location, but none had taken the trouble to fish them out. Elated New Englanders roped them and sent them up the cliff to join the rest of the armament."[4] Their verdigrised bronze tubes were still perfectly serviceable. Placed on platforms, they joined the bombardment of the Island Battery. Of the salvaged French guns the *Habitant* could have made the same lament he made for the powder captured with the *Vigilant:* "We were victims devoted to appease the wrath of Heaven, which turned our own arms into weapons for our enemies."

The lighthouse, salvation of many a ship, towered above the Provincial batteries around it. As they opened fire, the beacon became a token of destruction for the stronghold across the channel. Most of the gun crews by that time had become practiced artillerymen. Laying with precision, they pounded their target, whose retaliation was ineffective on their scattered and concealed positions. The fire of the New England mortars was particularly deadly. Their bombs soared high and swooped down to dismount Captain d'Aillebout's cannon and explode shatteringly in casemates. French soldiers were observed to flee and fling themselves into the sea to escape the frightful blasts of hurtling iron.

British naval gunners watched admiringly from their ships until they were called to stations to scoop in several French ships laden with food, molasses, and rum. In an attempt to supply

Louisbourg, they had made an untimely entrance in the last act of the drama.

Yankee cannoneers on the Point took full advantage of their higher elevation, and the range was only half a mile. The accuracy of their shooting steadily increased. In one day seventeen out of nineteen bombs from "The Big Mortar," king of the 13-inchers, plunged on the little fort. And that day, June 15, was the last for the Island Battery, for one of the shells penetrated and exploded in the magazine, which blew up with a tremendous roar.

Captain d'Aillebout, who had long and valiantly defended his post, could not but acknowledge that it was now completely untenable. Unable to lower his colors—they had been shot away—he displayed the white flag of surrender. Commodore Warren's marines landed and occupied the ruined fort.

The key was turned, the door flung wide. The fleet, cleared for action, prepared to file through into the harbor, while Pepperrell's guns boomed, continuing a furious cannonade on the Citadel of Louisbourg.

twelve

"And Great Was the Fall Thereof"

Inland the foremost Yankee battery, pushed forward to within 250 yards of Louisbourg's walls, kept pounding away. Others constantly closed the range. "They worked forward their batteries in a manner that almost savored of bravado, and which, as in the strife of line against column of later days, startled their machine-trained opponents." [1] The field guns, along with those of the Grand Battery, girded the bastions of the great Fortress with a ring of smoke and flame. Gaps yawned in the masonry of the Citadel and the redoubts. Debris heaped higher and higher, filling the moat. Only at night did the defenders dare attempt repairs. French cannon, struck by shells, reared muzzles skyward above shattered carriages. In the barrels of others, fired too long and too fast, appeared jagged, livid cracks, instant preludes to explosions that destroyed them and their crews. Six pieces, defending the West Gate, were silenced.

"Our Bumaneer held On, casting his Bums into the city," a diarist recorded. Gridley's artillerymen were using hot shot by then, balls heated to a red glow, grasped by tongs, and dropped down mortar muzzles onto powder charges. One of the besiegers wrote home indignantly that the practice made "the war much more terrible in North America than otherwise it would have been," though the houses were not close enough together for "this piece of humane malice [*sic*]" to have much effect. Hammers rang in the Provincial camps, where smiths were breaking up scrap iron into langrage, charges to sweep streets once assault had burst through the breaches; also manacles were being confidently wrought at the forges for prisoners.[2]

More French civilians left the doubtful shelter of houses, only one of which remained unhit, to take refuge in the stifling, crowded casemates. Fatigue, loss of sleep, and illness sapped the strength of the besieged. Another Swiss deserter reported powder low and provisions sufficient for no more than one month.

It was the powder shortage [3] and vanishing hope of relief that drove the inhabitants of Louisbourg to despair, not casualties, which were relatively light, nor the rigors of the siege.

"We could have borne all this," Intendant Bigot wrote, "but the scarcity of powder, the loss of the *Vigilant*, the presence of the squadron, and the absence of any news from Marin, who had been ordered to join us with his Canadians and Indians, spread terror among troops and inhabitants. The townspeople said they did not want to be put to the sword and were not strong enough to resist a general assault."

From the walls defenders saw large quantities of fascines being carried to the foot of the glacis to fill the ditch. Scouts reported that more than one thousand scaling ladders were lying ready behind the nearest hill. None could doubt that a concerted attack by land and sea was imminent.

Warren and Pepperrell were agreed that the time was ripe, and their plans were ready. The Commodore, hoisting a Dutch flag beneath his pennant as a signal, was to sail into the harbor with his fleet, which had increased to eleven ships, besides the Provincial cruisers. In addition to the captured *Vigilant*, the flotilla had been augmented by *Princess Mary*, *Hector*, *Chester*, *Canterbury*, *Sunderland*, and *Lark*, with a total armament of 210 guns. Bombardment of the town would be followed by a naval landing force. The General, answering the naval signal with three columns of smoke, would simultaneously advance to storm the city, drums beating and colors flying. For that assault a cannonade, with every Yankee gun firing at top speed, would open the way. Wrote an artillery officer commanding the most advanced battery, "By 12 o'clock we had got all our platforms laid, embrazures mended, guns in order, shot in place, cartridges ready, dined, gunners quartered, matches lighted to return their last favours."

Then, in the lull before the storm, drums rolled on the Louisbourg parapets on June 15. The drummer boys were beating the parley. Provincial officers passed word to hold fire along the lines. A party of Frenchmen under a flag of truce emerged, was met by the commander of the foremost battery, and was promptly conducted to headquarters. Stirring news spread among the besiegers. Governor du Chambon was asking the suspension of hostilities, pending the drawing up of articles of capitulation.

Surrender! It seemed almost incredible, offered after only 46 days of siege, so strong was the legend of the impregnability of Louisbourg.

Pepperrell and Warren, ashore for council on the impending assault, received the envoys and told them they had come only just in time, since a general attack was about to be delivered. It would be withheld, they promised, until detailed proposals were proffered, but those must arrive by eight o'clock the following morning. Meanwhile a cease-fire would be observed.

At the stipulated time Du Chambon's terms of surrender were presented but summarily rejected with an adamant demand for revision. Make it or suffer the consequences was the unveiled threat the envoys carried back. Du Chambon, believing he had no other choice, sadly complied.

His decision "touched the very life of my soul," he would avow in his report to the ministers of the King. A translation into English of that remarkable document is given in full in Appendix C. Like the letter of the *Habitant*, previously quoted, it is a first-hand account of the siege from beginning to end in the form of an attempt by the responsible official to explain his loss of a strong and vital fortress "which had been most costly to the King." The Governor glossed over his disregard of warnings and his failure to make adequate preparations, for which the blame, as can be read between the lines, was by no means all his own. The weak sortie to repulse the original landings is minimized as much as the defense of the Island Battery is extolled. But there is no exaggeration in Du Chambon's description of the state to which the fortifications of Louisbourg had been reduced by the enemy's cannonading, with the consequent inevitability of surrender. By asking for terms on the eve of a general attack that could not have been resisted, the Governor saved lives of soldiers and civilians that would have been vainly lost. A glorious last stand could have offered little redemption from the ruin of his career. His revised terms were sent at the stipulated hour.

With stern finality, firm in the assurance of victory, Pepperrell and Warren sent the Governor their answer.

Camp before Louisbourg, June 16th, 1745.

Sir,

We have before us yours of this date, together with the several articles of capitulation on which you have proposed to surrender the town and fortifications of Louisbourg, with the territories adjacent under your government to his Britannic majesty's obedience, to be delivered up to his said majesty's forces now besieging said place under our command.

Which articles we can by no means concede to, but as we are desirous to treat you in a generous manner we do again make you an offer of the terms of surrender proposed by us in our summons sent you 7th of May last, and do further consent to allow and promise you the following articles, Viz:—

First. That if your vessels shall be found insufficient for the transportation of your persons and proposed effects to France, we will provide such a farther number of vessels as may be sufficient for that purpose, also any provisions necessary for the voyage that you cannot furnish yourselves with.

Secondly. That all commissioned officers belonging to the garrison, and the inhabitants of the town, may remain in their houses with their families and enjoy the free exercise of their religion, and no person shall be suffered to molest or misuse any of them till such time as they can conveniently be transported to France.

Thirdly. That the non-commissioned officers and soldiers shall, immediately upon the surrender of the town and fortresses, be put on board some of his Britannic majesty's ships till they can also be transported to France.

Fourthly. That all your sick and wounded shall be taken tender care of in the same manner with our own.

Fifthly. That the commander in chief now in the garrison shall have liberty to send off two covered wagons, to be inspected only by one officer of ours, that no warlike stores may be contained therein.

Sixthly. That if there are any persons in the town or garrison which you shall desire may not be seen by us, they shall be permitted to go off masked.

The above we do consent to and promise upon your compliance with the following conditions.

First. That the said surrender and due performance of every part of the aforesaid premises be made and completed as soon as possible.

Secondly. That as a security for the punctual performance of the same, the island battery, or one of the batteries of the town, shall be delivered, with all the artillery and warlike stores thereunto belonging, into the possession of his Britannic majesty's troops before six of the clock this afternoon.

Thirdly. That his Britannic majesty's ships of war, now lying before the port, shall be permitted to enter the harbour of Louisbourg without any molestation, as soon after six of the clock this afternoon as the commander in chief of said ships shall think fit.

Fourthly. That none of the officers, soldiers, or inhabitants of Louisbourg, who are subjects of the French king, shall take up arms against his Britannic majesty nor any of his allies, until after the expiration of the full term of twelve months from this time.

Fifthly. That all subjects of the Britannic majesty who are now prisoners with you, shall be immediately delivered up to us.

In case of your non-compliance with these conditions we decline any farther treaty with you and shall decide the matter with our arms.

P. Warren, W. Pepperrell

Salvaging a shred of pride, Louisbourg's Governor put forward only one condition of acceptance: that his troops be allowed to march out of the fortress with their arms and colors.

One can picture the tolerant smiles of the navy and army commanders perusing that condition. It provided for no more than a brief display of martial panoply that could not cloak the bald fact of utter defeat. Warren remarked that "the uncertainty of our affairs, that depend much on wind and weather, makes it necessary not to stick at trifles." Let a last empty gesture be granted the French.

Both sides signed the articles on June 17. In the surrendered Fortress the *Habitant* penned a plaintive paragraph in his threnody.

"Would it be possible that we should sustain so great a reverse under the invincible Louis XV, and that, while so valiant a Monarch make the Powers who dare oppose him tremble, he allows his subjects in the colonies to be exposed to the violence of his enemies, and to be the only ones who succumb to the fortunes of war? Are we less his subjects?"

The British fleet and Provincial cruisers sailed into the harbor in stately processional, "which made a beautiful appearance." The ragged troops of the Colonies formed up and entered the Fortress by the Queen's Gate to triumphant music, an event duly recorded by a diarist. "When our Army Marcht to ye City, the Colours were flying, the Drums Beating, Trumpets Sounding, Flutes and Vials Playing. Col. Bradstreet att ye Head of the Army. The Gen., Lt. Genr'l and Gentry in ye Rear."

Bradstreet, the old Regular, bright sword at the carry; Pepperell in that bright scarlet tunic of his, the affability of the merchant submerged in the stern dignity of the soldier whose splendid command had achieved victory; more generals; then colonels—Gridley who had nobly upheld the traditions of the Ancient and Honorable Artillery Company of Boston; red-headed Vaughan, a trifle unsteady thanks to drafts from that same silver flask with which he had plied the Indian who scouted the Grand Battery for his taking; hard-fighting Gorham of the Rangers—they strode over the cobbles on into the Place d'Armes. On their heels followed tatterdemalion ranks, the farmers, students, woodsmen, artisans, and shopkeepers, the green volunteers turned gunners and musketeers, who had stormed the great Fortress, men destined not long thence to declare themselves citizens of the United States of America.

French music blared a reply to the Colonial band. Before the Citadel, in grim, glum silence, the commanders waited, arrayed in dress uniform. Governor du Chambon, oppressed by the knowledge that he must answer to the King for the loss of his costly, vital stronghold; the crafty Bigot, bearing a velvet cushion on which rested two symbolic, gilded keys to the city; Colonel

Verrier, the engineer, surely inwardly torn by bitter self-recriminations for those chinks in the armor of Louisbourg left open for years, for his veto of the destruction of the Grand Battery, abandoned intact to become a prime instrument for the enemy.

"Ye French men and women and children on ye Parade. They Lookt verry sorrowful." So observed that Colonial diarist marching in. Melancholy was stamped strongest on the troops of the garrison, drawn up around the square. Ranks stiff and precise, they made their last review a brave one, the French marine companies proudly wearing their grimy white, the Swiss their faded blue, the militiamen uniforms of sorts. The French belonged to no famed regiment of the realm, and the Swiss were mercenaries, yet they regarded themselves as regular soldiers. The expression on most of their faces was more than the crestfallen look of defeat—it was one of incredulity that they had been vanquished by this ill-armed, disorderly mob of *Bostonnais*.

Formal surrender was made "with all decency and decorum." Swords, offered hilt first by the Governor and his staff, were returned to them. Only the keys to the city were accepted, token of gates unlocked by Yankee guns.

Modestly but with justifiable pride evident, General Pepperrell made his report to Governor Shirley.

> May it please your Excellency, it is with the utmost pleasure that I now congratulate you and my country on the happy issue of our enterprise against Louisbourg, which was effected through God's goodness in the surrender of this strong fortress, etc., on the 16th instant, upon terms of capitulation then agreed to with the governor of said place by Commander Waldo and myself, a copy of which I have enclosed to your Excellency; and accordingly the fleet came into the harbor, and a detachment of our troops with myself entered the town yesterday and this morning. The French troops marched out and duly embarked on board the ships. We are with all possible speed removing everything from the camp into town and are taking an account of the state of the garrison, and of the store found here, which I shall send with this if it can be accomplished in season. We find our shots and bombs have prodigiously distressed and damaged the enemy. The circular battery is most entirely demolished; but I must omit particulars. Many of our army will be impatient to return home. I desire your

> directions on that point, also relating to Canso, etc., etc. I shall forthwith rush dispatches to the Duke of Newcastle to inform his Grace of the success of the situation.

Thus the amateur general made his modest report.

Surely, proclaimed rejoicing New England ministers, he and his tyro soldiers had proved themselves instruments in the hands of the Almighty when they humbled the mighty stronghold of papist France. Declared Parson Ebenezer Pemberton, preaching a long, resounding sermon, replete with Scriptural citations, to the Ancient and Honorable Artillery Company of Boston:

"THE wicked bid Defiance to Heaven, even when they stand in the greatest need of its assistance—they affront the *God of Battles,* when surrounded with that dreadful *Artillery* of His Wrath . . . Was it not God that conducted the Siege of Louisbourg, thro' numberless Difficulties and Dangers, and open'd the Gates of that City, to a few unexperienced NEW-ENGLAND MEN [?]"

An asterisk in the printed version of the Reverend Mr. Pemberton's sermon indicates footnote credit for the feat to William Pepperrell as commander.

thirteen

The Victors and the Spoils

French and English losses during the course of the siege were never precisely determined. Du Chambon reported fifty killed and eighty wounded. One New England journal raised French casualties to three hundred killed within the walls, a count rated high though inclusive of civilians.[1] Provincial dead were put at 130 and wounded at 300, with 30 of the deaths from disease.[2] That dire Horseman of the Apocalypse would carry off many more of the occupation troops, for the weather, which had remained providentially fine during the entire siege, now turned bad. The coming winter would prove a severe one, and crowded conditions and exposure were to swell the sick list and fill the burying grounds.

In the Louisbourg magazine, Du Chambon declared in extenuation of surrender, only 37 barrels of powder were left of the 16,000 pounds on hand at the beginning of the siege; all the 12-pound shot had been fired and almost all the 9-pound. An English check made the residue considerably more.[3] The besiegers' ammunition also had run low. The final bombardments had lifted artillery expenditure to a total, tremendous for the period, of nine thousand shot and shell and six hundred bombs.[4] Not a round was grudged. It was the cannon that had battered Louisbourg into submission.

As covenanted, the garrison marched out with the honors of war. Drums beat, colors fluttered from their staffs, and over shoulders slanted muskets shortly to be laid down. The column, filing between roughly arrayed lines of the victors, swung toward the docks. For a few minutes the brave spectacle hid the humiliation of the vanquished. Then disarmed soldiers, along with officials and a number of other civilians, boarded transports that carried most of them to France, some to Quebec. There was space for but few personal possessions, but Bigot represented as such the contents of the royal treasury, some two hundred thousand pounds, and so spirited it away from the victors.

Age-old custom, seldom denied, permitted the sack of a captured town, but the expedition's commanders, bound by terms and knowing they must winter at Louisbourg, were determined to prevent wholesale pillage and rapine. Toward that end Warren addressed the New England soldiers, exhorting them to behave like true Englishmen. Thereupon he presented the regiment at the Grand Battery with a hogshead of rum to drink his health, which was done with all the gusto of true Englishmen.

Yet it would take a great deal more than the Commodore's gift to divert thirsty, hungry, covetous soldiers from attempts to seize the spoils they believed they had justly won. Many came from meagre farms and communities where living was hard. It was dreams of the booty of Louisbourg that had inspired hundreds to volunteer. Patriotism and hatred of popery had played their part, but these men had not signed up to fight a war, hazarding life and limb at low pay, without expectation of looting the fabled wealth and luxuries of Louisbourg. Even Pepperrell's son-in-law had hinted to him that a handsome service of silver plate, to be acquired at a bargain or better, would be welcome.[5]

Surrender terms guaranteed the protection of the townsfolk and their property. "And Poore Termes they Bee too," declared a diarist, and he and his comrades prepared to ignore them. Before the fall of Louisbourg some of the younger men had begun bragging what they would do to the women once they got into the town, nor would they listen to the cautions of their elders.

" 'You can't go 'round raping women, even if they are papists. It ain't right.'

" 'Hell it isn't. Women in a captured city is always fair game. My Pa served under Marlborough. He knows what's what.'

" 'If that's the truth,' guffawed a pimple faced youth, 'I'm going to catch me a wench fifteen-sixteen years old, won't let her off the floor in a week.' "[6]

Some of the "brutal and licentious soldiery" may have quenched their fires at the brothels. More found themselves taking disgruntled tours of sentry duty before the doors of houses still occupied by inhabitants. Pillaging gleaned poor pickings. Before discipline was enforced, there was "excessive stealing in every part of town." But it garnered no more than thirty pounds sterling in cash, the contents of some wine cellars, cattle from the countryside, and assorted bar iron, cables, and spikes. The metal could be sold or used at home, if a man managed to pack it there. No wonder there arose "a great Noys and hubbub amongst ye Solders about ye Plunder: Som a Cursing, Som a Swarein."

The army's only valuable acquisitions were trophies. Bells, which had swung in the towers of Louisbourg, vanished to toll in colonial meetinghouses and schools. A silver cross from the Citadel chapel graced the walls of a Harvard hall for years, half forgotten, until it was identified. Cannon made appearances in colonial towns. Boston took a token in naming Louisbourg Square.

Probably the only fully sated member of the expedition was its senior chaplain, Parson Moody, the oldest man in the army. That fierce zealot, once in the town, rushed to the chapels, monasteries, and convents, unshouldered the axe he had carried so far, and wreaked havoc on the altars and images of the shrines, smashing the "emblems of the Anti-Christ."

Cross, looted from a Louisbourg chapel, today preserved at Harvard University.

Satisfaction of his iconoclastic fervor was not the only benefit. That evening Pepperrell tendered a dinner of celebration to Warren and his officers in lieu of a ball for the ladies of Louisbourg, which seems to have been abandoned. Perforce Chaplain Moody was invited to say grace—"to the great concern of those who knew his habitual prolixity, and dreaded its effect on the guests. At the same time, not one of them dared to rasp his irascible temper by any suggestion of brevity; and hence they came in terror to the feast, expecting an invocation of a good half-hour, ended by open revolt of the hungry Britons; when, to their surprise and relief, Moody said: 'Good Lord, we have so much to thank thee for, that time will be too short, and we must leave it for eternity. Bless our food and fellowship upon this joyful occasion, for the sake of Christ our Lord, Amen.' And with that he sat down." [7] An immediate clatter of knives and spoons by trenchermen betokened gratitude both to the Almighty for the fare and to the parson, who for once had not attempted to compete with eternity, for unwonted brevity.

It was the British Navy and the Royal Exchequer that reaped the rich harvest of victors' spoils. French colors, hauled down after the surrender, were craftily raised again over the town and the Island Battery by Warren's order, and the harbor mouth left open and unguarded. A procession of French East India Company ships from the South Seas, ordered to rendezvous at Louisbourg, sighted the white banners with golden fleur-de-lis and confidently sailed in. The elation of the skippers vanished when the fleet of perfidious Albion, gunports open, closed in around them and trapped them. Prize money reached a magnificent sum, estimated at one million pounds sterling. Its bulk was the cargo of a French frigate from Peru. Hidden under sacks of cocoa in her hold was a fortune in gold and silver ingots and coins. One-half the take was awarded the Crown. The other was proportioned among the fleet according to rank and rating. Warren was enriched by the lion's share, and "Admiral's eighth," amounting to sixty thousand pounds. Capture of the *Vigilant* (also engaged by Colonial cruisers) had been the nest egg for this golden hoard. The Navy treasure shower descended along the line, with 850 guineas jingling into the pockets and ditty chests of each and every seaman. Not a penny was allotted the Army, and "Noys and hubbub" of protest were completely ignored. Pepperrell, by the end of the siege had spent ten thousand pounds of his own funds, a sum that went unrepaid. That he could well afford it does not alter the inequity.

Who captured Louisbourg was a question indignantly but vainly asked. Britons were willing to grant that the capitulation of the Fortress had been forced by troops, but their sea flank, be it not forgotten, stood protected by His Majesty's men-o'-war. Unsupported by them, what would have been the fate of the Provincial cruisers from the broadsides of the *Vigilant?* So might the Senior Service have pointedly inquired. But what of the toil and tribulation of the landing and bringing the guns across the marshes; the blood on the Island Battery's beach; the long, intense bombardment from inshore and Lighthouse Point; the battle in the Gut of Canso; the Army's toll of deaths and wounds? *N'importe,* as the French might have put it. Valorous victory had to serve as reward without a share of prize money. "The Army beat the bush, and the Navy caught the bird."

However, Great Britain, in honor bound, stepped forward to cover most of the heavy expense of the expedition, which had sunk Massachusetts and other participating colonies deeply in debt, so deeply that, had they not been repaid, they would have been plunged into financial ruin. They were reimbursed to the extend of £183,649, heavy carts laden with 217 chests of Spanish dollars and a hundred barrels of copper coin rumbling up to the Boston treasury.[8]

So much for the monetary cost of war. Death and disability had to be largely written off until another era.[9]

Recognition was given the chief leaders. Warren was made a rear admiral. The able amateur soldier and diplomat Pepperrell was commissioned a colonel in the British Army with authority to raise a regiment of the line, which he did. In 1746 he was created a baronet, the first native American to be so honored. By 1755 Sir William was a major general, commanding troops on the frontier. He was promoted to lieutenant general in 1759 but saw no active service in that grade. A colonelcy and other distinctions were conferred on Governor Shirley of Massachusetts for his initiation of the expedition, and that official made a state visit to Louisbourg to view the result of his political handiwork and be presented with the keys to the city by Pepperrell.

A final reckoning of credits and debits was still to be cast up. When it was finally made three years later, the ire of New Englanders at being shut out of the prize money distribution was pale beside their fury at the settlement of the fate of Louisbourg by statesmen at the peace table.

News of the fall of the great Fortress, sent by a fast dispatch ship, reached Boston at one o'clock in the morning of July 3, 1745. The early hour stayed not the proclamation of the glad tidings by clanging bells and booming cannon that woke the city. Before dawn shouting townsfolk had filled the streets, and all day celebration never slackened, carrying on far into the night, with every lamp lit, bonfires blazing in the Common, and fireworks streaking across the sky. *Ames's Almanac* published a paean of triumph:

Bright Hesperus, the Harbinger of Day,
Smiled gently down on Shirley's prosperous sway,
The Prince of Light rode in his burning car,
To see the overtures of Peace and War
Around the world, and bade the charioteer,
Who marks the periods of each month and year,
Rein in his steeds, and rest upon High Noon
To view our Victory over Cape Britoon.

Jubilation followed in other cities and towns—New York, Philadelphia, and elsewhere. In Jamaica, New York, tubs brimmed with punch, doubtless appropriately spiked with rum from Jamaica in the West Indies. Voices chorused a song, quickly composed for the occasion:

Let all true Subjects now rejoice.
The seventeenth day of June
On Monday Morning in a Trice
We sung the French a tune.
A glorious Peace we shall have soon,
For we have conquered Cape Breton
With a fa la la.

Brave Warren and Bold Pepperrell,
Stout Wolcot, and the rest.
O British heroes, with Good Will,
Enter'd the Hornet's Nest.
A glorious Peace, *etc.*

A health let's to King George advance
That he may long remain,
The curb of Arrogance of France
And Haughtiness of Spain.
A glorious Peace, *etc.*[10]

"A glorious Peace." Those words would have to be eaten in due time and not to any gay madrigal rhythm of fa-la-las.

England, pervaded by gloom because of defeats by the French at Fontenoy and in other Continental battles,[11] was vastly cheered by news of the fall of the Fortress guarding the gateway to the St. Lawrence.

Louisbourg had to be held. It was inconceivable that the French would not attempt to retake it. In fact definite intelligence was received that a force of six thousand had been mustered in Canada to recover the Fortress and was on the march. The garrison was set to work strenuously to fill in the siege entrenchments, of which the enemy could make use, and to repair the breaches in the walls where additional guns from the warships were mounted. A boom was made ready to lower across the harbor entrance. To concentrate the defense, the Grand Battery, nemesis of the French when it had been abandoned intact, was dismantled. A grave warning of a naval assault kept the fleet constantly on the alert. Six ships of the line under the Duc d'Anville were known to have sailed from Brest June 22—weeks before word of the surrender could arrive—eluded the British blockade in home waters, and shaped a course for Cape Breton to relieve the Fortress. Surely they would not abandon their mission when they discovered it altered to recapture. A strong British squadron from the Channel, which had put to sea to reinforce Warren, might or might not intercept the Frenchmen.

Probably reports of preparations at Louisbourg deterred incursions, for none was made by land or, as yet, by sea.

No British troops could be expected for garrisoning the Fortress for months. Regiments which were to stage at Cape Breton for a sequel operation, the assault on Quebec, had been diverted to attack L'Orient, a depot of the French East India Company. Other regiments from Gibraltar, intended for Louisbourg, had sailed too late and were compelled to winter in Virginia.

As a result of this situation, Warren's fleet was ordered to remain to guard the harbor and make such patrols in outside waters as the worsening weather permitted. Pepperrell and most of his dismayed men faced the hard duty of keeping station on the ground they had won. Some seven hundred were designated to board transports and sail home to New England. They were the amputees and other seriously wounded and ill men, along with lumbermen needed for the thriving mast industry and a number of indubitable hardship cases like the owners of frontier homesteads menaced by Indians. Many who believed they also belonged in the hardship category were denied.

Gaps in the ranks were filled by replacements from Massachusetts and Rhode Island. The latter province, which had contributed no troops to the original expedition, though its ships had done good service, now made amends.

Few armies in history have failed bitterly to detest occupation duty. The thrill of battle and elation of victory vanish in the pangs of homesickness and the frustrations of monotony. Louisbourg veterans, no different from their predecessors and successors, groaned and griped. Disillusioned of the spoils, they branded the dream city a nightmare. It was only the presence of Pepperrell that prevented a disintegration of morale. The conscientious general had decided that it was his duty to remain in command. When money and supplies ran low, he contributed a large part of his personal fortune to make up arrears in pay and to purchase food and clothing. He endured the hardships of climate and scant shelter with his men and as a result, contracted rheumatic fever from which he suffered all his life and to which his death at 63 in 1750 was ascribed. Depite his efforts, as miserable autumn weather gave portent of the rigors of winter, the troops verged on mutiny. Only a raise of pay to forty shillings a month, promised by Governor Shirley, hastily summoned to Louisbourg for the emergency, prevented an outbreak.

Soldiers were put back to work then to clean up the town and repair the fortifications, and the labor, keeping them busy, lessened discontent. But it was necessary for martial law to be declared and strictly enforced. Men used to camping in the open were now quartered in lice-ridden, infected barracks. Sickness increased alarmingly: fever and the bloody flux—dysentery. A daily diet of pork brought on the dread scourge of scurvy; there was a dearth of fruits, vegetables, and spruce beer to counteract it.

Sickness struck as early as August. A diarist wrote, "After we got into the Towne, a sordid indolence or Sloth, for want of Discipline, induced putrid fevers and dyssentrys, which at length became contagious, and the people died like rotten sheep." The number of funerals rose to as many as 27 a day. Doctors were few and their small skill of little avail. To their efforts Puritan chaplains, their devotion comparable to that of the early Jesuits, added care of the ill and solace for the dying. Some, barely able to keep their own feet, insisted on continuing their rounds.

"No survivor ever forgot the miseries of that dire winter in cold and clammy Louisbourg." By April of 1746, 480 Provincials had died of disease, almost quadruple the toll of battle.[12] By spring, graves studded the cemetery outside the Maurepas Gate on Point Rochefort. There a monument, erected by the Society of Colonial Wars, now stands in commemoration.

Not until May did British line regiments and an artillery detachment arrive to take over the garrison duties. They were supplemented by the two New England regiments Shirley and Pepperrell had been authorized to raise, troops for whom recruiters' drums had been forced to beat long and hard and a bounty of four pounds per man offered. Undoubtedly letters home had passed the word that service in Louisbourg was no bed of roses. The appalling news of the hundreds of deaths from disease had spread. During the previous winter's high snows, when frozen ground had prevented burial, the dead and the living had been sheltered by the same roofs.[13]

Vice Admiral Townsend took over the sea command from

Warren, one of whose officers, Commodore Charles Knowles, became Governor of Louisbourg.

In England homage was being paid to the army that had stormed Louisbourg. "A glance at some of the English papers and periodicals of this year shows their warm recognition of the courage and endurance of Pepperrell and his New England men. Comparatively little attention was given by the writers of that day to Warren and his tars, and to their share in the enterprise, although known how essential it was; almost the whole praise was bestowed on the Provincial troops and their leader." [14] A member of Parliament went still further in tribute to the Yankee soldiers, declaring that "the colonists took Louisbourg from the French single-handed, without any European assistance,—as mettled an enterprise as any in our history,—an everlasting memorial to the zeal, courage, and perseverance of the troops of New England."

It could and would be said of the triumph that it was "a happy accident arising from a combination of peculiarly favorable circumstances," and that was true as far as it went. But those tyro soldiers, those scant-trained militiamen, had taken full advantage of the circumstances—which is a cardinal principle of the art of warfare—and had thereby won their astounding victory. No troops have ever more greatly deserved the laurels and the bays.

Their greatest acclaim awaited the passage of years and another war when the colonists remembered how they had achieved the seemingly impossible at Louisbourg and were emboldened to believe they might accomplish it again on a far larger scale; when Pomeroy, Gridley, and other veterans of 1745 marched to battle once more in 1775; when the shots fired at Lexington, Concord, and Bunker Hill resounded as distant but confident echoes of that first ragged volley by landing parties on the shore of Gabarus Bay; when American guns commanding British-held Boston opened a cannonade that woke the past thunders of bombardments that had breached the walls of the great French Fortress on Cape Breton Island; when the independence of spirit there engendered made a nation.

On captured Louisbourg history bestowed the worthy accolade: cradle of the United States.

fourteen
Trident of Neptune

Naval strength, not bastions, battlements, and batteries, was the safeguard of Louisbourg. So French ministries repeatedly emphasized, though they neglected to provide it. It was left to a perceptive Acadian priest to ask and pointedly answer the question: "What good is Louisbourg? It would be good if France were as strong at sea as England."

The great Fortress's mission, its whole *raison d'être*—protecting the fisheries and trade routes and standing sentinel at the gateway to French Canada—could not be fulfilled without men-o'-war based in its fine harbor and patrolling North Atlantic waters. Nor could the stronghold itself survive. Failing them, it had fallen. By their aid only could it be regained.

At the time of its construction Louisbourg had stood as a symbol of the far-flung, unsurpassed colonial empire of France. The East and West Indies and other dominions were perforce dependent on naval power. France had mustered 281 warships to England's 277 at the beginning of the eighteenth century. They were manned by able seamen of Brittany and Normandy and from the fishing fleets, men yielding nothing to the British tars who were beginning to realize the destiny of a maritime nation. Truly, wrote a French poet of the period, "*Le trident de Neptune c'est le sceptre du Monde.*"

Decline set in gradually but unmistakably. The ocean deity, so evidently Francophile at first, showed inclinations to bestow his seagoing pitchfork on a stately goddess, pictured on the

Colonials' Louisbourg flag as Britannia ruling the waves—and thereby the world.

The land wars of Louis XIV and Louis XV had drained the realm's manpower and other resources. Victories by the Army were won at the expense of the Navy. In Britain the Navy was rated the Senior Service; in France it became increasingly junior. British officers and sailors were spurred by incentives of prize money and other booty, rewards that grew scarcer for the French. Great preference in the French Navy was given to officers of noble birth; the British allowed commoners to rise to high command and in them found its foremost admirals. To avoid risks was a traditional French naval policy. Take them—and bring them off—demanded the British Admiralty, or face charges of neglect of duty, with penalties ranging from dismissal to death. In consequence, British commanders almost always fought to the finish. There were too many French leaders who saved their ships to fight another day or, overwhelmed by adversity, gave way to utter despair.

Sailors of both nations served under the same conditions of human misery: "the foul air 'tween decks of packed transports, the hundred thousand common seamen who died of sickness or deserted from floating hells, while but a thousand of their comrades fell in actual battle, the crowded mess tables where sailors were fed more like dogs than like men, who if we are to believe the novelist Smollett, subsisted on rations consisting of 'putrid salt beef . . . salt pork, which though neither fish or flesh tasted of both; hard bread or biscuit which, like a piece of clockwork, moved by its own internal impulse, occasioned by the myriads of insects that dwelt within it, and butter, served out by the gill, that tasted like train oil thickened by salt.' "[1] But it was the British crews, bulked out by landsmen dragged aboard ship by press gangs, who better endured and more successfully survived the dreadful circumstances. And superior British gunnery told in many a battle.

As stout and seaworthy as "the wooden walls of England" were the ships of the line and frigates built by the French. But, once off the ways, the Gallic warships suffered sorry neglect. Hulls were left foul, holds unscoured. Poor food, badly stowed, decayed until it became inedible. The Army's demands and grafting officials left scant funds for the dockyards, which relapsed into such inefficiency that imperative repairs were botched.

Thus developed deterioration of French naval might, a condition even Napoleon Bonaparte would fail to redeem, thus sowing the seeds of his own downfall. For the fate of the First Empire, that of Louisbourg and other colonial outposts stood as unregarded signboards.

King Louis averted his eyes, turning a proud gaze toward his armies on the battlefields of Europe. He paid little heed to his able Minister of Marine, Jean-Frédéric Maurepas, behind whose frivolity of spirit lay a keen intellect thoroughly understanding the peril of scanting sea power. During his term of office, he succeeded to only a minor extent in arresting the decline of the Navy which 1758, the year of the second siege of Louisbourg, would see reduced to 71 vessels mounting 4,790 guns, opposed by Britain's 131 ships with an armament of 8,733 guns. *Après moi le déluge,* Louis was to foretell, and that floodtide would sweep over the fleets of France.

No small contribution to catastrophe was made by a lady of the Royal Court, definitely not a lass who loved a sailor.

Madame de Pompadour did not become the mistress of Louis XV until 1745. Consequently Louisbourg's capture that year cannot be scored against her. Her influence on the King, inimical to matters maritime and colonial, had not yet been established. But the lady worked fast. Her sway may have become strong enough to affect to some degree the naval attempt to retake the Fortress the following summer, and she certainly was a factor in the neglect of Louisbourg's maintenance after it had fallen again into French hands.

A fortune-teller had predicted to Jeanne-Antoinette Poisson when she was nine years old that she would be a king's mistress; her age allowed time for a procession of royal inamoratas before her. When the soon-to-be-created Marquise de Pompadour made the grade, she was 24.

Once installed, she triumphed over competition which no longer included the Queen. Maria Leczinski, daughter of the exiled King of Poland, had presented Louis with twin daughters punctually nine months after their wedding night. Eight subsequent offspring induced the Queen to complain that she was always "in bed, or pregnant, or brought to bed." To keep the King at bay she proclaimed her boudoir out of bounds on the days of major saints. Such occasions not proving plentiful enough, she added the days of lesser holy ones until Louis, banned by a calendared saint of whom he had never heard, flew into a temper and ordered his valet to provide a pretty housemaid as a substitute.[2]

For Pompadour and her predecessors the result was a series of field days, sanctified or otherwise. These the lady of the historic hairdo largely reserved to herself once the fortune-teller's prophecy had been fulfilled. "She absolutely extinguished all the other women at the Court, although some were very beautiful." A discriminating courtier paid her a glowing tribute: "Not a man alive but would have had her for his mistress if he could. Tall, though not too tall; beautiful figure; round face with regular features; wonderful complexion, hands and arms; eyes not so very big, but the brightest, wittiest and most sparkling I ever saw."

When the King was sick of love, she not only stayed him with flagons and comforted him with apples, in the biblical phrase, but provided numerous other devices to dispel his besetting ennui. The chase, cards, the theatre, frequent changes of residence, and costly building operations were in her repertoire of royal diversions. Before her time Louis had had his fill of the last mentioned in constructing Louisbourg but he was ready to be entertained by monumental works again. The King and his mistress were little interested in the maintenance of that distant Fortress, out of sight and out of mind, or in its support by the French Navy. When Maurepas begged for naval funds, Pompadour told him not to upset the King.

Such was her sway over the sovereign that "she made and unmade Ministers, she selected Ambassadors, she appointed generals, she conferred pensions and places. Upon her rests the responsibility for that sudden change of traditional policy of France toward the House of Hapsburg which enabled the vindictive Maria Theresa to fan the ashes of the War of the Austrian Succession into the devouring flame which ravaged the Empire for seven long years."[3]

As the Army, not the Navy, was Louis's pride, so was it Pompadour's penchant. Generals were on the scene, but admirals (less dashing fellows) were often absent on cruises—remote and forgotten like Louisbourg. It was clear on whom honors would be heaped by the King, abetted by the influence of his left-hand queen.

Since 1743 Maurepas had vainly pleaded with the King to strengthen Louisbourg, and he placed responsibility for the poor condition of its defenses on the monarch's indifference. During the critical period preceding the fall of the Fortress, its disregard cannot, as has been acknowledged, be attributed to Madame de Pompadour, who had not yet come to power. It is equally true that decay of the Navy had been in progress before her rise. Yet when she came to share the throne, unofficially but indubitably, her designs made themselves felt overseas and on them. Spurred by resentment and the inclination of his mordant wit, Maurepas made matters far worse by writing scurrilous verses about the lady, which could not be done with impunity. Shown them, she was enraged and took her revenge by wrecking the Minister's projects as best she could. Frederick the Great of Prussia also made the mistake of lampooning the King's mistress and thereby surely fed fuel to the implacable enmity displayed by France in the Seven Years' War.

To the French proverb on the trident of Neptune may be added an English dramatist's observation that hell hath no fury like a woman scorned.

Neglected defenses were Louisbourg's lot not only under the French but also during the English occupation following its surrender in 1745.

It was no secret that burning resentment had been aroused in France when her mighty North American fortress had been captured by despised militia from New England. Her honor had to be retrieved despite deep embroilment in the Seven Year's War. Belatedly steps were taken. Reliable intelligence was received by Britain and her colonies that a great fleet, nearly half the French Navy, was being assembled in the summer of 1746, at Brest, to win back Louisbourg.

Regardless of the threat, Louisbourg's Governor, Commodore

Knowles, pursued a policy that was not only *laissez-faire* but also *laissez-aller*. The stronghold, he declared, was not worth keeping; its fortifications were badly designed and worse built. Nor did he hesitate to tell the Home Ministry so, understating the Fortress' strategic value and adding that the cost of putting the place in good condition would run to five or six hundred thousand pounds. The climate he cursed as frightful—frost or fog nine months of the year—and it made for little more comfort that buildings were warmer in the winter than before, as coal was being mined on the island for the first time.

Knowles let slide repairs of the defenses, begun by Warren, Pepperrell, and Shirley. He sniffed at the advice of Shirley, who while Royal Governor of Massachusetts told the Prime Minister that should Louisbourg be strengthened, the Crown would have an absolute hold on the colonies if ever the time should come that they grew restive and disposed to throw off the yoke of their mother country. "That possibility," Shirley, no seer, added, "seems to me some centuries further off than it does to some gentlemen at home." [4]

Commodore Knowles, "a testy person," was having troubles with New Englanders of the garrison. "Banditti" was his term for such troops. While he was still in naval command, he had tried to impress Boston mechanics for his crews and had been forced to give them up when mobs attacked his officers.[5] His prejudice flamed hotly when the shivering garrison took to drink "to battle the elements in this damned place." It reached a point where, the Commodore claimed, every man in the New England army from the General down was either trading in rum or downing it—or both. Rum (only ninepence per gallon) flowed so freely that by Knowles' count one thousand men a day were found drunk. Taking steps to curb the wholesale sprees, the Governor ordered all the sutlers' liquors impounded in casemates under guard, which did little good until the considerable secret stores ran out.

The Governor was compelled to enforce a drastic stoppage of liquor rations which he made the grave error of combining with a cut in pay, funds in the war chest having run low. At once the garrison broke out in open rebellion. Knowles' officers managed to parade the seething troops to hear him. What happened then is related in his report to the Duke of Newcastle.

> In a few hours after the whole garrison was in a general mutiny & the troops [demanded] returned their provisions into store in tumultuous manner & swore that they were no longer soldiers. It was impossible to discover any leader, for in an instant there were more than a thousand assembled together; as I thought, no time was to be lost to prevent the threatening danger I immediately order'd them under arms & met them upon the parade & informed them it was His Majesty's Order & that nothing but the exigencies of the state for money to carry on the War could occasion this stoppage being made. They demonstrated regiment by regiment that they were ready to obey his Majesty's commands with their lives, but they must perish in this climate if those stoppages were made, that it was scarce possible for them honestly now to supply themselves with necessarys and the Common Refreshments of Life in this Scarce and dear place but would be absolutely so with those deductions & that therefore, if they had not their full pay they could be no longer soldiers, all reasoning proving ineffectual, and perceiving many to be heated with drink, I found myself obliged to order their pay & provisions to be continued to them till His Majesty's further Pleasure should be known, when they huzza'd & said they would serve faithfully. I told your Grace in several of my former letters that I dread the consequence of such an order being issued & I may now rejoice that nothing worse happened, for I will venture to affirm that had four hours been neglected to have given them satisfaction no reasoning would have been able to have stopped their rage & force we had not to quell it with.

Louisbourg was ripe for the retaking.

The great French fleet, with a strong expeditionary force aboard, had put to sea. Indians were attacking the blockhouses which were protecting the coal mines on Cape Breton Island. The Viceroy of French Canada, deeply concerned for Quebec, now that Louisbourg was in English possession and the St. Lawrence waterway open to invasion, was bending every effort to regain the safeguard. Lieutenant Colonel Marin was poised to make another thrust from Acadia.

Though Governor Knowles was carelessly oblivious, a state of alarm gripped the New England colonists, alarm so grave that it has been justly compared to that which had seized their forebears 150 years earlier when the Spanish Armada appeared in the Channel. Massachusetts troops, marching on the French works at Crown Point, were hastily recalled. The streets of Boston were thronged by eight thousand militia, called up from the countryside, while Connecticut alerted six thousand to spring to arms. More cannon were emplaced to protect Boston harbor, whose entrance was obstructed by sunken hulks and a boom, for that city and Annapolis Royal were reliably reported as French objectives after Louisbourg. Then, as subsequently became known, the Gallic warships and troop-crammed transports were to sweep south along the American coast, laying waste cities and towns and finally ravaging the British West Indies. Such were the proportions of the menace. Never had France launched a mightier effort in its rivalry for the New World. Even partial success could reverse the tide of conquest and shake the English hold.

Could Britain's fleet block that of France? If not, could the colonials defend themselves both from attacks along the seaboard and inroads by the French of Canada and the Indian allies who would throng to join them once victories crowned their arms? Men asked those questions with deep anxiety and doubt.

In the pulpit of Boston's Old Church the Reverend Thomas Prince faced his apprehensive congregation and fervently besought divine aid to avert the approaching peril. That occasion was to inspire a poem by Longfellow, "A Ballad of the French Fleet":

A Fleet with flags arrayed
  Sailed from the port of Brest
And the Admiral's ship displayed
  The signal: "Steer southwest."
For this Admiral D'Anville
  Had sworn by cross and crown
To ravage with fire and steel
  Our helpless Boston Town.

There were rumors in the street,
  In the houses there was fear

Of the coming of the fleet,
And the danger hovering near.
And while from mouth to mouth
Spread the tidings of dismay,
I stood in the Old South
Saying humbly: "Let us pray!

"O Lord! we would not advise;
But if in thy Providence
A tempest should arise
To drive the French Fleet hence,
And scatter it far and wide,
Or sink it in the sea,
We should be satisfied,
And thine the glory be. . . ."

Even to the staunch and resolute, determined to fight for their homes, it seemed that salvation could come from God alone when the dire news arrived that the French fleet had evaded British blockading squadrons and was making all sail westward.

The poet who had written, "*Le trident de Neptune c'est le sceptre du Monde,*" might have proclaimed the name of the French Vice Admiral's flagship as the happiest of omens. It was *Trident.*

fifteen

Death of a Fleet

Fourteen sails of the line, twenty-one frigates, transports with three thousand veteran troops aboard (added to the naval complement they brought the total to seventeen thousand men), fireships—such was the huge French fleet gathered at Brest in the summer of 1746 to recapture Louisbourg and take vengeance on the British colonies of the American coast.[1] Four more large warships from the West Indies were ordered to join it at Chibucto, Nova Scotia. Nearly half France's Navy, it was a force, magnified by rumor to the size of the old Spanish Armada, whose memory still lingered in English minds.

Tradition and Court influence and intrigue had given its command to De Roye de la Rochefoucauld, Duc d'Anville, of the celebrated Montmorency family. Not yet forty, he was young for the post of High Admiral. Physical strength and charm of manner along with a famous name—those he possessed, but they were overwhelmingly discounted by lack of experience and of a stout heart in adversity, as events would prove. Appraisal of his qualities ran the gamut from glowing to ominous. "A nobleman of great experience and ability"; "Great reliance was placed upon his courage and skill"; "Worthy to be loved and born to command" were encomiums harshly contradicted by other evaluations. "An illustrious nobleman but an incompetent sailor"; "Without any sea-service he was made Lieutenant General of the Naval Armaments of the King"; "While distinguished for a highly cultured mind he appeared to have had no experience at sea, though he had entered the Naval service of France at an early date."[2] When history's vote was cast, the "nos" had it.

The Duke's second in command was Vice Admiral d'Estournel, no landsman like his chief but equally unstable. Only third in line and thus without a strong voice in the fleet's leadership was the able La Jonquière.

France's neglect of her Navy stacked the cards higher against the expedition. It is not on record that d'Anville protested or took any steps to remedy the condition of his ships: foul bottoms, poorly stowed provisions where spoilage would soon begin, dirty, cramped quarters breeding disease. Either he was unaware of or ignored those grave hazards. Blithely he set sail on a cruise which proved to be a large-scale replica of the ill-starred voyage of Coleridge's Ancient Mariner.

At Rochelle, the first port of call, headwinds delayed the fleet so long that it was June 20, 1746, before it could put to sea again. Unrest among officers and crews developed since, with the Duke sailing under sealed orders, their destination was known to no one else. When pressed he weakly disclosed his mission, only to double their discontent. Retaking Louisbourg, its legend of impregnability little lessened for Frenchmen by its capture, was a forbidding prospect. In the Bay of Biscay a gale roared down on the flotilla.

> And now the Storm-blast came, and he
> Was tyrannous and strong.
> He struck with his o'ertaking wings . . .[3]

With many of its sails split, with spars and bowsprits carried away, the fleet was scattered. More precious time was lost before it could be reassembled and proceed, delayed by the slow sailers. A dead calm off the Azores was the next stroke of bad luck.

> Down dropped the breeze, the sails dropped down . . .
> Day after day, day after day,
> We stuck, nor breath nor motion,
> As idle as a painted ship
> Upon a painted ocean.[4]

The calm was broken by a squall. Lightning flashed through a pall of dark, scurrying clouds. On one ship six men were killed by a bolt. Another struck an ammunition box on the 70-gun *Mars;* it blew up, slaying ten men and injuring twenty-one. A leaky store ship which began to sink was abandoned and burned. Then a virulent pestilence swept the fleet, until the able-bodied were outnumbered by the sick and hard put to man the vessels.

Near the dreaded Sable Island shoals off the coast of Nova Scotia a thick, blanketing fog shrouded them. They sailed blindly into a second storm, more frightful than the first. Battered by waves towering mast-high, a transport, colliding with a frigate, went down with all on board. Two warships narrowly avoided a crash in the fury of the tempest which raged through the night. When it subsided at last, a flotsam-strewn sea gave testimony of the victims it had engulfed. Three of the ships of the line had barely weathered the cataclysm. Mastless and rudderless, the *Argonaut* rolled helpless. All starboard guns on the upper deck of the wallowing *Caribou* had been jettisoned. The badly damaged *Trident* and other survivors groped through another fog in search of vanished vessels, including d'Anville's flagship, the *Northumberland.*

Never had prayer seemed more completely answered than when the Reverend Mr. Prince of Boston, beseeched Providence for a tempest "to drive the French fleet hence." Longfellow's ballad speaks again for the preacher when tidings of the disaster reached Massachusetts.

This was the prayer I made,
  For my soul was all on flame,
And even as I prayed
  The answering tempest came;
It came with a mighty power,
  Shaking the windows and walls,
And tolling the bell in the tower,
  As it tolls at funerals.

The lightning suddenly
  Unsheathed its flaming sword,
And I cried: "Stand still, and see
  The salvation of the Lord!"
The heavens were black with cloud,
  The sea was white with hail,

And ever more fierce and loud
  Blew the October gale.

The fleet it overtook,
  And the broad sails in the van
Like the tents of Cushan shook,
  Or the curtains of Midian.
Down on the reeling decks
  Crashed the o'erwhelming seas;
Ah, never were there wrecks
  So pitiful as these!

Like a potters' vessel broke
  The great ships of the line;
They were carried away as a smoke,
  Or sank like lead in brine.
O Lord! before the path
  They vanished and ceased to be,
When thou didst walk in wrath
  With thine horses through the sea!

By no means was malignant fortune through with havoc on d'Anville's armada. The Admiral's flagship and two accompanying men-o'-war safely made the harbor of Chibuco (the future Halifax) by virtue of having captured an English sloop and forced one of her crew to pilot them in. But the four big warships from the West Indies were not there to keep the rendezvous. They had arrived earlier and waited vainly for the Admiral, who was known to have left Rochelle nearly three months previously. Having given up, they had sailed for France two days before he appeared.

D'Anville lacked the fortitude to withstand the bludgeoning of fate any longer. So far as he knew, his three ships in the harbor were all that were left. Disease was killing off crews by the hundreds; more than a thousand shallowly buried skeletons would later be found along these shores. Provisions were nearly spent. Distraught, the King's Admiral retired to his cabin, where his body was found dead of apoplexy or, said some, of suicide.

When D'Estournel and his storm-wracked ships limped in shortly afterwards, the weight of command descended upon him as a crushing burden. Abandon the enterprise and sail back to

France, he urged a council. Its vote having gone against him, the Vice Admiral bolted himself in his cabin. Groans from within brought officers who hastened to break open the door. They beheld him dying in a pool of blood. He had braced his sword against his breast and fallen on it.

The death of the two admirals spread dismay among the seamen, their morale already in shreds. Aboard the flagship *Northumberland* a mutinous crew clamored to go ashore. She was haunted, they declared, by the ghosts of their shipmates—yet another parallel to the voyage of the Ancient Mariner. There was no choice but to give them their way; in any event the ship was a near wreck. She was scuttled and joined other vessels, no longer seaworthy, at the bottom of the harbor.

La Jonquière, made of sterner stuff than his seniors, succeeded to the command and strove to carry on, still hoping to assault Annapolis in lieu of Louisbourg. Although the ravages of pestilence continued, he sailed for the former stronghold, the wake of his ships dotted with corpses heaved overboard. A third storm proved to be the last straw for even that indomitable man. Homeward pennants were hoisted. In the passage the starving crew of one straggling ship devoured all the rats in the hold and were about to turn to cannibalism on five English prisoners when interception of a Portuguese vessel with sheep aboard, which the sailors ravenously ate raw, spared a crowning horror.

Remnants of the fleet narrowly escaped an English squadron to make port safely in Brittany. More than 2,300 dead of plague, buried at sea or on land, were reported, the fatalities swollen by the toll of those drowned in stormy seas. The saga of catastrophe would verge on the incredible were it not so well attested.[5]

Vast relief and rejoicing spread along the coast of America at the destruction of that mighty armament of the enemy. "Certain it is that there were many in self-righteous New England who would have held it impious to doubt that God had summoned the pestilence and the storm to fight the battle of his modern Israel." [6]

Even a calamity of such frightful proportions failed to dampen French ardor to regain Louisbourg. Another fleet was equipped and manned; though not equal to its predecessor, it was still formidable. With the staunch La Jonquière in command, it sailed from Rochelle on May 10, 1747. Four days later it was encountered by a stronger English fleet, one of whose admirals was an old Louisbourg antagonist, Warren. In a hard-fought battle, the French sustained a decisive defeat, with nearly eight hundred killed in the action. Six warships were captured, La Jonquière himself among the many prisoners.

How the Duc d'Anville reached Louisbourg after all is a curious footnote to history.[7]

His remains had been buried on an island in the harbor where his tragic cruise ended. In 1749 it was decided that the Duke should be "transferred among his people"—to Louisbourg. Brought thence by a frigate, the body was reinterred at the foot of the altar of the Royal Chapel.

In the span of almost two centuries the tomb was lost beneath the crumbled ruins of the Fortress. Then were commenced excavations leading to its restoration. Original plans, which had been preserved in France, guided diggers of 1932 to the bones of the Duke on the top of three tiers of burials. They were positively identified by means of a small circular opening in the skull, the fitting piece of which was found nearby. Research [8] had disclosed that D'Estournel had ordered an autopsy, including trepanning to still rumors that the Admiral had died of poison.

Written of a greater figure in the annals of Louisbourg was Thomas Gray's immortal line:

> The paths of glory lead but to the grave.

Those over which an evil fate led De Roye de la Rochefoucauld, Duc d'Anville, were darkly inglorious.

Parson Pemberton's sermon, not preached until 1756, revived the chorus of thanksgiving for divine deliverance. The fall of Louisbourg, he thundered to the Ancient and Honorable Artillery Company, had given "a mighty Shock to the ambitious Designs of the *French King*, fir'd his Breast with Resentment, determined him to take a severe Revenge."

> To this End, he soon collected a formidable Force, design'd not only to recover his Loss, but scatter Destruction thro' the

coasts of NORTH-AMERICA. We all remember how greatly we were surprised when we heard their Fleet had actually sail'd to execute this fatal Scheme—No wonder every Face gathered Paleness, every Heart was seiz'd with Terror. We had every Thing to fear, which the Bigotry of Rome—the Tyranny of France—the Rage of provok'd Enemies, could contrive or inflict. Had they succeeded, we had nothing to expect, but to see our Cities in Flames—our Habitations demolished—our Virgins defloured [sic] —our Street delug'd with Blood—and the Temples of our God prostituted to Superstition and Idolatry.

BUT, though destitute of human Assistance, our *Help was in the Name of the Lord, who made Heaven and Earth.*—God sent a contagious sickness among them, which dispirited their Generals, and exceedingly diminish'd the Number of their Forces:—Unwilling to return, without executing some Part of their intended Mischief, they summon'd all their Strength, and determined to make a resolute Attack on some of our *Eastern Settlements*—God sent forth his Commission to the Winds, they heard his Voice, and immediately gathered into a mighty Storm; and scattered their floating Castles, *upon the Face of the great Deep.* —This dissipated all their Hopes;—a small Remnant only return'd to their native Country, to tell the melancholy Story of their Losses and Disappointments.

THUS, in the Day of our Extremity, *the Name of the Lord alone was exalted. His right Hand* obtain'd for us an early Victory over our Enemies. Our Lives were preserv'd—our Liberties maintain'd—our valuable Enjoyments secur'd—Not by our own *Swords and Bows,* but by the signal Interpositions of Heaven.

sixteen

Price of Peace

Two great French fleets had perished in disaster and defeat in attempts to recapture Louisbourg and keep the sea-lanes open to Canada. Though force of naval arms had failed, there remained an unexpected recourse for winning back the Fortress, one that was to fill its conquerors with angry dismay and carry far-reaching consequences.

The bloody War of the Austrian Succession, begun in 1740, was drawing toward its end. Approaching the scope of the global conflicts of the twentieth century, it had spread over three continents and two oceans, involving eight nations and their dependencies. As in other wars before and afterwards, it was difficult to distinguish the victors from the vanquished. Queen Maria Theresa of Austria still sat on the throne of her ravaged realm, but she had lost the province of Silesia to Frederick the Great of Prussia, whose kingdom's star had begun to rise. Spain's booty was no more than a few Italian towns. The chief belligerents, England and France, casting up gains and losses, could reckon many lives and vast treasure in the latter category. In the former, French armies under the great Marshal Saxe had made conquests in the Netherlands. In India France had seized Madras and other British colonies. England had scored more heavily at sea and had triumphed on a number of European battlegrounds. Defeat of the French-supported Pretender to the British throne, Charles Edward Stuart, and his Scots at Culloden had ended a serious internal threat for Great Britain. Yet in the give-and-take of the war tally the capture of Louisbourg by New

England colonists, guarded by Warren's fleet, loomed largest for the contenders.

Therefore when peace commissioners met in 1747 to formulate the Treaty of Aix-la-Chapelle, which was to be signed October 18, 1748, possession of the Cape Breton Fortress became the crux of the negotiations. To regain that key stronghold seemed as vital to France as had its establishment. Upon Louisbourg depended, more than ever the preservation of New France. Despite the earlier loss of Newfoundland and Acadia, the guardian of the St. Lawrence had kept that waterway open. With that barrier down, how long could Quebec and Montreal survive? French Canada's links to the south, the valley of the Ohio and the Mississippi hinterland, were being increasingly menaced by English settlers pushing westward. If the northern anchor of those chains was destroyed, Louisiana would be isolated. The long-disputed waters of the Gulf of Mexico and the Caribbean would then be more securely hedged by "the wooden walls of England." Britannia's naval preponderance there could well add the rich islands of the French West Indies to her own.

Louis XV declared that only the miseries of his people, bled white by the war, persuaded him to consider peace. It was by no means peace at any price he was prepared to accept but "peace with honor," and honor, that elastic word, demanded the return of Louisbourg to France. On His Majesty's insistence, commissioners put forward that condition on a grant-it-or-fight basis. Despite his humanitarian protestations, the King plainly was as willing to submit his subjects to further sacrifices as the English Ministry was reluctant again to plunge an equally exhausted country into conflict.

Convinced that Louis was not bluffing, the English commissioners yielded. Article 5 of the Treaty provided that "all conquests which have been made since the commencement of the war . . . shall be restored without exception." The *fleur-de-lis* would fly over Louisbourg again. There was, of course, a *quid pro quo* or what passed for it. France for her part gave back Madras and other Indian trophies, along with various Dutch and Belgian towns, and agreed to dismantle the fortifications of Dunkirk and to abandon support of the Scottish rebels. But for public opinion in both nations there was little question who had won the peace. In France far-off Madras went unmourned. Remote Louisbourg, neglected till it was lost, was welcomed back, a stain on French arms wiped away.

The news that Louisbourg was to be relinquished shocked the British people. It was in vain for the Ministry to claim that the best possible bargain had been made, that, though it might be a bad one, it was far better than resumption of the war. In bitter irony the *London Evening Post* published a ditty to be sung to the tune of "Derry Down":

> Cape Breton's expensive, as well hath been prov'd,
> And therefore the *Burthen* is wisely remov'd;
> Which *Burthen French Shoulders* we settle again on;
> And *add*—our own *Stores,* our *Provisions,* and *Cannon.*

It also rankled that British hostages were required to be sent to Paris as surety for the completion of the transfer. Yet indignation at home paled before the furious resentment aroused across the ocean. The New England colonies in particular clamored against a *fait accompli* they could do nothing to reverse. They had bought Louisbourg with their blood, and here it was being handed back to the enemy in a diplomatic horse trade none of the doubtful benefits of which they shared. What if the money cost of the undertaking, which had bankrupted them, had for the most part been refunded? Outlays would begin to mount again, as French depredations on the mainland, with Louisbourg and Quebec as bases, were inevitably renewed. Once more militia would have to be called up and in increasing numbers. Again outlying settlements would ring with the war whoop as the Indians were incited to murderous raids by their long-time allies. There would be more trouble with the stubborn Acadians, still French at heart despite their oath of allegiance. Yankee commerce, which had been in a fair way to eliminate competition, would suffer.

Deep distrust of the mother country was bred in New England and the other colonies. The guns of the great Fortress they had stormed frowned down on them again. Although the future held in store a second English assault upon Louisbourg, profound disillusionment over the restoration of 1748 never vanished from American minds. It clung as closely as the confidence in their own martial prowess built up in the Colonials by their capture of Louisbourg. And both elements blended as potent components of the powder train that exploded in the Revolution.

The take-over at Louisbourg was accomplished with due ceremony, with British correctness and French *savoir faire* and *politesse*. Arriving men-o'-war, shepherding crowded transports, boomed salutes, answered by the Fortress batteries. French troops —twenty-four companies of infantry of fifty men each and one company of artillery—landed and marched through the gates into the Place d'Armes that summer day of 1749 in a reversal of the panorama of four years before. Trumpets sounded, drums rolled, and muskets snapped to present arms. With sour looks the drawn-up British battalions stared at the smug faces of the "mounseers." Well, let them have this God-forsaken post and such joy in it as they could muster through the long, frigid winters. Governor Peregrine Thomas Hopson turned over the Fortress to his successor, Navy Captain Charles Desherbiers, who took possession of Isle Royale and its dependencies in the name of the King of France. White and golden banners soared up staffs to replace the Union Jack.

From the transports uprooted *habitants* flocked back to their homes, chattering with indignation at the disrepair in which they found them. Yet at Louisbourg they were home again, and even a sojourn in France had not broken old ties. They took up disrupted lives, encouraged by provision made by Intendant Bigot of two hundred cows and the promise of rations for two years from the King's Stores. Boats were bought from the English, others were built, and fishermen put to sea. The population increased as exiles returned from French Canada.

Then dawned a day of evanescent glory for Louisbourg under Desherbiers and the following Governor, Jean-Louis, Comte de Raymond, who took office in 1751. A man of some ability but arbitrary with subordinates, De Raymond was adept at currying royal favor. He made the most of an opportunity to ingratiate himself at Court by staging a grand celebration in honor of the birth of another son to King Louis, the Duc de Bourgogne. An account, probably written by the Governor himself, describes festivity such as Cape Breton never had seen, a glittering affair that caused the gubernatorial salary to be overdrawn to meet its expense.[1]

On Sunday 28th of May this important news was announced at day-break by a salute from all the artillery of the place and the King's ships, the frigates *Fidèle* and the *Chariot Royal*, which had dressed ship.

M. le Comte de Raymond gave a dinner to the staff, the engineers, the officers of artillery, and to the other principal officers, to the Conseil Supérieur, the Baillage, the Admiralty, and to the ladies of the place.

He had two tables with 50 covers, served in four courses, with as much lavishness as elegance. They drank in turn freely every kind of wine of the best brands, to the health of the King, Queen, and Dauphin, Mme. la Dauphine, M. le Duc de Bourgogne, and to the Royal Princesses.

Many guns were fired, and the band increased the pleasure of the fête.

About 6 o'clock, after leaving the table, they repaired to the King's chapel to hear vespers. At the close of the service, the Te Deum was sung to the accompaniment of all the artillery of the town and of the ships.

They then went in a procession, as is the custom in the colonies, to the Esplanade of the Maurepas gate.

The governor there lit a bonfire which he had had prepared; the troops of the garrison, drawn up on the ramparts and the covered way, fired with the greatest exactness, three volleys of musketry, and the artillery did the same. After this ceremony, the Governor distributed several barrels of his own wine to the troops and to the public.

The "Vive le Roi" was so frequently repeated, that no one could doubt that the hearts of the townspeople, the troops, and the country folk, which this festival had attracted, were truly French.

He had given such good orders in establishing continual patrols in command of officers, that no disorder was committed.

About 9 in the evening, the governor and all his guests went to see set off the fire-works and a great number of rockets, which he had prepared, and were very well done.

On his return home, the ball was opened, and lasted till dawn; all kinds of refreshments, and in abundance, were handed round. His house was illuminated with lanterns placed all round the

> windows, looking on the rue Royale and the rue Toulouse.
>
> Three porticoes, with four pyramids, adorned by triple lanterns and wreaths of flowers, rare for such a cold climate, were erected opposite the rue Royale.
>
> At the opposite angle, where the two roads cross, two other pyramids were also illuminated; and on the frontal of the three porticoes were painted the arms of the King, the Dauphin, and the Duc de Bourgogne.
>
> At the end of the same street, opposite the three porticoes, were also represented, by means of lanterns, three large fleurs de lys and a "Vive le Roi," very visibly placed on a border above.
>
> Between these two principal illuminations is situated the large gate of the Government House, which was also adorned at the columns and cornices, by triple lanterns, as high as the retaining wall of the garden. These illuminations were charming in their effect and lasted till the end of the ball; all the houses in the town were lit up as well as the frigate *La Fidèle.*
>
> The government house being too small to accommodate all the distinguished members of the colony, M. le Comte Raymond gave a big dinner the next day to the clergy and the Sunday following to several ladies, officers, and others who had not attended the first fête.
>
> It can be said that the Governor spared nothing for these festivities and that he gave on that happy occasion very evident proof of a rare generosity.

For the populace and the garrison there was an humble share in the gaiety, such as wine donated to toast the royal offspring. The soldiers' satisfaction in having ousted the English and in measures to insure that Louisbourg remained French still endured. Fortifications were strengthened. New works were built at the lighthouse on the site where colonial cannon had bombarded and reduced the Island Battery. One hundred guns now barred the entrance to the harbor.

Yet a fault from which the Fortress had suffered from the first appeared again to undermine it. Incompetent engineers were guilty of slipshod work on new structures and on repairs to the old. Of the golden stream of livres pouring again into Louisbourg much was squandered. One visitor avowed its defenses more resembled ancient ruins than modern fortifications. The drain increased with demands for money to finance the fishing fleet and shipbuilding and for subsidies to the Indians. Little went to improve the equipment and living conditions of the troops. They were still quartered, two to a bunk, in dirty, musty barracks. When their ill-made, shoddy uniforms had to be replaced, they were forced to buy through their officers, who bilked them.

Some reforms were put through when Michel le Courtois de Surlaville arrived to assume military command under Raymond. That efficient officer, holding his first review, was shocked by the garrison's soiled white uniforms—the color should be changed, he declared—and by its sloppy, disorderly performance of the manual of arms and primary evolutions. Promptly he ordered more drill, with cadets and higher officers to conduct it instead of noncoms. He curbed officer graft on supplies, and it no longer cost a private six months' pay to buy a new pair of shoes. In demanding better quality in clothing and other improvements,[2] he listed 66 "follies" which he ascribed to Governor Raymond, a procedure which neither endeared him to higher authority nor promoted his chances of getting results. A number of accomplishments nevertheless stood to his credit, and the general tone of the garrison was brightened when new troops of a better class were added. However, Surlaville is said to have taken a cut on canteen revenues as did other officers. And his tour of duty at Louisbourg was too short for lasting achievements.

Training and discipline, fair treatment, pride in the uniform, and consequent high morale—these make a good soldier. Absence of enough of those requisites at Louisbourg in the 1750s would sound the same knell for the Fortress as in 1745.

In the facade which caused Louisbourg to be acclaimed the Athens of the French colonies other familiar flaws appeared. Officials' peculations were resumed. Bigot had been transferred to Quebec, greener fields where he was reaping a far richer harvest. While the new Intendant, Prévost, could not hold a candle to him, he strove to fill his coffers with percentages of royal appropriations. Smuggling flourished again, most of it by British ships. English Joshua Mauger used a circuitous but effective route for dutiable goods. He smuggled from France to Louisbourg, thence to Halifax, and on through Nova Scotia to adjoining colonies, never scrupling to sell the Micmacs tomahawks for use on his own countrymen. Dying a wealthy man in

England, he left his fortune to his daughter who married a French nobleman and perished with him under the guillotine in the French Revolution.[3]

Though smuggling, connived at as formerly, was of no great concern to Governor Raymond, he was confronted by gathering difficulties. When he sought to build up the defenses of the Fortress by strengthening outposts and constructing more redoubts and roads, he was balked by the military, whose cooperation ought properly to have been reliable. Trouble developed in his personal staff. His secretary, Thomas Pichon, formerly an army commissary in France, was engaged like other officials in feathering his own nest. While that practice was condoned if not too flagrant, Raymond suspected his secretary of adding to his revenues by selling information to the enemy.

An affair between Pichon and a Louisbourg lady—one of those scandals that blaze up in the confines of a garrison town and prove a disrupting influence—gave the Governor an excuse to act. Pichon, whose gallantries in Paris had been so notorious that fathers warned their daughters against him, met Raymond's censure with the airy reply that it was no crime to love and be loved. However, the Governor shipped him to a French stronghold in Nova Scotia, Fort Beauséjour, where the former secretary became—or continued to be—a spy for the English and a useful one. Still masked after British capture of the Fort, he pumped French prisoners. Before his cover could be broken, he sailed for London with his gains, including a specially made, rich mink coat which he may have employed advantageously in an intrigue with a lady high in Court circles.

Notwithstanding faults, failures, and dissensions within, Louisbourg was France's to have and to hold. And it was still the "tough nut to crack" Ben Franklin had called it in 1745.

But forgotten again except by a small minority, whose cautionings went unheeded at Versailles, was the primary essential for defense. Neptune still wielded that trident-sceptre for Louisbourg's weal or woe. A noted naval historian, commenting on the Treaty of Aix-la-Chapelle, has written, "France was forced to give up her conquests for want of a navy, and England saved her position by her sea power, though she had failed to use it to best advantage."[4] While France had won back Louisbourg despite her naval inferiority, she could not keep it unless that disadvantage were remedied. No effective measures were being taken to do so. In French fleets and navy bases the same sorry conditions prevailed: shortages of armament, rigging, and other supplies; miserable maintenance, and wastage. Promotions were made through influence and bribery. "Honor and modesty were turned into ridicule." [5] By 1756 the French Navy, fallen still further below parity, could oppose but 45 ships of the line to England's 130.

Once more the handwriting could be read, not on the walls of Louisbourg, but on the horizon beyond the sea that girded the Fortress.

seventeen

Check and Countercheck

Scarcely was the Fortress repossessed by France when it became apparent that in the New World peace lay as uneasy as proverbial heads that wear a crown. Commissioners were still wrangling over the boundaries of the vast mainland area west of Cape Breton. All but insoluble was the question of where English Nova Scotia ended and French Canada began, for the claims of both nations were as wide as they were vague. France strove to maintain a coastal foothold, essential to winter communication between Louisbourg and Quebec, while England was equally determined to prevent any inroad on her Acadian conquests.

Moving toward check and countercheck, the hands of statecraft resumed shifting the pieces on the board: those red pawns, the Indians; the white ones, the Acadians; and the black bishops, the French missionary priests. Knights were marshaled, and above all loomed the castle that was Louisbourg.

Countering it, an opposing citadel was placed on the board in June, 1749, when the British founded Halifax on the fine Nova Scotian harbor of Chibucto. Transports brought 2,500 settlers, their number soon to be swelled. Palisades and redoubts rapidly rose, their ramparts manned by troops who had recently evacuated Louisbourg. By 1752 garrison and population amounted four thousand souls. As swift and effective reaction, the establishment of the fort and naval base which would become the capital of Nova Scotia, ranks high. Halifax would play a powerful part in the coming struggle. It furnished British fleets safe and spacious anchorage with means to recoup from the rigors of voyages across the Atlantic or up from the West Indies, within easy striking distance of Louisbourg. Only the smaller port of Canso, its blockhouse and town burned out, was closer.

France met the telling gambit of Halifax with a single individual, but that one man held such power that he was able to raise, arm, and lead a fifth column in the heart of the enemy's country.

Abbé Louis Joseph le Loutre, Vicar General of Acadia and missionary to the Micmac Indians, returned in 1749 to continue those interrupted labors which have been referred to in an earlier chapter. Parkman vividly describes him as "a man of boundless egotism, a violent spirit of domination, an intense hatred of the English, and a fanaticism that stopped at nothing. Towards the Acadians he was a despot; and this simple and superstitious people, extremely susceptible to the influence of their priests, trembled before him. . . Three successive governors of New France thought him invaluable, yet feared the impetuosity of his zeal, and vainly tried to restrain it within safe bounds."[1] Under the lash of his fierce sermons threatening excommunication, the devout Acadians shed their sworn allegiance to England and forgot the fair treatment accorded them since the conquest of 1710 when their land had been formally transferred by France to the British Crown. This "Moses," the code name given Le Loutre by the British because he claimed that he would lead the Acadians from the land of bondage, drove his flock to revolt by the menace of divine wrath if they resisted him, herded them wherever it suited French purposes, and sacrificed them on the altar of patriotism. Thus was a doomed people forced to set foot on the path that led to banishment and distant exile.

No less were the Indians made instruments and victims by Le Loutre and his staff of black robes. Their flagging enmity to the English inflamed, they took the warpath again. They were surreptitiously provided with powder and ball, money, blankets, liquor, and other presents, quantities of which were sent from Louisbourg. Documents signed by Governor Desherbieres and Intendant Prévost so attest, while cautioning that the source of supplies had to be kept secret lest the peace be broken. Distribution was made through Abbé Le Loutre, a ready paymaster of scalp bounties, particularly for those taken near Halifax. He compelled Acadians, disguised as Indians, to accompany the Micmac war parties; should any be taken prisoner, they were adjured to declare they were acting of their own accord.

Finally, but not until after he had accomplished many of his designs to the best of his considerable ability, Le Loutre himself was captured by the English. He escaped, slipped aboard a ship bound for France, was again taken at sea, and was confined for eight years on an island. Before his imprisonment ended, he narrowly escaped retribution. One of his guards, a British soldier who swore the priest had tried to scalp him in America, was barely prevented from bayoneting him.

The covert conflict spread far and wide beyond the environs of Louisbourg to develop as the last phase of the French and Indian War. Across the Alleghenies the hollow truce was shattered when French and English columns clashed, and the English were driven back in hasty retreat. An able young officer named George Washington, marching to the rescue with Virginia militia, was penned up by the enemy in Fort Necessity and forced to surrender. He was back in action again with the British retaliatory expedition under Braddock when that general met his disastrous defeat and suffered a mortal wound at the hands of a French and Indian force on the Monongahela in 1755.

In Europe the Seven Years' War broke out in 1756. As in the previous war, England and France were engaged on three fronts. Frederick the Great of Prussia, Britain's ally, was winning brilliant victories over Austria and France, but on other fields French arms held their own. In India a British army defeated the Hindus at Plassey. While at sea the fortunes of war swayed back and forth, British naval might began to build up when in 1757 a strong Prime Minister, William Pitt, returned to office. Wielding maritime and land power in masterly fashion and supporting allies with subsidies, Pitt moved to overwhelm his chief adversary on three continents.

The New World saw forts held or lost, with the French at first prevailing in Montcalm's capture of Oswego and Fort William Henry and his repulse of the British from Fort Carillon (Ticonderoga). To England's alarm more French troops landed in

America, including the Artois and Bourgogne Regiments to reinforce the garrison at Louisbourg.

Then the perceptive Pitt focused his attention on the key Fortress with all the concentration Governor Shirley of Massachusetts had displayed when he organized the expedition of 1745. British warships closed in. A fleet of fifteen vessels under Admiral Boscawen cruised the Gulf of the St. Lawrence to bar French ships from Louisbourg and Quebec, but the blockade was broken by French squadrons, totaling nineteen sail, which safely made Louisbourg's harbor, greatly augmenting its defenses. Tightening of the cordon thereafter prevented all but a few supply ships from slipping through.

However, in September, 1757, it was rent asunder by just such a terrific tempest as had smitten d'Anville's armada. Although scattered, all the storm-tossed ships of the British patrol, some dismasted and forced to jettison guns, managed to weather the gale, finding refuge at Halifax, except for the 60-gun *Tilbury*, which was wrecked on the rocks of St. Esprit, south of Louisbourg, her captain and half her crew drowned. "The French sent prompt assistance to the survivors as they feared the Indians might find them first and kill them. The Indians did find them, unprotected and half dead with the hardships they had suffered, but treated them well, 'which,' says the French narrator, 'surprised us.' "[2]

Such was the fury of the storm that even the shelter of Louisbourg's harbor could not save French ships from a severe battering. Despite four anchors down for each craft, numbers were wrenched loose by high winds and seas and cast ashore. However, all were refloated. After repairs the badly damaged flagship *Tonnant* was able to sail for France with a report.

Winter lowered its shield of storms and ice and snow in front of Louisbourg, but spring would raise it.

Chevalier Augustin de Drucour had been appointed Governor, succeeding De Raymond and destined to be the last for France. Arriving in 1754, he was granted ample time to prepare for the assault he could not fail to have foreseen—more time than and warning as plain as those vouchsafed the inept Du Chambon.

His, too, was the advantage of being able to learn from his predecessor's blunders.

Louisbourg still stood accounted the strongest fortress in French or British America. That it had once fallen—and to a harebrained, fortune-favored expedition of Yankee Colonials—gave no assurance that it would succumb again, since it was stronger than ever. Some of its inherent weaknesses still existed, but others had been corrected. The Free Companies of Marines and Swiss mercenaries, prone to mutiny, had been replaced by 3,080 regular soldiers; the battalions of Artois, Bourgogne, Cambis, and Volontaires Etrangers, with two companies of artillery and twenty-four of Canadian troops. Militia, organized from the four thousand inhabitants, were supplemented by Indians. In the harbor lay five ships of the line and five frigates with an armament of 544 guns and a complement of some three thousand men, brought by Admiral du Bois de la Motte. Unfortunately there was disease aboard, and it spread through the town to some extent before dying out.

Two hundred nineteen cannon and seventeen mortars were manned on the ramparts of the main fortress and at the outworks, with forty-four more pieces in reserve. Defenders were determined that those of the Grand or Royal Battery would not again be spiked in foolish abandonment. The other guardian fort of the harbor entrance, the Island Battery on its rocky islet, seemed safe from such bombardment from across the channel as had forced its surrender in 1745. French guns were mounted on fortified works near the lighthouse at the site to which the colonials had dragged theirs. High ground inland still commanded the main Fortress, but a vigilant watch was kept on the craggy shores that might give an invading army access to the heights. Munitions crammed the magazines and food the storehouses, sufficient for more than a year. To be sure, a long siege would dangerously deplete both; as always Louisbourg remained dependent upon the sea lines of supply. Thus far the Navy, abetted by storm, had kept them open.

Such was the optimistic view of the Fortress's situation, one that could not be fully justified. There were those who denounced the fortifications as wretched, the garrison as inadequate, and the stock of provisions as far too low. English warships swooped down to make prizes of French shipping, including a frigate bringing money and recruits for Louisbourg. Outposts were raided, fishing villages burned.

Once more Louisbourg stood in grave peril.

Spring 1758, and the curtain of fog, rain, and snow squalls lifted from time to time to reveal billowing sails to Louisbourg lookouts. English men-o'-war were back on blockade, but they could not yet maintain a tight one. There were days when gales drove them off, scouring Cape Breton seas clear, but the patrol ships always returned, sometimes venturing to within cannon shot of the harbor entrance batteries.

Again a three-front war was underway. In India the British prevailed, but in Europe, despite resounding victories by their ally, Frederick the Great of Prussia, they had met serious reverses, which were also being inflicted in the New World at the hands of the great French general, Montcalm. At sea where the war was being brought to focus on Louisbourg, Britannia ruled the waves. One French fleet, bound for Isle Royale, was cornered and shut up in the harbor of Cartagena. A second, attempting to relieve it, suffered defeat. When the first fleet emerged, it was chased back to France. The admiral of a third fleet did reach Louisbourg, but, fearing he might be blockaded like the squadron already there, sailed on to Quebec with most of his best warships.

British strategy had isolated Louisbourg. What if the Fortress was stronger than ever, one million pounds sterling having been spent on its works according to British intelligence—that it was reported to be better armed and garrisoned by troops of superior quality—that the French could be presumed to have filled gaps in its defenses demonstrated by the siege of 1745? Since it had fallen to colonial militia, it was confidently predicted that it could not withstand British Regulars, whether or not the French had learned past lessons as it appeared they had, for the shores of Gabarus Bay were manned against landings, and guns on Lighthouse Point seconded the cannon of the Island Battery.

Some Colonials would join the besieging force: Gorham and his rangers; Lieutenant Colonel Meserve—he of the stone-boats that had brought cannon across the marshes—in command of a detachment of ship's carpenters and fated this time to die of smallpox; the Royal Americans (60th Rifles) with many Swiss and Germans in their ranks; a few privateers. But this was a predominantly British operation, with the fleet commanded by Admiral Edward Boscawen, dubbed "Old Dreadnought" and "Wrynecked Dick" by his tars, the army by General Jeffery Amherst. An admiral of skilled seamanship and a troop commander of bulldog tenacity, both left names on the land; the former to an inland New Hampshire town, the latter to a Massachusetts one, site of a college whose lilting song proclaims that,

> Lord Jeffery Amherst was a soldier of the King
> And he sailed from across the sea.
> To the Frenchmen and the Indians he didn't do a thing
> In the wilds of this wild countree.

Both were to be overshadowed by one of Amherst's three brigadiers, James Wolfe. In the service since he was fifteen, the tall, thin officer, then 31, had, despite poor health, displayed a brilliance that would cause him to be rated "one of the most outstanding figures in the entire British army." He was as demanding of troops as he was considerate of their welfare. At Louisbourg he would establish a brew-house and issue quantities of spruce beer, an antiscorbutic, also taking along casks of it when he sailed for Quebec. Not one of his men was incapacitated with scurvy.[3] Wolfe, standing above the two other brigadiers, Whittemore and Lawrence, would be selected to lead the chief assaults. At once impetuous and cool and calculating, Wolfe had been early marked for promotion by Pitt. When the English Court branded the young Brigadier mad, King George II, "sleepy old drone from the Georgian hive," roused to declare: "Mad, is he? Then I only hope he'll bite some of my other generals!" If Wolfe did not bite them, at least he shouldered ahead of them, as he did with the other two brigadiers, both of whom were veterans of American wars. Although he considered Amherst unnecessarily cautious, Wolfe gave him a subordinate's loyalty and prompt obedience, justifying the confidence that had awarded him the leading role in the Louisbourg assaults. As a result of that dashing leadership, it was Wolfe, not Amherst, who would command the subsequent expedition against Quebec.

It was a mighty fleet that sailed from England in February 1758, bound for Halifax as a base for the expedition against Louisbourg. Totaling two hundred sail—twenty-three of the line, seventeen frigates, transports, and hospital ships—it was manned by crews numbering fourteen thousand men and it mounted 1,842 guns. Aboard were eleven thousand troops, later augmented to fourteen thousand. All other efforts had been subordinated. Lord Loudon, whose American campaign had been marred by failures and defeats, was relieved by Pitt and his supplies were made available to Amherst.

The spacious harbor of Halifax was crowded when Boscawen after a slow voyage made port May 12. Troops were put ashore for training, including amphibious operations. They comprised the following regiments: 1st Royals, 15th, 17th, 22nd, 28th, 35th, 40th, 47th, 48th, and 58th Foot, Frazier's Highlanders, and two battalions of the Royal Americans. Wolfe rated the Highlanders especially high, the Americans low, though he was to revise his opinion of those seasoned Indian-fighters. The artillery train was equipped with a powerful array of ordnance for the bombardment of Louisbourg. Brass pieces consisted of twenty-six 24-pounders, six 6s, and one 3, with two 13-inch mortars, two 10s, seven 8s, ten 5½s, and thirty 4⅔s; of iron pieces there were eight 32-pounders, twenty-five 24s, four 6s, and one 13-inch mortar. There were two 8-inch and four 5½-inch howitzers. Ammunition provided was 43,000 rounds of roundshot, 2,380 of case, 41,762 shells, and 4,888 barrels of powder.

Ginger and sugar were issued to counteract "the evil effects of American water," though many a soldier of the line doubtless would have preferred an increase in the rum ration. Quaint also were some of the orders published to instill discipline, courage, and confidence in the troops.

> No care or attention will be wanting for the subsistence and preservation of the troops, such as our situation will admit of. There will be an Hospital, and in time it is hoped there will be fresh meat for the sick and wounded men. . . . The least murmur or complaint against any part of duty will be checked with great severity, and any backwardness in sight of the enemy will be punished with immediate death. If any man is villain enough to desert his colours and go over to the enemy, he shall be ex-

> cepted in the capitulation, and hanged with infamy as a traitor. When any of our troops are to attack the French regular forces, they are to march close up to them, discharge their pieces loaded with two bullets, and then rush upon them with their bayonets; and the commander of the Highlanders may, when he sees occasion, order his corps to run upon them with their drawn swords . . . A body of light troops are now training to oppose the Indians, Canadians, and other painted savages of the Island, who will entertain them in their own way, and preserve the women and children of the Army from their unnatural barbarity . . . Indians spurred on by our inveterate enemy, the French, are the only brutes and cowards in the creation who were ever known to exercise their cruelties upon the sex, and to scalp and mangle the poor sick soldiers and defenceless women. When the light troops have by practice and experience acquired as much caution and circumspection, as they have spirit and activity, these howling barbarians will fly before them . . . The tents will be slightly intrenched or palisaded, that the sentries may not be exposed to the shot of a miserable-looking Mic-Mac, whose trade is not war, but murder . . . As the air of Cape Breton is moist and foggy, there must be a particular attention to the fire-arms upon duty, that they may be kept dry, and always fit for use; and the Light Infantry should fall upon some method to secure their arms from the dews, and droppings of the trees when they are in search of the enemy.[4]

Finally all was in readiness. Vessel after vessel cleared Halifax harbor, ships of the line, frigates, and transports crammed with troops, cannon, ammunition, and stores. Through the dark of the night of June 1, 1758, Louisbourg lookouts beheld glimmering globes like St. Elmo's lights in a sea storm, the masthead lanterns of invaders. Morning, and a dense fog blotted out vision. "Then a light sea breeze came in from the Atlantic. The curtain drew back at its touch. And there, in one white, enormous crescent, all around the deep-blue offing, stood the mighty fleet, closing in for the final death-grip on its prey." [5]

From the crowded decks, grenadiers and light infantry, artillerymen and seamen who would help haul and man the guns, pioneers and sappers stared shoreward. The fabled Fortress yonder, the beaches and fields before it, the hills behind it, and its outlying batteries were about to become the theatre of conflict for the most powerful and numerous army ever engaged on an American battlefield, save only, a century later, in the Civil War.[6]

eighteen

Amphibious Operation

Brigadier Wolfe, like some British officers before and many after him, carried a cane. While scabbarded sword and holstered pistol at belt were disregarded, the stick, hung over arm by crook or cord, was a token of nonchalant coolness under fire. That of the red-headed assault leader wrote history on the eighth day of June, 1758, when from one of the landing boats thronging Gabarus Bay he waved and leveled it at a crucial point.

This was the third attempt to put troops ashore through rolling breakers and boiling surf in weather whose gusty winds, fog, and rain alternated as extra hazards. Twice Amherst had ordered his grenadiers and light infantry into boats bobbing alongside the transports. They sat there miserably, drenched with spray, stomachs growing queasy, while Boscawen's scout craft tested the tossing seas and reported that heavy-laden boats would fill and sink long before they could reach shore. Back up rope ladders the soldiers climbed, certain that another trial would be made at the earliest possible moment. There was pressing need for haste since the expedition was behind schedule. Louisbourg had to be taken before the gales of September came to its rescue, driving away the fleet and an army that dared not risk being marooned in the open on the island under winter snows.

Along the crescent beach the French waited confidently behind their defenses, bristling abatis, and lines of entrenchments

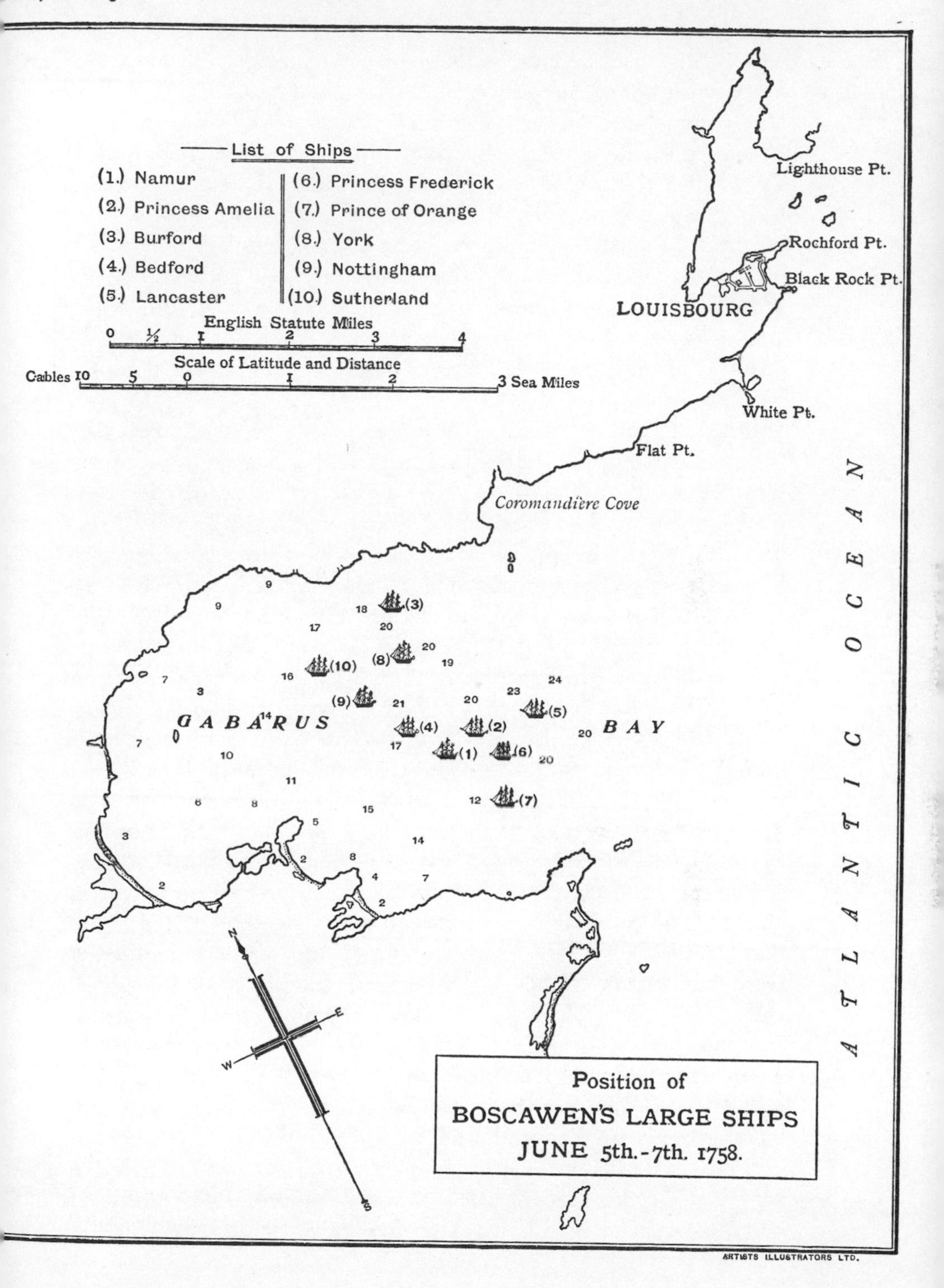

Position of
BOSCAWEN'S LARGE SHIPS
JUNE 5th.-7th. 1758.

ARTISTS ILLUSTRATORS LTD.

where guns and swivels, masked by evergreens, were emplaced to cover the shore. Sited along a bluff fifteen feet above the beach, they commanded an excellent field of fire. Heavier pieces in the Grand or Royal Battery were laid to blast landing boats out of the water if they came within range. Governor Drucour, realizing how vital it was to deny the invaders a beachhead, had avoided the mistake of his inept predecessor, Du Chambon. No weak, extemporized force manned the shore line, but two-thirds of the veteran garrison of Louisbourg with orders to hurl the British back into the sea. The Governor was determined to prevent the enemy this time from landing guns and bringing them to the high ground overlooking the Fortress's walls.

British frigates, standing in to range on the shore defenses, suffered damage in the stormy seas, but a moderation of the weather on the night of the 8th saw all assault troops ready in the boats before daybreak. Risky though it still was, Amherst sent them in in three columns under the warships' covering fire. Wolfe's column, spearhead of the main attack, sped into La Coromandière, nesting place of the cormorants, to be called Kensington Cove by the British. The other two made feints toward different landing places to distract the enemy's attention. Seamen bent hard to the oars of boats heavy-laden with redcoats.

But the defenders of La Coromandière were ready and undiverted. Batteries let Wolfe's flotilla come on until it was well within range. Then every gun from 24s to 6s and swivels boomed. Spurting musketry blazed the length of the abatis and entrenchments. "The French gunners had held their fire to good purpose, for now the effect of the battery of guns opening up in an instantaneous cannonade was devastating. In showers of spray and plumes of smoke, boats splintered and upturned and men were hurled into the sea where they floundered helplessly in their heavy uniforms. Sailors holding out oars and throwing ropes to the spluttering, choking soldiers, were peppered by French sharp-shooters as they tried to pull them back on board and were washed off their feet by sudden rushes of cascading water thrown up by exploding shells." [1]

Wolfe, a bold and daring man but no rash one, signaled to sheer off in the face of such devastating fire. Reluctantly his column began to turn back. And then came the break.

Three boats either failed to see or ignored the signal. They dashed for a half-tide ledge, entrance to a half-hidden inlet. Once there had been a French post there, but there was none now. It was the chink in the beach's armor. Three young officers of the 35th Regiment, Lieutenants Thomas Hopkins and Thomas Brown and Ensign Allan Grant, led their men ashore. Shortly they were reinforced by Major George Scott's light infantry and rangers.

Disappearance of the boats into the inlet and a sudden outburst of firing from that direction told Wolfe his chance had come. Up he stood in the sternsheets of his craft, whose flag had been shot away. He needed something else to serve for a signal. The cane flourished above his red head, pointed at the inlet, lifted again, swept forward. A great commander had instantly recognized and seized opportunity. His column swung inshore after him, flashing oars churning up the water.

Other trains of boats turned to dart for their quarters of the beach. A feint was made at Lorembec beyond Lighthouse Point to distract the enemy further. The frigates warped in closer and redoubled their fire. Guns of the larger ships engaged the Fortress at long range.

Meanwhile Scott and the men of the entered wedge staved off a heavy counterattack, taking their losses until Wolfe clambered up the rocks behind them at the head of boatload after boatload of troops. The beachhead won had to be enlarged and consolidated or it would be wiped out.

French artillery boomed a bass accompaniment to the rataplan of musket fire as other boat columns swerved shoreward. A British sergeant rose in the bow of a boat and shouted, "Who wouldn't go to Hell to hear such music for half and hour?" He was granted a shorter audition, for a bullet drilled him, and he keeled over, dead. In spite of swampings and drownings, the assault poured ashore. As Wolfe carried the nearest battery with a bayonet charge, the French fell back to their second line of resistance. It was outflanked when a new landing force suddenly emerged from the battle smoke and enfiladed it. In a fighting retreat the white-clad regiments withdrew to the shelter of the walls of Louisbourg. The landing had been achieved in four hours of swift action, with each side suffering about one hundred casualties.[2]

No sortie in force was made to destroy the lodgments, the still tenuous lines of British infantry. "Fort mentality," a phrase which would later be coined to describe an old military failing, held the French in its grip. They clung to the security of the battlements. An all-out sally scouring the beach clean, whatever the sacrifice, might have saved Louisbourg, for no British cannon were yet ashore. Without them the French batteries, including those floating in the harbor, the warships, could not be reduced. As before, big battering guns were the keys to Louisbourg.

History repeated itself with several striking variations on the theme of the first siege.

The landing of artillery was the same *coup de main* the untried New Englanders had accomplished. But the British, unlike the Colonials, did not have to sleep in the open or in crude huts; tents and small-arms ammunition and stores had been ferried in previously. Wind and high seas for a time enforced a period of inactivity. "A most terrible day," was a repeated entry in Amherst's journal. Then a lull allowed light field pieces to be brought ashore, with implements and fascines sent via Lorembec. Followed a few heavy guns, two 18-inchers and two 13-inch mortars. Before the rest of the heavies were beached, the total of smashed boats rose to one hundred, with drownings and injuries mounting.

In the interim Wolfe was busy throwing up redoubts and establishing battery positions. As the cordon was drawn tighter around Louisbourg, a flaring conflagration illumined the night. Again the French had abandoned the Royal Battery, about to be isolated, for Drucour, with odds of three to one against him, could spare no men to hold it. But this time the fortification was left gutted by fire, with no guns to be turned against the town. Wolfe thereupon occupied the outwork and led a march of 1,300 infantry and a detachment of light guns that completed the encirclement of the Fortress and the harbor when he reached Lighthouse Point. Cannonading from the town ramparts, the warships, and the Island Battery could not halt him. When the French finally made a sally with three hundred men, he was

EXPLANATION

POSITION OF SHIPS FROM MAY 18TH TO JUNE 20TH.

A. *Bienfaisant.*
B. *Prudent.*
C. *Entreprenant.*
D. *Célèbre.*
E. *Capricieux.*
F. Position of same ships from 20th to 30th June.
G. Unused Royal Battery.

1. Lighthouse Battery of 7 guns erected by Wolfe on 19th June.
2. Battery to fire on ships erected 21st June.

strong enough to meet it. Though the first rush overran his front line trenches, the Brigadier ran up to rally his men and drive the enemy back through the gates.[3]

By the 18th more artillery, 24s and 12s, were ashore. Only one gun of the former calibre was lost in the surf. Then the problem of transporting the guns to the high ground of Green Hill over intervening marshes faced the invaders, as in 1745. The know-how of a professional British army came to the fore. Colonel Meserve, sickening of smallpox of which his son also would die, was not called upon for stone-boats. Nor was use made of a "cart" devised by Amherst, a "machine" Wolfe called it. (This may have been a gun conveyance mounted on broad rollers.) Instead, engineers surveyed the most practicable route through morasses, rocks, sand, and bush, and pioneers constructed a road. It was a slower process than the Colonials' method, but the result was a good, solid throughway.

Yet once more draft had to be manpower, no animals being available, and it proved to be womanpower as well. Among the parties who tugged on the drag ropes, one thousand strong with frequent shift changes, were several hundred laundresses, a number being allowed to each British regiment by regulations, and carried as "married and on the strength."[4] Heavy fire from Louisbourg disconcerted them no more than it did the men.

Sailors and marines from the fleet also pitched in. "Wry-necked Dick" Boscawen stinted no aid for the sister service. Thirteen years earlier Warren, in contrast, had deemed the Navy's duty toward the New England militia done when he guarded the seas, helped with the landings, and fired on the forts. He had lent three master gunners to supervise green artillerymen and had turned over surplus powder from the captured *Vigilant*. Except for a cask of rum for the men to drink his health, that was his entire contribution, and he had royally repaid himself and his crews by appropriating all the money from French prizes.

So the cannon rolled into ready emplacements around the Fortress and ringed it with fire. Others were dug in among the ruins of the Royal Battery. At the Lighthouse Point Battery, also abandoned, Wolfe filled the embrasures with guns brought by sea in a feat duplicating that of the Colonials. Landed with diffi-

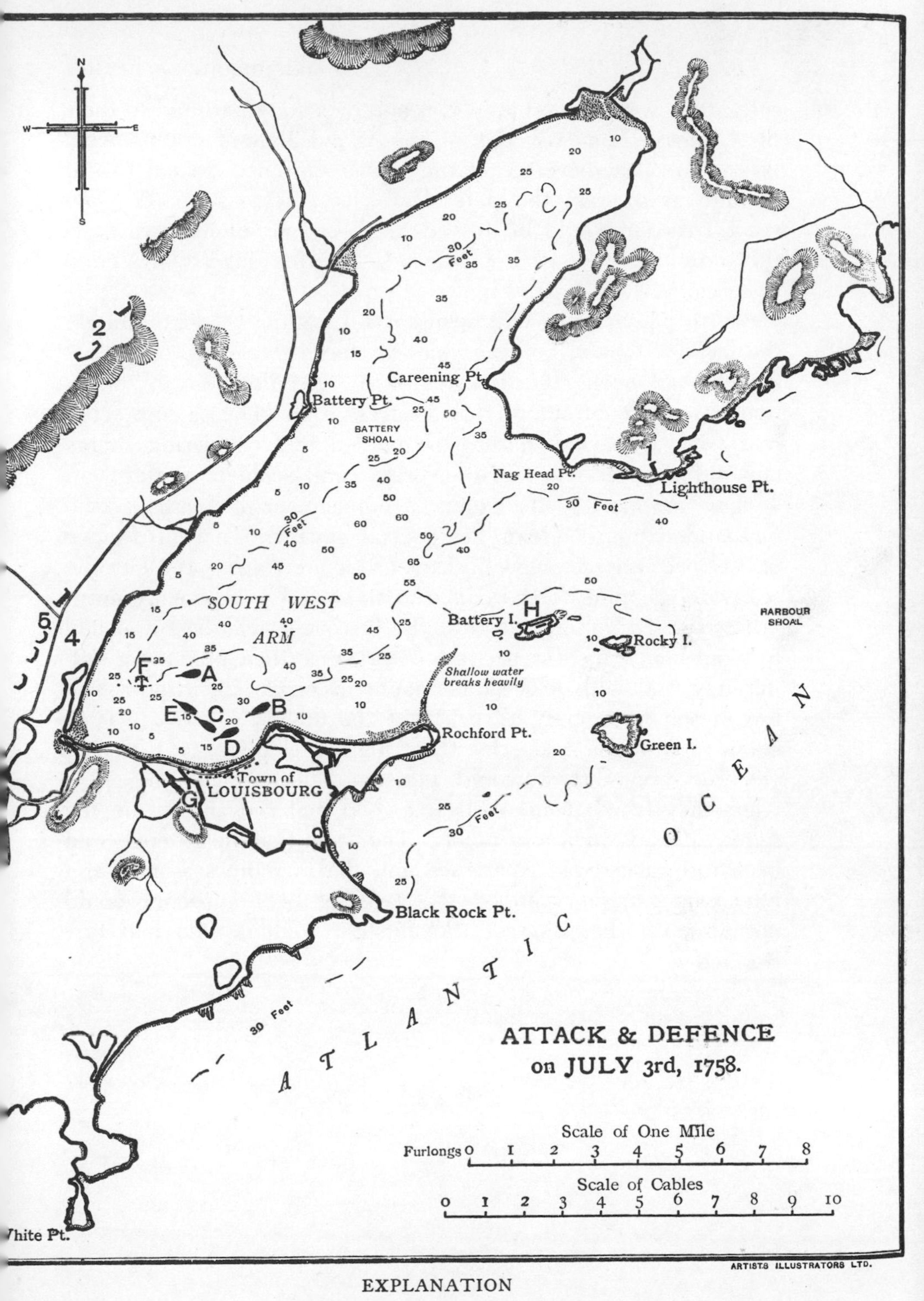

EXPLANATION

POSITION OF SHIPS, JULY 2ND

...faisant.
...lent.
...eprenant
...bre
...icieux
} Burned July 21st.

F. *Aréthuse.*
3. Battery erected against this frigate.
G. Works to destroy which batteries were erected at 4.

H. Island Battery destroyed June 25th.
1. Wolfe's Battery.
2. Battery of 6 guns and a mortar.
5. Battery of two heavy mortars.

culty, they were hauled up a cliff and over rough ground to their site. A brisk bombardment of the Island Battery commenced. Boscawen's fleet hovered off the harbor entrance, poised to run through as soon as the defenders' pieces were silenced. Governor Drucour would be forced to order four of his own warships sunk in the narrow channel, blocking ingress for large vessels of the enemy.

British preparations had been careful, cautious, and thorough, the means at hand being ample—far more than the New Englanders had been able to provide. A two-mile crescent of entrenchments confronted the Fortress. Blockhouses protected rear areas from Indian inroads; only a few wandering sailors and outpost sentinels were surprised and scalped. Watch was kept by the alert Wolfe against a detachment of Acadians who had landed from St. Jean. Prospect of naval succor from France or Quebec was remote. Boscawen's scout ships patrolled the sea, vainly hoping for a chance to sight and prize enemy craft.

The few New Englanders of the first siege who had returned to Louisbourg for the second observed British operations admiringly and with a certain amount of envy but without any loss of self-esteem. By all evidence the mighty Fortress was in a fair way to be taken by their mother country's scarlet-clad veterans—troops they would christen "lobster-backs" in 1775 when they faced them. Well and good, but they had done the same with less men and power. The facts that the French had been forewarned by experience and that a more seasoned and numerous garrison manned the defenses of Louisbourg could not diminish the pride of the amateur soldiers who had first stormed it.

nineteen

The French Frigate

Aboard the *Aréthuse* anchored at the western end of Louisbourg's harbor, a cannon boomed and recoiled against its breeching ropes. At the masthead a spotter watched the ball soar and descend to scatter a group of British road-makers. He shouted down to Captain Jean Vauquelin, his commander. Others of the frigate's 36 guns chimed in, pounding away until the work was halted, to be resumed only under cover of night or fog. Soldiers on the Fortress's ramparts turned from cheering the bombardment to glare at the remaining naval vessels, five ships of the line and four other frigates standing silent well off shore, and brand them cowards.

Commodore Desgouttes had desired to take his fleet to sea while a way through the blockade was still open. Whether he was well advised is a moot question. The warships, though not strong enough to risk a pitched battle, might have harried and distracted the English fleet, although those which had earlier left Cape Breton waters and sailed up the St. Lawrence to Quebec had not returned to Louisbourg's aid. Bottled up in the harbor, Desgoutte's ships had been vulnerable targets for such enemy guns as could be brought to bear. However, Drucour believed they could be of great service to the defense as floating batteries and held them in port for that mission. The Commodore, obsessed with saving his vessels from damage, utterly failed him. Clumsily maneuvered, they masked one another's fire. Instead of moving in close enough for effective cannonades, they crept under the protection of the Fortress guns to the Army's intense contempt.

Only the *Aréthuse* maintained the best traditions of His Most Christian Majesty's Navy, undermanned though she was with a crew of only fifty. The gallant Vauquelin frequently shifted moorings to blaze away at the British whenever he could take them under fire. So well did he hold up their advance and stave off attack that Louisbourg was given time for hasty repairs to the works. At length Wolfe in grudging admiration had to halt his left approach to deal with the *Aréthuse*. Erecting a costly epaulement a quarter-mile long and nine feet high to protect his pioneers from the frigate's broadsides, he established two batteries, one of six guns and another of two mortars. They concentrated on the *Aréthuse*, holed her, and forced her to withdraw beyond a range where her guns could reach the enemy. Only then did Vauquelin propose to the Governor that, since his craft could no longer hinder the foe, he be allowed to run the blockade carrying dispatches to France. Desgouttes had the gall to demur; the frigate might still be useful in the harbor, he protested. Whereupon the Captain bellowed at his superior officer:

"Yes, by God, if you will give me one of your men-of-war of the line that are laid up doing nothing, you will see that I will do much more yet than I have done hitherto with a frigate!" [1]

Marquis Desgouttes, looking down his aristocratic nose at the former merchantman skipper, refused. Then Vauquelin, granted Drucour's permission, patched up the *Aréthuse* and took advantage of a favorable wind and fog to thread his way through the British fleet and sail safely to France. One of Boscawen's first acts after the Louisbourg surrender was to inquire for the frigate captain of whose escape he was unaware; a man who had comported himself so valiantly should have been put in command of a ship of the line, declared "Old Dreadnaught." Two years after the siege Vauquelin was again across the Atlantic, as commodore of a small squadron on the St. Lawrence in support of the vain French attempt to retake Quebec. While his other vessels fled before the British, throwing guns overboard or running aground to be burned, Vauquelin fought his flagship to the last round and even then refused to strike his colors. Captured, he was accorded the distinguished honor he so well deserved.

Of the warships remaining in Louisbourg's harbor, Drucour, as previously related, had four sunk in the entrance channel when the fall of the Island Battery seemed imminent. Since Desgouttes could seldom be induced to bring the others into action (he secretly ordered two of them to run the blockade at first opportunity), the Governor finally stripped them of part of their crews and guns to reinforce the garrison and its armament. They lay anchored and impotent under the battlements, soon to play a last act in the drama in which their role had been so inglorious. For the Marquis Desgouttes a dark epilogue to that finale would be written: deprivation of naval command and dismissal, degradation from the ranks of the nobility, a jail sentence of twenty years.

After the *Aréthuse* had escaped to France, another vessel attempted to run the gantlet from beleaguered Louisbourg. Drucour, deciding it was essential to send dispatches to the Governor of New France at Quebec, chose the fast sloop *Echo* for the mission and took the opportunity to put his wife and several other ladies aboard to spare them from the increasing dangers of the bombardment. It may be assumed that the charming and determined Madame Drucour obeyed her husband's order under protest, convinced her place was at his side. There it soon proved to be in fact, for while the *Echo* won through the blockade, the fog which had hidden her lifted to reveal her too soon to a pair of enemy warships. They pursued and overtook the fleeing sloop. *Echo*'s captain fought them off as long as he could, then surrendered. The British returned the Governor's unfluttered and unreluctant lady and her companions to Louisbourg with all consideration.

There ensued rounds of wartime courtesies that match the celebrated exchange, factual or legendary, at the Battle of Fontenoy, when ranks of British and French musketeers faced each other at fifty paces; the commanders doffed their hats to each and bowed, the Briton calling over, "Gentlemen of the French Guard, fire!" His opposite number, demurring politely, replied, "Fire yourselves, gentlemen of England. We never fire first."

Flags of truce frequently halted Louisbourg hostilities, and messages and gifts passed back and forth. Drucour offered to send his own skilled surgeon to attend wounded British officers. An envoy from Amherst entered the gates with letters from French officers and prisoners. The Governor asked to be allowed to send out several soldiers to act as their orderlies, along with a supply of spare clothing, a tender which met prompt British acceptance. When Drucour asked for a refuge for his wounded, Amherst proffered a neutralized warship or the Island Battery, which had been captured; the Governor expressed his appreciation but felt he could accept neither.[2] Between interchanges, the guns resumed firing, and the English observed that regularly a skirt fluttered on the Louisbourg ramparts behind the embrasures. It was Madame Drucour, who every day advanced with burning linstock and fired three guns for the honor of the King, thus enshrining herself among history's heroic artillerywomen. Again a white flag waved in the British lines for a personal message from General Amherst for Madame Drucour. Would the Governor's lady accept his compliments for her courage and a basket of West Indian pineapples? The lady would and graciously begged the General's acceptance of a tub of fresh butter and a case of wine—no less than fifty bottles of champagne, some say.[3] That prompted a gift of more pineapples, one spoiled, a French diarist noted. Courtesies continued when during a truce three British officers escorted a lady into the French lines, where she was introduced to the officer commanding that sector, a Captain Joubert, whom conversation revealed to be her distant cousin. Might she be permitted to pick some of the greens in the vicinity for salad? But certainly, *chère cousine*.[4]

Amenities gave way to an increasing cannonade. British preparations had been deliberate and thorough. By July 22, eight new batteries with an armament of 37 pieces—guns from 32s to 12s, 13- and 8-inch mortars—were playing on the town alone. That day two more batteries, guns, mortars, and many coehorns, were advanced to blast the French out of the covered way. Exclusive of ships' armament, more than two hundred cannon ringed Louisbourg. French ordnance, numbering 218 guns and 11 mortars at the beginning of the siege, was steadily being silenced. Walls tottered and fell under some; others, exposed by blasted parapets, could not be manned. Battered by British pieces, stone buildings of Louisbourg crumbled under the pounding, and wooden ones burst into flame. "Burning the Town is spoiling our nests," Amherst wrote in his journal, "but it will probably be the shortest way of taking it."

The storm of shells buffeting the Fortress rose to the intensity of a tempest.

twenty

Ring of Iron

The cannonading of Louisbourg in 1758 ranks high among great siege operations during the four centuries that gunpowder gave artillery a leading role. On a remote island of the New World, guns of old antagonists confronted each other, flaming and thundering at ranges which narrowed from a mile or so to a few hundred yards, in resumption of duels fought for many scores of beleaguered forts and walled towns in Europe. French genius in gunnery, bright since blazing victories in the Hundred Years' War, was rivaled by the British, steadily risen in power from that day at Crécy when small bombards boomed amid the whirring flights of arrows that shattered the charge of armored knights.

The Royal Artillery, founded in 1716, carried on tradition and proved its might at Louisbourg. Its performance overshadowed but could not minimize that of Colonial gunners in 1745, handicapped by inexperience and other factors. On the record of the veteran R.A. stood none of those all-too-frequent premature bursts, due to such causes as overcharging, that killed New England crews around their guns. No longer was grudging support all the British Navy gave. General Amherst had complete cooperation from Admiral Boscawen from the landings onward. Those field expedients and extemporizations to which the Americans had been compelled to resort were avoided by a professional army with trained artillerymen, sappers, and pioneers in addition to its elite infantry.

At the start of the siege the French, as noted, manned 218 guns and 11 mortars, their ammunition supply seemingly ample. The British brought 149 pieces—guns, howitzers, and mortars—with 43,000 roundshot, 2,380 case (shrapnel), grapeshot, and carcasses (bombs filled with an inflammable substance), and 4,888 barrels of powder. These figures are exclusive of ships' armament, some of which was put ashore by both sides. Weight of metal thus at first favored the defenders but did not long do so, for their guns were steadily knocked out of action.

As a ring of iron was slowly riveted around the Fortress and its outworks, Frenchmen, watching from ramparts, marveled at British thoroughness and its deliberate pace. No battery was emplaced until its position had been well protected by redoubts and entrenchments. The same procedure was followed as each was moved forward. Working parties, though using fog and night cover whenever possible, still suffered casualties from French fire, but when they had finished the guns were so stoutly sheltered that they were little hampered by counterbattery.

From June 19, when Wolfe occupied and armed the abandoned Lighthouse Battery and opened on the Island Battery across the channel, the reports of British cannon presaged the crack of doom. The eager Brigadier poured a hail of shells on the rocky islet and the shipping behind it, fire returned with equal warmth. Against its strongest battery behind stout parapets and a double ditch he concentrated six 24s. Gunners were driven from their posts on the rampart and forced to take cover behind rocks below. The battery was silenced on the 25th and the rest of the outwork's guns soon thereafter. There was no need to storm it with a landing party as the Colonials had attempted at such heavy loss. The way into the harbor was opened, but the British Navy was not yet ready to risk running in and facing crossfire from Louisbourg's cannon and the broadsides of French warships.

Meanwhile British batteries were closing in on the main Fortress—some sited on Green Hill opposite the Citadel and only half a mile away, another that pounded the West Gate, one on the mound the English would call Gallows Hill less than three hundred yards from the Dauphin Bastion, still more encircling

Louisbourg with converging fire. Big 32s and 24s battered the walls. Thirteen-inch mortars and later, as the range shortened, coehorns, lobbed bombs over battlements onto roofs and into streets.

The French stood to their guns, and Amherst did not stint his praise of them while admiring the work of his own artillery. "The Enemy," he wrote in his journal, "likewise fired very well on them and threw their shells extreamly well. One shot went just into the Muzzle of a 24-Pounder and stuck there as if it had been forged to be rammed in." Other observers also described the French cannonade and musketry as very hot and inflicting no inconsiderable losses in the British trenches—blazing away not only at sight but even when sound betrayed movement or digging at night or in fog.

Masonry crumbled under the impact of large-calibre projectiles. Breaches opened, but they were not yet practicable for assault. The British began to push light pieces up the foot of the glacis toward a point where they could enfilade the covered way of entrenchments that defended approaches to the Fortress. But it was the high-angle fire of mortars and howitzers, their shells and carcasses soaring over walls and dropping into the town, that dismayed the people of Louisbourg and gave them a foretaste of the aerial bombings of the future. Dreadfully effective in that circumscribed area, it often forced the citizenry and soldiers not on duty to seek safety in the dark, stuffy casemates. Although the cannonade was by no means incessant, there were days when from 120 to 130 bombs plunged down on roofs and streets. Enemy fire was the more harrowing because it was delivered at unexpected moments.[1] When British gunners sighted the smoke of a fire curling up from some quarter, they were quick to deluge the vicinity, knowing it would provide a good target of fire-fighters and refugees. One daily bombardment *was* regularly timed. Between eleven and two o'clock, when the garrison assembled in the Citadel for mess, the structure was plastered with such harassing fire that none could eat in peace.

Numbers of the houses not burned or smashed were torn down to furnish wood to repair defenses, and the task was performed with spirit though streets were being raked.

As the siege wore into July, shells burst over the wooden barracks around the Place d'Armes. Those within the Queen's Bastion, which were especially inflammable, were ordered evacuated, the troops finding what scant shelter they could behind the walls of houses built against the ramparts. No sooner had they left their former quarters than a fire bomb set them ablaze. "A fearful scene ensued. All the English batteries opened upon it. The roars of mortars and cannon, the rushing and screaming of round shot and grape, the hissing of the fuses and the explosion of grenades and bombs mingled with the storms of musketry from the covered way and the trenches; while by the glare of the conflagration, the English regiments were seen drawn up in battle array, before the ramparts, as if preparing for an assault." [2]

Flames threatened the casemates under adjacent ramparts in which the wounded, the women, and the children were cowering. In fear of suffocation from billowing smoke—timber barriers before the entrances had been ignited—all who could move "rushed out, crazed with fright, and ran hither and thither with outcries and shrieks amid the storm of iron."

Surgeons, attending the wounded, were compelled to desert their charges and take cover when a shout of *Gare la bombe!* was raised. Otherwise they might well have been struck down, leaving no skilled hands to aid the increasing number of maimed. Drucour must have sadly regretted that he had not accepted the British offer to allow evacuation of the injured and sick.

A shell through the roof of the King's Bastion, which formed the front of the Citadel, detonated among a group of soldiers and started a fire. In half an hour it consumed the chapel and all the north part of the building. Fire brigades, working under heavy shelling called down by the smoke, could save only the end of the structure occupied by the Governor's apartments.

The British bombardment did not neglect the warships in the harbor. Since the departure of the hard-fighting little *Aréthuse,* they had for the most part lain anchored under the Fortress guns, the inept Commodore Desgouttes making not even his former contribution to the defense. He had stripped them of all but skeleton crews when on the night of July 21 a well-aimed shell struck the deck magazine of the *Célèbre,* of sixty guns, and exploded it with a roar. Sparks from leaping flames caught in the rigging of the *Entreprenant,* fire spreading thence to the *Capricieux.* The few seamen aboard strove vainly to extinguish raging blazes on the three vessels. They abandoned them as loaded guns, touched off by the heat, began hurling broadsides into the town and at one another. British batteries added their thunder to the din, with the red glare silhouetting splendid targets of opportunity, as artillerymen call them—the flaming craft and packed boats being rowed frantically away from their sides. The three men-o-war burned to the water's edge and sank as hissing hulks. Of all the French fleet only the *Prudent* and the *Bienfaisant* remained, and their fate was about to be sealed.

An account of the daring naval exploit of July 25 will have a familiar ring for readers of C. S. Forester's novels, whose hero Hornblower specializes in achieving its like. At midnight two divisions of boats, 25 in all and carrying six hundred sailors, entered the harbor, rowing with muffled oars. Concealed by deep darkness and fog and with a cannonade by shore batteries diverting the enemy's attention, they steered toward the Grand Battery so as to make an unexpected approach to their quarry from the landward side. One division, drawing alongside the *Prudent,* was challenged by a deck sentry. His hail was answered in French that they were boats from the town and coming aboard. The deceived guard was overpowered before he could alarm the crew asleep below. British tars hoisted anchors, made fast cables, and tried to tow the warship away, but she was fast aground. Setting her afire, they had rowed off when her crew, roused at last, managed to make its escape before the blazing *Prudent* went to the bottom.

The second division, failing to surprise the *Bienfaisant,* swarmed over her bulwarks and subdued her crew in a short, sharp struggle with losses on both sides. Finding her well afloat, they commenced towing her out of the harbor. By now Louisbourg had been alerted, and Governor Drucour himself had rushed to the shore guns of Batterie de la Grave and was directing their fire on the captured warship. Illumined though she was by the flames of her burning sister ship, she was safely extricated and moved under the lee of the Lighthouse Battery while British cheers echoed over the waters.

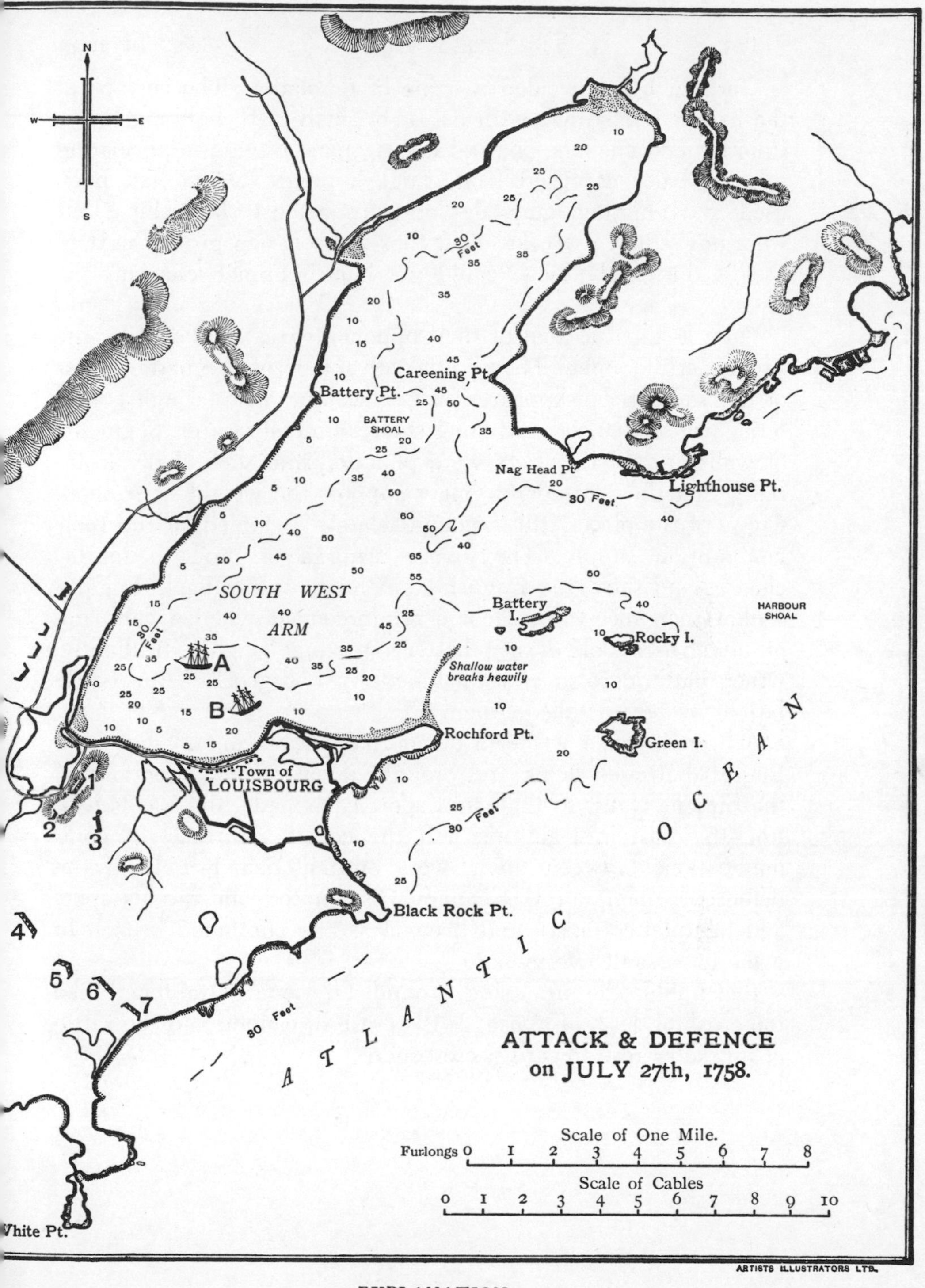

EXPLANATION

Bienfaisant, captured 25th July.
Prudent, burned 25th July.

1. Battery 6 guns, 22nd July.
2. Battery mortars.

3. Battery of 4 guns only used on July 26th.
4, 5, 6, 7. Batteries firing on July 22nd.

Morning light revealed a scene of desolation. The surface of the harbor was strewn with debris of small craft, bobbing buoys from slipped anchors, charred masts, spars, rigging—and floating tobacco bales captured from English prizes, which had been used to strengthen gunwales of ships against shot, ships that were now sunken wrecks. That those vessels had proved next to useless during the siege could not banish French chagrin.

Valor as great as that of their opponents was displayed by the French artillerymen. Their initial advantage of the better cover of the ramparts disappeared as the well-protected English batteries were advanced and flung shells into embrasures. Segments of walls crumbled; others were pounded into such shaky instability that they would no longer support the weight of cannon. Crews of the pieces still in action steadily dwindled, as did their ammunition supply. They were using scrap iron in mortar charges and salvaging English cannonballs to fire back. Regular artillerymen received welcome reinforcement when a company of merchants took over a battery, serving its guns brilliantly. Other batteries also were manned by bourgeoisie. But battle fatigue began to tell on them all.

A French officer wrote in his journal, "Each cannon shot from English batteries shook and brought down immense sections of the ruinous walls, so that, in a short cannonade, the Bastion du Roi, the Bastion Dauphin, and the courtin [curtain] of communications between them, were entirely demolished, all the defenses ruined, all the cannon dismounted, all the parapets and banquettes razed, and became as one continued breach to make an assault everywhere."

Inexorably, the iron ring around Louisbourg tightened like the crushing jaws of a vise, as the crash of cannon and the rattle of musketry rose toward a crescendo.

twenty-one

Fall into Oblivion

Prospect of succor for Louisbourg from the French Navy had completely faded. Of several sorties attempted from the Fortress, only one had been briefly successful. Because of lowered morale no more were risked. A diarist caustically wrote, "The soldiers were so used to profusion that they would not make nor go upon a sally unless they were half drunk." His observation on the officers was pessimistic. "When they were not upon duty they assembled together and gambled so very high that to see them one would have thought that they were certain of the future inutility of their money." [1]

There remained a resource which had failed the Fortress in 1745—help from an expedition from the mainland. Such a force had been assembled by Boishébert, a noted leader of Indians, and for it Governor Drucour had established a depot of provisions and ammunition on the Miré River before the siege began. But that cache had been gutted by the missionary Maillard and a band of Micmacs on their flight from Louisbourg the day the British landed. When Boishébert with Acadians and Indians arrived, the empty depot served as an excuse for inaction. Beyond a few raids on British outposts nothing was done. The first hint that Louisbourg might be at the point of surrender sent the partisans scurrying to safety. So vanished the last forlorn hope.

Sappers dug more parallels, closer to the walls, in classic siege procedure. Guns were emplaced in them, and the range for many was now only two hundred yards. Where the English lodgment at the foot of the glacis had been secured, trenches burrowed on into the covered way to afford sweeping musketry along its length that made it indefensible. Three hundred bombs a night dropped into the town. One of the twelve encircling batteries, a six-gun unit, raised its rate of fire to the height of six hundred rounds a day. A Frenchman despairingly recorded: "Not a house in the whole place but has felt the force of their cannonade. Between yesterday morning and seven o'clock tonight from a thousand to twelve hundred shells have fallen inside the town, while at least forty cannon have been firing incessantly as well." [2] Such brutal punishment could not much longer be endured by a garrison and townsfolk many of whom were suffering from that shattering of nerves subsequently to be termed "shell shock." One-fourth of the besieged were incapacitated by wounds or exhaustion. The rest fought on.

Destruction of the town was the first British objective. Now that it was far advanced, the big battering guns concentrated on breaching the ramparts. They opened gaps, tons of masonry tumbling into the moat. Assault troops with scaling ladders mustered in the trenches. "The fleet was waiting for the signal to file in and turn a thousand cannon against the walls."

One after another, surviving French guns fell silent—were knocked out by direct hits, became impossible to serve because of shaky bases, or ran out of ammunition. At last, only three pieces of all the powerful armament that had defended Louisbourg continued to fire. To Governor Drucour their slow, spaced reports resembled the mournful firing of a funeral salute.

On July 25 he made a tour of inspection of the circuit of the fortifications and could not doubt that the stronghold was *in extremis*. At once he called a council, all of whose members but one voted for capitulation. A white flag soared up over the Dauphin Bastion, and emissaries crossed the lines to ask for terms. Amherst's and Boscawen's reply was uncompromising—surrender the whole garrison in one hour or suffer assault by land and sea. On a second plea, the British sternly reduced the granted time to half an hour.

The Governor saw no other course but to refuse. Only a year

before, the colonial defenders of Fort William Henry had been massacred by rum-crazed Indians, unrestrained by Canadian troops, though Montcalm's French soldiers had risked their lives to save the prisoners.[3] Burning resentment might well visit retribution on Louisbourg. Better a fight to the last with no quarter given than supine submission to slaughter, Drucour decided, and sent out a third flag of truce with his defiance.

As the messenger departed, Intendant Prévost and other civilians begged the Governor on behalf of the inhabitants to reconsider and surrender on any terms. The official presented a memorandum that declared that the citizenry would "be delivered over to carnage and the rage of the unbridled soldiers, eager to plunder, and impelled to deeds of horror by pretended resentment at what had formerly happened in Canada." Yielding, Drucour dispatched an officer who ran after the flag shouting, "We accept! We accept!"

British demands stood prepared. They required the immediate surrender of Louisbourg, all Cape Breton Island, and Isle St. Jean, with all the public property they contained. At eight o'clock next morning the gates were to be opened and French arms laid down before the conquerors. Drucour was given special assurance of good treatment of the townspeople by an accompanying note.

> Sir,—We have the honour to send Your Excellency the signed articles of Capitulation.
>
> Lieutenant Colonel d'Anthony has spoken on behalf of the people in the town. We have no intention of molesting them; but shall give them all the protection in our power.
>
> Your Excellency will kindly sign the duplicate of the terms and send it back to us.
>
> It only remains for us to assure Your Excellency that we shall seize every opportunity of convincing you that we are, with the most perfect consideration, Your Excellency's most Obedient Servants.
>
> E. Boscawen
> J. Amherst

As no mercy had been promised Indians and Canadians in the Fortress, the former prudently paddled away in canoes that night and escaped. The latter either followed them or mingled with the townsfolk undetected.

At midnight the articles were signed. Disciplined troops in the British batteries, entrenchments, and camps remained quietly alert, forbidden celebration until after the take-over. It was Louisbourg that was astir all night. Officials, busy with documents, tried to shut their ears to the racket from the jammed cabarets where soldiers drank hard to drown their humiliation and leave as little liquor as possible for the hated English. As crowded was the parish church, scene of scores of hastily performed marriages. "The priests spent the whole night in marrying all the girls of the place to the first that would have them for fear they should fall into the hands of heretics." [4] To the dread of rape, so often the fate of the women in a captured city, and the hope that wives would be less vulnerable than unmarried girls was joined the belief that married couples would stand a better chance of being allowed to stay in Cape Breton.

The Dauphin Gate swung open on the morning of July 27, and British grenadiers and light infantry marched into the desolate, ruined town. At noon the formal ceremony of surrender took place, witnessed by the whole population. An imposing group of British generals and admirals faced Governor Drucour, who advanced, saluted, and tendered his sword to Boscawen. His officers followed suit, but the soldiers, weeping tears of rage, broke their muskets. Behind them their burned colors smoldered.

For the second and for the last time the great Fortress had fallen.

English casualties in the siege amounted to 195 killed and 329 wounded. The occupying army counted 10,813 fit for duty. Four hundred eleven Frenchmen had been killed; of the 5,637 survivors 1,790 were wounded or sick. The usual ratio of the heavier cost of an offensive was reversed; yet it might not have been so had it been necessary to storm Louisbourg. That necessity had been obviated by the long, deadly bombardment.

The Royal Artillery had expended 18,700 roundshot, 3,340 shell, 766 case shot, 156 rounds of fixed ammunition, 50 carcasses, and 1,493 barrels of powder. One can picture touring gunners surveying the tremendous havoc they had wrought with satisfaction and sometimes a tinge of pity.

Drastic orders scoured Louisbourg of all the French, military, naval, and civilian. Few saved many of their possessions. The *habitants* and 5,637 soldiers and sailors boarded transports which sailed out of the harbor into the Atlantic, Madame Drucour, valiant symbol of the defense, standing at the stern of one to wave her white scarf in final farewell. How the curse of Louisbourg followed them is described by Wood in *The Great Fortress*.[5]

> The combatants were coldly received when they eventually returned to France, in spite of their gallant defense, and in spite of their having saved Quebec for that campaign. Several hundreds of the inhabitants were ship-wrecked and drowned. One transport was abandoned off the coast of Prince Edward Island (Isle St. Jean), with the loss of two hundred lives. Another sprang a leak as she was nearing England; whereupon to their eternal dishonour, the crew of British merchant seamen took all the boats and started to pull off alone. The three hundred French prisoners, men, women, and children, crowded the ship's side and begged that, if they were themselves to be abandoned, their priest should be saved. A boat reluctantly put back for him. Then, leaving the ship to her fate, the crew pulled for Penzance, where the people had just been celebrating the glorious victory of Louisbourg.

France, in dismay at the loss of her sea link and in deep apprehension for her New World colonies, addressed a desperate appeal to other powers. It went unheard in the paeans of triumph and resounding celebrations in England and America. London was illuminated, as Parliament voted the nation's thanks to Boscawen and Amherst. Such rejoicings were dimmed by those across the ocean. Halifax, as if foreseeing the future that the fall of Louisbourg was about to confer on her, would welcome detachments of the victors with bonfires, salutes, and toasts that consumed sixty thousand gallons of Jamaica rum.

The following triumphantly jingoistic verse is preserved in the Louisbourg Museum.

A NEW SONG WROTE ON THE TAKEN OF LOUISBOURG

Prepare British Boys,
Your Hearts for new joys.
For Cape Breton and Louisbourgh's taken;
Our Cannons dire Thunder,
Has made France knock under,
And Louis, and Louis has scarce sav'd his bacon.

Nor to Gallia alone,
Is our Valour made known,
Ev'ry Nation before us shall fall:
Both the Indies can tell,
What they know but too well,
And Africk, and Africk gives up Senegal.

Let the Bullies of France,
Now be slow to advance,
Since our old British courage revives:
When e're wee attack them,
We'el hack them, we'el thwack them,
They never, were never so thwack'd in their lives.

Then my Jolly Boys sing,
To GEORGE our great King,
To his Council, his Army, and Navy:
Who have humbled the Monsieurs,
And prov'd them vain bouncers,
And made, and made grand Monarch cry peccavi.

New England shared the general joy, though enthusiasm was somewhat tempered by the fact that Yankee troops, so triumphant in 1745, had taken little part in this siege. It was Philadelphia, despite its staid Quaker citizens, that staged the most elaborate celebration, an altogether remarkable display of fireworks and a series of tableaux.

A floating castle, to represent England appearing before Louisbourg, was erected on the River Delaware, opposite Philadelphia, which represented Louisbourg. From the right of the castle rose a tower pierced by three tiers of guns, and bearing the inscriptions: "Boscawen" and "Amherst"; from the left a tower bearing the inscriptions, "Hardy" and "Wolfe"; and from the centre a citadel supporting a majestic statue of "George Rex," a perpendicular wheel of fireworks, a similar representation of the sun, a triangular wheel, and a St. George's flag on a spire. The curtain bore the inscription, "Charles Frederick, King of Prussia," above two ten-gun tiers of guns; below them was the inscription, "General Lawrance"; and on the gate appeared the names of "Pitt and Whitemore," enclosed by fluted columns with a full entablature.

The tableau opened with a rocket from the castle, replied to by a cannon from the shore, and a salute of the statue of the King on the citadel with twenty-one guns and three cheers, while the bells rang "God Save the King." A second rocket was then fired from the castle, the flag of France was hoisted over Philadelphia, and a vigorous bombardment of the castle began. The castle as hotly bombarded Philadelphia, which offered a vigorous defence with cannon and shell, and defeated an attempt to carry it by storm by springing a mine. The engagement continued with great determination on both sides for some time; but, after sustaining a vigorous bombardment, the besieged at length surrendered, the French colours were lowered, and the flag of England again floated over the city. The rejoicings over the capitulation then began. A swarm of rockets ascended from Tower Amherst on the floating castle: a *feu de joie* with rockets followed; a horizontal wheel of fireworks in the Whitemore gate of the castle and the perpendicular wheel on the citadel were lit and set in motion amid joyful strains of music; and a swarm of rockets burst from Tower Wolfe, followed by the lighting of the sun, and the triangular wheel on the citadel, and a brilliant *feu de joie* of rockets. A flaming Indian, equipped for war, then issued from Whitemore's gate, with the motto, "Britons Strike Home!" suspended from his mouth, amid the chiming of all the city bells and the spirited rendering of "Britons Strike Home" by the bands. This was followed by a brilliant discharge of rockets, water-rockets, and a general discharged volley of cannon; and the unique display concluded with three cheers from the immense number of spectators that thronged the water front.[6]

It was reluctantly conceded that it was too late in the season to advance to the assault of Quebec. Louisbourg's resistance had given the capital of French Canada grace and time for preparation. Heartened by Abercrombie's bloody repulse from Fort Carillon (Ticonderoga) by Montcalm, the French made good use of the respite.

Amherst and Boscawen soon went home to gather their laurels. The energetic Wolfe, given well-deserved command of the forthcoming expedition, began his usual thorough plans while in garrison at the Fortress in whose capture he had played such a leading part. Spruce beer vats bubbled in the production of the beverage that would ward off scurvy from his troops. In an order of the day he announced the formation of the Louisbourg Grenadiers, made up of elements of the 22nd, 40th, and 45th Regiments in tribute to their gallant conduct during the siege. The new unit proudly received its colors from his hand.

One of his veterans, Sergeant Edward Botford, well known as a soldier poet, busied himself composing a campaign song which would continue to be a favorite of British troops through the American Revolution. The morale it inspired was long to outlive its author who would fall before Quebec. Entitled "Hot Stuff" and set to the tune, "Lilies of France," the ditty ran:

Come, each death-doing dog who dares venture his neck.
Come, follow the hero that goes to Quebec;
Jump aboard of the transports, and loose every sail,
Pay your debts at the tavern by giving leg-bail;
And ye that love fighting shall soon have enough;
Wolfe commands us, my boys: we shall give them Hot Stuff.

Up the river St. Lawrence our troops shall advance,
To the Grenadiers' March we shall teach them to dance.
Cape Breton we have taken, and next we shall try
At their capital to give them another black eye.
Vandreuil, 'tis in vain you pretend you look gruff,—
Those are coming who know how to give you *hot* stuff.

With powder in his periwig, and snuff in his nose,
Monsieur will run down our descent to oppose;
And the Indians will come; but the light infantry
Will soon oblige *them* to betake to a tree.
From such rascals as these may we fear a rebuff?
Advance, grenadiers, and let fly your Hot Stuff!

rary of Congress

English medal struck on capture of Louisbourg.

> When the forty-seventh regiment is dashing ashore,
> While bullets are whistling and cannons do roar,
> Says Montcalm: "Those are Shirley's.—I know the lapels."
> "You lie," says Ned Botwood, "we belong to Lascelles'!
> Tho' our clothing is changed, and we scorn powder-puff;
> So at you, ye b------s, here' give you Hot Stuff."

Halifax, soon visited by Wolfe, stood as flank guard for the Quebec invasion. It was the destiny of that new city, with its citadel and fine harbor, to serve as the instrument that wrote finis for Louisbourg, to decree the doom of the great Fortress in irrevocable accents, to all intents forever.

twenty-two

Rack and Ruin

Within a year and a half after the capture of Louisbourg—in February, 1760—Prime Minister Pitt informed General Amherst, Commander in Chief in North America "that after the most serious and mature Deliberation being had . . . the King is come to a Resolution, that the Fortress, together with all the works, and Defences of the Harbour, be most effectually and entirely demolished."

It was Louisbourg's death warrant, signed by George II.

Delenda est Ludovicoburgum. It echoed Shirley's pronouncement of sixteen years before but with an emphatic finality never contemplated by the Massachusetts Governor.

Meanwhile Wolfe and his army of nine thousand men had sailed in two hundred transports, convoyed up the St. Lawrence by fifty men-o'-war, one-quarter of the Royal Navy; had landed to scale cliffs to the Plains of Abraham in his last march on the path of glory, and had joined battle in which both he and French General Montcalm were killed. Quebec had fallen, and in that year of 1759 New France in the North was all but finished.

The garrison left behind in Louisbourg, monotonously safe, had endured two dull, bleak winters. Toward the end of the second arrived those tidings from London that spelled relief. British troops would man many a Canadian and American fort thenceforth but never again the stronghold on lonely, remote Cape Breton Island.

One hundred skilled sappers and miners were dispatched to Louisbourg in the summer of 1760. Large details of infantrymen aided them in the strenuous work of the Fortress's condemnation, pushed forward every day except Sundays and the King's birthday. Forty-seven galleries were driven beneath the walls, drifts well shored up with timber to prevent cave-ins, the last stock of lumber being obtained from torn-down houses. Barrel after barrel of powder was placed in 45 chambers and fuses laid. From the ramparts 230 guns had been removed for shipment to Halifax. Cut stone from the Citadel, the hospital, and the gates would also be transported to be used in public buildings of the supplanting settlement.

On sunrise of the appointed day charges were detonated. A succession of roaring explosions smote the skies, surpassing the bombardments of both sieges in din and effect. "Black clouds of smoke suspended over the city, often veiling her in dense gloom, and fragments of her falling towers plunged into the water of the port." In a distant echo of Joshua's trumpets blaring before Jericho, the last mine blasted on October 17, tumbling the great fortress in utter ruins, its walls overthrown, its moat filled with debris.

> No more th' ear,
> Nor th' tormented air, nor earth could bear,
> Nor that deep-throated engine, erst presumed
> Impregnable, such mighty shocks sustain,
> But all to shivers rent, lay scattered o'er the plain.
> Loud shouts succeed: Huzza! God save the King! [1]

Sic transit gloria Ludovicoburgi.

The capture and demolition of the Fortress further dimmed the resplendence of the King who had founded it. Though Louis XV would long survive his famed stronghold, the words spoken by another monarch, Solomon of Israel, arose to plague him. "He that hath no rule over his own spirit is like a city that is broken down, and without walls." [2]

Plunder, as well as salvage, gutted Louisbourg. A bell from the chapel tolled in Montreal. The swinging sign from the Golden Lion Inn adorned a hostelry in Placentia, Newfoundland. Carved chimney pieces and mantles reappeared in Halifax,

Boston, Salem, and Charleston, South Carolina. From the dark hole that had been the Governor's wine cellar, presumably ransacked thoroughly before the destruction, were dug up years later hundreds of fat bottles, the contents of some in an excellent state of preservation.[3] Long after tons of Caen stone and quantities of usable wood had been taken, treasure-hunting divers pillaged the sunken vessels in the harbor with little or no official hindrance. Probably unreported hauls of chests of coins, prize money, and other trove were made. Certainly a number of cannon and cannonballs, increased in value by time, were raised and removed for sale before the enforcement of regulations that saved some for a restoration. Much had been lost beyond recovery before vigilant supervision was tardily established.

When the historian Parkman visited the ruin-strewn site of Louisbourg, he sat on the broken cornerstone of the Citadel, watched a few sheep graze on fields intersected by rows of stone that once were streets, and gave himself over to musings from which he would pen an eloquent epitaph for the mighty Fortress.[4]

> Green mounds and embankments of earth enclose the whole space, and beneath the highest of them yawn arches and caverns of ancient masonry. This grassy solitude was once the "Dunkirk of America"; the vaulted caverns where the sheep find shelter from the rain were casemates where terrified women sought refuge from storms of shot and shell, and the shapeless green mounds were citadel, bastion, rampart, and glacis. Here stood Louisbourg, and not all the efforts of its conquerors, nor all the havoc of succeeding times, have availed to efface it. Men in hundreds toiled for months with lever, spade, and gunpowder in the work of destruction, and for more than a century it has served as a stone quarry; but the remains of its vast defences still tell their tale of human valor and human woe.
>
> Stand on the mounds that were once the King's Bastion. The glistening sea spreads eastward three thousand miles, and its waves meet their first rebuff against this iron coast. Lighthouse Point is white with foam, jets of spray spout from the rocks of Goat Island; mist curls in clouds from the seething surf that lashes the crags of Black Point, and the sea boils like a caldron among the reefs by the harbor's mouth; but on the calm water

> within, the small fishing vessels rest tranquil at their moorings. Beyond lies a hamlet of fishermen by the edge of the water, and a few scattered dwellings dot the rough hills, bristled with stunted firs, that gird the quiet basin; while close at hand, within the precinct of the vanished fortress, stand two small farmhouses. All else is a solitude of ocean, rock, marsh, and forest.

William C. MacKinnon of flourishing Sydney, which became the metropolis of Cape Breton Island, added a threnody for the fortress that had been.[5]

De Raymond stands on a rampart's height
That overlooks the city's domes,
Those domes then glorious to the sight,
But now some fisher's homes.
Oh she that was the fairest gem
In haughty Bourbon's diadem,
That glittered on his regal brow,
Such was she then—what is she now?

I stand on a grassy plain—I see
Nothing around that recalls to me
That city, the queen of the western sea.
There the bay's glassy waters sleep—
Here graze amid grey ruins, sheep—
Beyond yon cliff, old azure ocean
Resound in his eternal motion;
While on its high and rugged steep
That o'erhangs the howling deep,
The sailor's beacon claims devotion—
And looks like baron's donjon keep.

Her pomp is gone, her streets are lone,
Her ramparts are with grass o'ergrown,
Her lordly palaces o'ergrown with rank decay,
Her knightly halls are filled with sand
And levelled to the foam-worn strand;
Her busy crowds—her warrior bands,
Her chieftains—where are they?

De Raymond's arms are dark with rust,
Lord Montmorency's pennon dust,
And De la Mothe,[6] her hope's last trust,

Long shattered lies his shield.
Her dust from sea-born towers driven,
Is scattered on the wings of Heaven,
And worships holy places given,
With storm and war all rent and riven,
To creatures of the field.

The dead past had not buried its dead for a Canadian of French extraction, Pascal Porier, who visited Louisbourg in 1912 and deeply mourned its vanished glory.[7]

> The Englishman who comes from Toronto or Liverpool, serenely regards the somber panorama, and finds it entirely natural that the French citadel fell, since England was determined to capture it, and that the world was created for England.
>
> The American, disturbed despite his efforts to remain calm, finds it altogether astonishing that Louisbourg was able to resist so long, when it was Pepperrell and his New England troops that besieged it.
>
> The Frenchman, after having, in a swift vision, seen passing before his eyes the image of the fortress reported impregnable, regards the mass of debris tumbled at his feet and demands, with the bitterness of the prophet Jeremiah weeping over the ruins of Jerusalem: How solitary is the state of the city once thronged with people? All its gates are overthrown; the streets of Zion weep.
>
> So indeed speak the stones you tread; there are tears in the depths of the casemates which stare up at you with great cavernous eyes; one still hears distinctly the shouts of victory, mingled with shrieks of malediction, ringing on the crest of the bastions. And these voices, shouts, and tears merge with the great voice of the ocean, which eternally grinds the stones of the walls of Louisbourg, crumbled and dragged through the abyss of the waves.
>
> Spectacle of infinite sadness! The knell that tolls in the distance is the funeral lament of French doom in America.
>
> Of the citadel itself remains but a mass of ruins worn away and covered with dust . . . The Puritans of New England resolved to capture it for the greater glory of God, out of hate of Papists, and in the interests of their maritime commerce.

The slow processional of the years passed over Louisbourg, desolate, all but deserted. A few settlers came from Placentia in Newfoundland. Fishermen still plied their trade in surrounding waters.

The moving finger of history "having writ, moved on" to inscribe the pages of the American Revolution, adding footnotes that were the due of the Fortress that had stood on Cape Breton. There, too, reverberated "the shot heard round the world," for the farmers at Lexington and Concord and comrades taking arms could not fail to remember the deeds of their forebears at the storming of Louisbourg, and the vivid memory of the first siege emboldened its aging veterans marching to the Battle of Bunker Hill. Once more the limelight focused briefly on the northern island when one of the streams of Loyalists, fleeing the United States, was directed to Louisbourg. Their settlement of flimsily roofed huts—a ship bringing lumber for repairs had been wrecked—clung to the site through a miserable winter. Then the emigrants gave up and moved to Sydney.[8]

Unredeemed, Louisbourg's relapse ran through another hundred years. Now and again came a rare visitor or salvage seeker. Grass overgrew the rubble of land reverted to private ownership. "Dilapidated shacks dotted it here and there, and cattle, sheep, and horses roamed the unkempt fields where Frank and Briton and American had won immortality a century before."

Postscript

That an immensely formidable fortress once stood at Louisbourg, that the French dominance it represented had been dreaded and hated along the American coast as far south as the mouth of the Delaware, that its essential subjugation had twice imperatively called the colonies and their mother country to arms—all these facts were long as widely forgotten as if Louisbourg had never been. Louisbourg had been expunged from the face of the earth, scarcely one stone left above another,[1] and its memory lived only in the pages of history, history it had so strongly dictated in the brief span of its half-century's existence.

It is still true today that for many its renown holds no significance. A Bostonian may walk through Louisbourg Square, vaguely wondering why it is so called or ignoring its placards except as an address. The name of that highly capable Colonial general, Sir William Pepperrell, survives for many people only (with an "r" dropped) as that of a textile firm; a Massachusetts town uses the same misspelling, "Pepperell." In Boscawen, New Hampshire, a roadside sign is needed to inform passersby why the village was christened in honor of a British admiral for his part in Louisbourg's second siege. Amherst collegians sing on of Lord Jeffery, but verse and chorus omit reference to the Cape Breton stronghold he stormed. *Sic transit* . . .

Belatedly, enduring tokens of remembrance began to be given other than in annals. In 1895 the Society of Colonial Wars in the

Commonwealth of Pennsylvania raised a shaft on the ground in commemoration of the Provincial forces, the British fleet, the French defenders, and their heroic dead of 1745. Not until 1928 were the Fortress remnants and a large part of the battleground outside the walls designated a National Historic Site. "During 1935-36, a spacious museum facing the site of the citadel was erected by the Government of Canada to house the exhibits and mementoes which have been presented by public spirited citizens, as well as relics which have been unearthed in the ruins of the fortress." [2] Creation of a National Historic Park followed in 1940. An increasing number of tourists started to flock to Cape Breton.[3]

The summer of 1958 saw the celebration of the two hundredth anniversary of the second siege by the Fortress Louisbourg Bicentenary Committee. Participants wore period uniforms of France, Britain, and the colonies. Indians appeared, complete with wigwams and birchbark canoes. Music was furnished by singers in old French costumes and by Highlands pipers. Television showed anachronisms: modern warships of the British, Royal Canadian, and United States Navies, along with jet planes. Three of the vessels provided diving and salvage facilities which were graphically demonstrated by the recovery from the bottom of the harbor of a cannon of the French 74-gun ship of the line, *Le Prudent*, burned during the British night raid. A troop landing was made in Kensington Cove where Wolfe's men had won their beachhead.[4]

First to press for the restoration of the Fortress was Major Walter Crowe, a resident of Sydney, Cape Breton Island, and publisher of its newspaper, *The Record*. He was inspired by the remarkable reclamation work done on Fort Ticonderoga, which, however, stood more or less intact and had only fallen into disrepair. In demolished Louisbourg a start had to be made from scratch.

In 1908 the Nova Scotia legislature incorporated a board of trustees with Major Crowe as president. Other members were Lord Strathcona, the Earl of Amherst, descendant of Lord Jeffery; Viscount Falmouth; Everett Pepperrell Wheeler of New York; Sir Frederick Borden, then Canadian Minister of Militia; Senator William MacDonald of Glace Bay; Sir Robert L. Weatherbe, then Chief Justice of Nova Scotia; Hon. George H. Murray, then the Province's Premier; Warden Henry C. V. LeVane of Cape Breton County, and David J. Kennelly, coal operator and railroad man who owned the Fortress site. The Canadian Government provided substantial annual grants for excavations.

Restoration was based on documents of primary importance. The original 1720 plans for the Fortress had been preserved in the Paris archives of the French Ministry of Marine, surviving both the Revolution and the German siege and occupation of 1870-1871. The Canadian Government obtained copies which offered engineers the incalculable advantage of being able to locate redoubts, buildings, streets, and so on almost to the inch. Thus became possible the accuracy and authenticity that rules the project. They are evident in the painstaking Harper Report of 1960.[5] Its preliminary investigations and excavations extended from salient features to such details as which streets were cobbled, which graveled.

The Louisbourg Restoration Committee estimates the work will require twelve years for completion (about two-thirds to be finished by 1967), with an expenditure of twelve million dollars. Its span will extend far beyond the 57 acres of the site of the fortified town, covering a total area of twenty square miles northeast and southwest of the present town. Thus it will include landing points, battlegrounds, and battery emplacements of both the 1745 and 1758 sieges.

Within Louisbourg the following will be totally reconstructed: the King's Bastion; the 360-foot long, three-story Château St. Louis, which housed the Governor's apartments, a chapel officers' quarters, and barracks; the elaborate Dauphin Gate. Several private buildings will be restored along with wharves used by the Navy and thriving commerce and fisheries. Outside the walls will be built again the causeway to the Dauphin Gate, historic path of entry for victorious troops into the fallen Fortress. The famed lighthouse will tower once more on its point across the harbor. There will be partial reconstruction of the Grand or Royal Battery, twice ingloriously abandoned to besiegers. Field headquarters, gun positions, redans, redoubts, and entrenchments, long since obliterated, will take form. Redeemed and preserved will be the cemetery on Rochefort Point where lie French, British, and American soldiers, slain in combat, amid the nearly nine hundred New Englanders who perished of disease while garrisoning the captured stronghold. It stands as a tribute to honored dead such as those that dot great battlefields across the world.

With work delayed by severe winter conditions, completion, following the extensive excavations already made, is a matter of years. Yet when the Fortress of Louisbourg rises again from its rubble and ashes, it will rival other great North American restorations—Ticonderoga, Williamsburg, and the rest. And the shade of Louis XV, if a French monarch were willing to quote a British bard, could proudly declare:

"After me cometh a Builder. Tell him, I too have known." [6]

Appendices

APPENDIX A

Governors of Isle Royale (Cape Breton) *

Costebelle, Phillippe de, appointed January 1, 1714; died between September 21 and October 10, 1717.

L' Hermite, acting during absence of Costebelle, 1714; 1715.

St. Ovide, acting during the absence of Costebelle, 1715; November 23, 1716, to September 21, 1717.

Brouillan, Joseph de, first King's Lieutenant at Isle Royale; appointed Governor, November 16, 1717.

Bourville, M. de, acting during absence of Brouillan, 1730; 1731; November, 1737 to 1739.

Forant, Isaac Louis de, appointed, April 1, 1739; arrived, September 10, 1739; died at Louisbourg, May 10, 1740.

Bourville, M. de, acting during absence of Forant, May 10, 1740, to November 2, 1740.

Du Quesnel, Jean Baptiste Prévost, appointed September 1, 1740; arrived November 2, 1740; died at Louisbourg, October 9, 1744.

Du Chambon, Dupont, acting following death of Du Quesnel, October 9, 1744, to June, 1745.

Le Moyne de Chateauguay, Sr., appointed, January 1, 1745; illness prevented him from assuming post; died at Rochefort, March 21, 1747.

Warren, Peter, August, 1745, to June 2, 1746.

Knowles, Charles, March 14, 1746, to November 30, 1747.

Hopson, Peregrine Thomas, November 30, 1747, to July 12, 1749.

Desherbiers, Charles, appointed January 1, 1749; arrived at Louisbourg, June 29, 1749; took possession, in the name of the King of

* From *Canada and Its Provinces*, XXIII, 335.

France, of Isle Royale and its dependencies, July 23, 1749; left Louisbourg, September 13, 1751.

Raymond, Jean Louis, Comte de, appointed March 1, 1751; arrived, August 4, 1751; left October, 1753.

D' Ailleboust, acting during absence of Comte de Raymond, October, 1753, to August 15, 1754.

Drucour, Augustin de, appointed February 1, 1754; arrived, August 15, 1754; left, August 15, 1758.

APPENDIX B

The Louisbourg Lighthouse *

In the year 1731, the first Lighthouse on the Island of Cape Breton was commenced at the entrance of Louisbourg Harbor. This too, was the first concrete fireproof building in North America. The date of this first Louisbourg Lighthouse, 1731, was twenty-five years before the building of the far famed Eddystone Lighthouse in England, in 1756, which was also made of cement.

The principal ingredient of the concrete used at Louisbourg was cement, which the French made from limestone burned in kilns, and slacked for twelve months. This was mixed with perhaps, lava, slag, or some other material now unknown. The use of cement, almost universal in the present day, was practised, to some extent, ages ago in North Africa, in Egypt, and notably by the Romans.

Old plans of the first Louisbourg Lighthouse, still in existence, show its round castle-like tower to have been sixty-six feet high, made up of four turrets. The walls, at the base, were about six feet thick. There were three main landings and also the lantern landing. Ascent was made by means of a circular stairway embedded in the main walls of the tower.

This pioneer Louisbourg Lighthouse, begun in 1731, was completed

---

* Albert Almon, *Louisbourg—The Dream City of America* (Glace Bay, Nova Scotia: 1934), pp. 56-57.

in 1733, and the light in its lantern first kindled on the first of April 1734, now just two hundred years ago. The fuel used for the light was coal, brought from any of the different coal mines at Morien and Spanish River. The coals were burned in an iron pan set up on a tripod in the lantern. The light was visible out at sea, at the not inconsiderable distance of six leagues.

After the Lighthouse had served its purpose for something over two years, an accident occurred on November 10th 1736, when the lantern caught on fire and was burned; the tower, being fireproof, was not injured. It was seen to be necessary that a fireproof lantern should be made, and also advisable that an improved mode of lighting be devised. Consequently a method of Oil Lighting was installed. For this purpose a special lamp was constructed, similar in design to a much smaller one that had been in general use by the French. And, singularly, one of these small design oil lamps was found about thirty years ago, in the Burnt Mines, New Aberdeen, that were known to have been operated by the French in 1750. By this new system light was supplied from a number of pots, fed through wicks, which passed through copper tubes, located in a copper circle. This form of lighting, it may be assumed, was the original "Naked Light," the oil being constantly open to flame.

For purposes of safety, in installing the new lighting system in the lantern of the lighthouse, provision was made by sustaining the rings on pieces of cork (or floats) when, should fire take place, it would burn through, letting the rings fall into the oil, where they would immediately be extinguished. Another phase of "Dousing the glim."

This new lighting process is made to seem very real in view of the finding of the little lamp noted above, and more particularly by the recent finding, in the ruins of the old foundation of the Lighthouse, of old oaken staves of the very barrels which contained the oil for lighting purposes. The staves were just as sound as when the wood came from its original tree.

What marked another very great step in advance in this lantern reconstruction of 1737, was that the use of glass was necessary in connection with the oil lighting system. References to that fact have been found in old Louisbourg official reports. One such mentions that "They are waiting for Glass for the Lighthouse," and another, "The glass has arrived for the Lighthouse Lantern."

The final fate of the famous, strongly built, old Lighthouse, "The sailor's beacon," that "looks like baron's donjon keep," and was so primitively lighted, is not now known. The lantern, however, was shot away during the siege (1758) . . .

APPENDIX C

Governor Shirley's Proclamation of the Louisbourg Expedition *

BY HIS EXCELLENCY WILLIAM SHIRLEY, ESQR. CAPT. GENERAL & GOVERNOR IN CHIEF IN AND OVER HIS MAJESTY'S PROVINCE OF THE MASSACHUSETTS BAY IN NEW ENGLAND.

A PROCLAMATION

Whereas ye great and general court or assembly of this Province upon due consideration of the present state and circumstances of the French settlements upon ye Island of Cape Breton have judged it expedent to attempt the Reduction of that place to the Obedience of the Crown of Great Britain & have voted a sutible enchouragement for the enlistment of three thousand vollintiers for that service; and whereas ye said assembly have desired I would issue forth my proclamation for such enlistment under such proper officers as I shall appoint;

I do therefore hereby with the advice of his majestys Council publish and declare for the enchouragement for all such able bodied effective men as I shall enlist as soldiers into his majestys service for that expidition that they shall receive twenty five shillings in new tenor bills per month as there wages and that one months pay shall be advanced to them in hand that each soldier shall have a blanket allowed him, that they shall be discharged from ye service as soon as the expedition shall be over, and that they shall be exempt from all impress to any military service for two years next to come and to that intent that all persons purposing to ingage in this service may have their elextion of the Captains in whose companies they would enlist I shall order the names of the Captains and other officers whome I shall Commissionate to be transmitte to ye Chief Officer of each Regiment or militia.

I do hereby command ye sherriffs of ye respective counties within this province to take effectual care that there be delivered without delay to ye Chief military Officer in each town as many of ye said proclamations as there military officers in such town and that each Captain immediately after receiving ye same call his company together and that ye said Captains keep the said proclamation in there hand and suffer no copies to be taken thereto and that after all necessary use of ye said proclamation has been made that they return them to

* Spelling and punctuation are those in the original draft.

ye respective sherriffs who are hereby required to take a list of ye proclamations to delivered and to whom—Delivered & that they send them into ye Secretay's Office of ye said List with ye proclamations so delivered up.

GIVEN at ye Council in Boston ye 26th day of January 1745 in ye Eighteenth year of ye reign of our sovereign LORD GEORGE ye second by ye grace of GOD of Great Britain, France and Ierland KING defender of ye etc.

W. SHIRLEY

By order of his Excellency ye Governor
with ye advice of ye Council

J. WILLARD. SECR.

GOD SAVE YE KING

APPENDIX D

Benjamin Franklin and Louisbourg *

To John Franklin

MS not found; reprinted from extract in Sparks, *Works,* VII, 16-17.

Philadelphia, [May?], 1745 [1]

Our people are extremely impatient to hear of your success at Cape Breton. My shop is filled with thirty inquiries at the coming in of every post. Some wonder the place is not yet taken. I tell them I shall

* Letter to his brother John in Boston, from *The Papers of Benjamin Franklin,* III, 26-27.

1 Sparks printed this letter incomplete and dated it only "Philadelphia, 1745." Smyth (*Writings,* II, 283) assigned the date March 10 on the basis of his interpretation of BF's "ecclesiastical mathematics," but this is clearly too early. BF printed the first news of the expedition's departure from Boston, March 24, in the *Gazette,* April 12, and that of the arrival of most of the troops at Canso, the rendezvous, April 10, in the *Gazette,* May 2. Inquirers at BF's shop could hardly have begun to "wonder the place is not yet taken" much before the middle of May at the earliest. Actually Louisbourg's capitulation took place on June 17 and was announced to the Pennsylvania Council on July 11. *Pa. Col. Recs.,* IV, 764.

be glad to hear that news three months hence. Fortified towns are hard nuts to crack; and your teeth have not been accustomed to it. Taking strong places is a particular trade, which you have taken up without serving an apprenticeship to it. Armies and veterans need skilful engineers to direct them in their attack. Have you any? But some seem to think forts are as easy taken as snuff. Father Moody's prayers look tolerably modest.[2] You have a fast and prayer day for that purpose; in which I compute five hundred thousand petitions were offered up to the same effect in New England, which added to the petitions of every family morning and evening, multiplied by the number of days since January 25th,[3] make forty-five millions of prayers; which, set against the prayers of a few priests in the garrison, to the Virgin Mary, give a vast balance in your favor.

If you do not succeed, I fear I shall have but an indifferent opinion of Presbyterian prayers in such cases, as long as I live. Indeed, in attacking strong towns I should have more dependence on *works,* than on *faith;*[4] for, like the kingdom of heaven, they are to be taken by force and violence; and in a French garrison I suppose there are devils of that kind, that they are not to be cast out by prayers and fasting, unless it be by their own fasting for want of provisions. I believe there is Scripture in what I have wrote, but I cannot adorn the margin with quotations, having a bad memory, and no Concordance at hand; besides no more time than to subscribe myself, &c. B. FRANKLIN

The general interest in the Louisbourg expedition which existed in the Middle Colonies, expressed in the foregoing letter from Benjamin Franklin to his brother John in Boston is reflected in the following reprints, also made available through the courtesy of Yale University, repository and publisher of the papers. That interest was represented by contributions of money and, in some cases of arms, though not of men and ships.

---

[2] Rev. Samuel Moody (1676–1747) of York, Maine, although "much impair'd by old Age," accompanied the expedition which his neighbor from Kittery Point, William Pepperrell (1696–1759), commanded. After the capitulation he preached the first Protestant sermon ever delivered at Louisbourg ("the citadel of Popish darkness"). *Sibley's Harvard Graduates,* IV, 356-65.

[3] This was the date on which the Massachusetts General Court approved Shirley's proposal for the expedition. Charles H. Lincoln, ed., *Correspondence of William Shirley* (N. Y., 1912), I, 169-70.

[4] Moody and Pepperrell were both enthusiastic supporters of the Great Awakening. George Whitefield preached at Portsmouth to the "Gentlemen bound on the Expedition" while it was being organized. *Pa. Gaz.,* April 12, 1745.

In the June 6, 1745, issue of Franklin's *Pennsylvania Gazette,* he printed the following "Plan of the Town and Harbour of Louisbourgh" with an explanatory key, the first news illustration he had ever used in his paper. Four days later his friend and former associate, James Parker, published the same map and key in his *New York Weekly Post-Boy.* In the issue of May 10, Parker had printed an extensive essay by an unknown author (perhaps Vice Admiralty Judge Robert Auchmuty of Boston). Franklin picked up that article in the *Gazette* of May 23:

PHILADELPHIA, June 6. 1745.

As the *CAPE-BRETON* Expedition is at preſent the Subject of moſt Converſations, we hope the following Draught (rough as it is, for want of good Engravers here) will be acceptable to our Readers; as it may ſerve to give them an Idea of the Strength and Situation of the Town now beſieged by our Forces, and render the News we receive from thence more intelligible.

PLAN of the Town and Harbour of ***LOUISBURGH.***

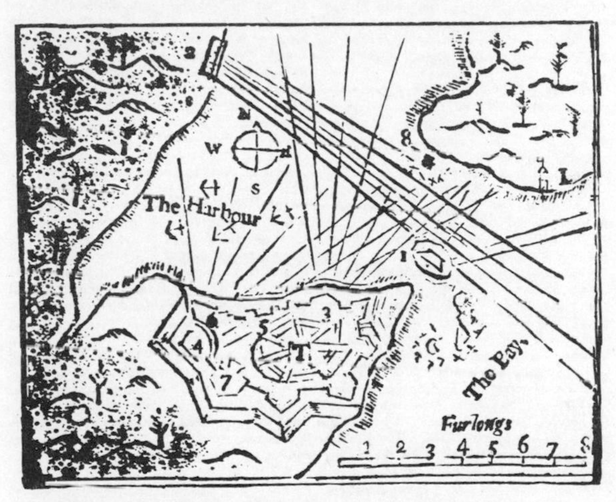

EXPLANATION.

1. The Iſland Battery, at the Mouth of the Harbour, mounting 24 Guns,-----Pounders. This Battery can rake Ships fore and aft before they come to the Harbour's Mouth, and take them in the Side as they are paſſing in.
2. The Grand Battery, of 36 Forty two Pounders, planted right againſt the Mouth of the Harbour, and can rake Ships fore and aft as they enter.
3. The Town N. Eaſt Battery, which mounts 18 Twenty four Pounders on two Faces, which can play on the Ships as ſoon as they have entered the Harbour.
4. The Circular Battery, which mounts 16 Twenty-four Pounders, ſtands on high Ground, and overlooks all the Works. This Battery can alſo gaul Ships, as ſoon as they enter the Harbour.
5. Three Flanks, mounting 2 Eighteen Pounders each.
6. A ſmall Battery, which mounts 8 Nine Pounders. All theſe Guns command any Ship in the Harbour.
7. The Fort or Citadel, fortified diſtinctly from the Town, in which the Governor lives.
8. A Rock, called the Barrel.

T The Center of the Town. L The Light-Houſe.

Every Baſtion of the Town Wall has Embraſures or Ports for a Number of Guns to defend the Land Side.

The black Strokes drawn from the ſeveral Batteries, ſhew the Lines in which the Shot may be directed.

BOSTON, May 6.

We have Accounts from Albany, that they have received Intelligence from Canada of a Body of French and Indians setting out from thence, under one Monsieur Bilaire, as Commander in chief, and a Son of Monsieur Lanoo's, and one Monsieur Artel who are to have the Command under him.—That the Party is to consist of 5 or 600 Men, and is designed, as some of the Albany Indians say, against Annapolis Royal, and others of 'em report, against the Checasia Indians; which last seems only a Blind. Likewise that they had other Intelligence about the middle of April, that within a few Days there was to be a great Meeting of Indians in Lake Champlen, where they were called by the French from their Hunting; from all which Accounts, it can't be reasonably doubted but that the French were meditating another Attack against Annapolis Royal, in which they expect to be joined by a Naval Force from France sometime this Month. But there is the utmost probability, that our present Enterprise against Cape-Breton will either cause the Enemy to desist from making their Attempt against Annapolis-Royal, or frustrate it; so that whatever may be the Success of the present Expedition in other Respects, there seems the utmost Probability of its producing these good Consequences, viz. the Recovery of Canso with our Fishery there, and Preservation of Annapolis Royal, at least for the present.

May 13. On Friday last the Schooner Montague, one of the Ordnance Tenders, arrived here Express from Annapolis Royal, and brought Advice, that Governor Mascarene had received undoubted Information, that 600 French and Indians came in the Winter from Canada to Chegnicto, being the same which were seen passing on the Skirts of New-England, and arrived at Menis on the 19th April last, part by Land, and part by Sea in the Vessels they found up the Bay; that they had with them 12 Officers, an Engineer and a Surgeon, and were come in Expectation to join the Forces which the French intended should come with Monsieur Duvivier from France and Louisburg; and that two Men of War were expected to be early on our Coast to prevent any Succours from being sent to the Garrison. That upon the Report of Part of the New-England Fleet's being seen off the Eastern Coast of Nova Scotia, their Thoughts at Menis were various, some thinking 'em to be the Fishery, others a Force going to take Possession of Canso: That since the News of the Canadeans being arrived at Chignicto, which the Garrison had received five Weeks ago, there had been a grand Expectation among all the Settlements in Nova Scotia, of a very vigorous Attempt upon his Majesty's Garrison at Annapolis Royal; and that a secret Correspondence was discover'd to have been carried on between the Inhabitants of Annapolis River about the Fort and those of the Bay, for which several of the former had been seized and were now confined in Prison; But that as that Fort was now in good repair as to its Out works, there was no fear of the Enemy's doing much harm to the Body of the Place with their Firelocks.——And upon the Whole, those Letters add, "that "if the Enemy's Projects had not been defeated by "those of this Government, the Garrison might "have had a great deal of Work this Spring."

Yesterday his Majesty's Ship Princess Mary sail'd from Nantasket Road, in order to join Commodore Warren off Louisburg, to the great Satisfaction of all the Wellwishers to the important Expedition, who had been under much Concern that that gallant Ship has been so long from her Station, at this critical juncture.

As Cape Breton at present engages the Attention of our Readers, perhaps the following short Account of the Importance of that Place, will not be disagreeable to many of them.

The Island of Breton, or as the French call it, the Isle Royal, lies between Newfoundland and Nova Scotia, and is about 30 Leagues long, and near 10 broad. The Soil is but indifferent, but the Coast is full of good Harbours, in most of which the French have small Settlements and Stages for the Fishery; but there are no Fortifications of any Consequence except at Louisburg. This Town is about three quarters of a Mile long, and nearly oval. It is regularly fortified on the Land Side, and the Harbour is defended by several Batteries.

This Island was given to the French by the [wise] Treaty of Utrecht, and by the Advantage of it they have carried on a prodigious Fishery, annually employing 1000 Sail of Vessels, from 200 to 400 Tons, and 20,000 Men. It is computed that they cure five Millions of Quintals of Fish, Communibus Annis: And in 1730. they carried to Marseilles only, twenty two hundred Thousand Quintals.

From hence it plainly appears to have been a vast Nursery of Seamen, and a prodigious Addition to the Riches and Strength of France, and that the Reduction of it must be a proportionable Increase of the Number of British Seamen, and of the Wealth of Britain, and the British Dominions in America: for the French, if removed from thence, have no other Shelter for their Fishery, nearer than Old France, and must therefore of Necessity drop it in a great Measure.

From the Situation of the Island, it commands the Navigation up the great River St. Lawrence, and so cuts off all Communication with Quebeck, by which Means the whole Country of Canada must in a little Time fall into the Hands of the English, if they are once master of Cape Breton.—Some of the many Consequences of which are as follow.

The French Sugar Islands would lose the chief Vent for their Rum and Molasses, and the Supply of Lumber and Provisions they now have from Canada; and the English Islands would gain both. Great Britain must have a boundless Vent for all Kinds of their Manufactures, and command the valuable Trade in Fur, with all the Indian Nations,---And those of them who live near the English Settlements, will have no French Missionaries to stir them up to a mischievous and expensive War.

While on the other Hand, so long as the French keep Possession of that Place, all the British Plantations in North America, will be liable to perpetual Annoyance from their Parties and Indians by Land; and all the British Navigation to and in America, from their Privateers and Men of War, as we have sufficiently experienced the last Summer.

The only Reflection I shall make on these Facts is, that every Man who loves his Country, ought to pray for the Success of the present Expedition.

The following letter from Franklin, forwarding Pennsylvania's Louisbourg contribution, is reprinted through the courtesy of Joseph W. P. Frost, who owns the original.

To Colonel Nathaniel Sparhawk at Kittery

I received yours by Mr. Baynton with the money as therein specified; and have since delivered it to Mr. Warren (who is now here) with Mr. Pepperrell's letter of which please advise Mr. Pepperrell. I am

Your most humble servant
B. Franklin

Philadelphia June 15, 1748

Nathaniel Sparhawk (1715–1776) was a merchant of Portsmouth and Boston; he married the daughter of Sir William Pepperell in 1742. The Pepperell referred to is probably Andrew (d. 1751), business partner of his father, Sir William, from 1744 until his death. Baynton may be John Baynton (1726–1773), a merchant of Philadelphia. Warren has not been identified.

APPENDIX E

Letter from Governor Du Chambon to the Minister at Rochefort *

Monseigneur,

As you requested in your letter of the 20th of this month, I have the honor of giving you an account of the attack and surrender of Louisbourg.

On last March 14, we noticed a ship among the pieces of ice which had broken off in the bay. This ship appeared to be about three or four leagues from port and was moving toward the southwest. By afternoon it was out of sight.

On the 19th, we saw—still on the other side of the pieces of ice—a snow sailing parallel to the iceberg which stretched from Escartary

* September 2, 1745, from the Archives of the Ministry of Marine; Jill Adams and Nouailles Degoue are the translators.

to St. Esprit. Several hunters and soldiers who had been wintering in the woods reported having seen two ships which had changed direction at Menadou; others had heard canon fire near St. Esprit. Consequently, I gave warning to the inhabitants of all coastal villages near town to get ready to obey any signals I might give them.

In addition, I called together all the residents of both the town and the harbor of Louisbourg, dividing the former group into four companies, and telling the others to repair to the Royal Battery or to the battery of the harbor island upon a signal from me.

On April 9, we saw through a clearing in the fog four ships among the ice floes near Pointe Blanche. One of them fired a few cannon shots, which were returned by one shot from the island, and as the ship answered right back, we assumed that they were French ships which were trying to get through the ice floes to port. They took advantage of every lift in the fog to get closer to the harbor so that we were almost sure that they were not privateers but Frenchmen.

However, being still in some doubt as to whether the ships were French or English, I sent an order to Mr. Benoît, commanding officer in Toulouse, to dispatch a reliable man to Canceau to find out if there were ships there, if anyone was working there, or if there was any particular activity on the Isle Royale.

Mr. Benoît sent Jacob Coste, a resident, with a soldier and an Indian in the hope of taking a few prisoners there. These three men landed at Grande Terre near Canceau, where they were fortunate in taking four English prisoners. However, on their way back, the prisoners overcame our three Frenchmen one night while they were asleep, and we received no further news either from them or from the enemy.

On the 22nd, I was informed by two men who had come by land from Toulouse, that they had heard cannon fire at Canceau and that work was being done to restore that island. A third man who arrived that evening told me of a battle he had witnessed on the ship *St. Esprit*, in which three large ships had come down upon four others which were along the coast. Firing started immediately and had lasted well into the night. This led us to believe that we had ships along that coast.

On April 30, we saw seven ships among the ice floes—four warships, two corvettes, and a brigantine with neither flag nor pennant—which hovered around the islands at Dion.

These ships, flying a white flag, were visible for several days between Pointe Blanche and Port de Noue. Then, as the ice cleared from the coast, we saw, heading for port, a ship which finally landed with ease. This ship, coming from St. Jean de Luz, was commanded by M. Janson Dufoure, who informed us that on the previous day he had been pursued by three ships of which one, a 24-cannon frigate, had caught up with him, but that he had escaped after a skirmish involving three volleys of cannon and musketry.

At dawn on the 8th, we could see all the ships upwind and southwest of the port. We gave an alert, and, according to plans, the residents of Lorembec and La Baleine, being nearest the town, took up their prearranged positions as did the townsfolk. The same day we saw those ships seize two of the King's coasting vessels from Toulouse, loaded wtih firewood for the troops. They also took a shallop laden with game from the Isles Madame.

Having been in doubt until that day as to whether those ships were English or French (the ice had blocked the entrance to the harbor since the day they had appeared all together), I had taken the precaution of preparing with M. Bigot two ships which, if necessary, could be dispatched to France to let His Majesty know the situation in the colony; so as soon as the capture of the coasting vessels and the reports of our escaped crews from ships at Canceau confirmed our suspicions that they were English, we took advantage of fog and a dark night to send off, on May 10, *La Société* under Captain Subtil with letters reporting the state of the colony, and telling of the ships blocking the harbor. As for the other ship which had been prepared, we had to sink it since, after the enemy's raid, it was impossible to get it out.

The enemy ships being just outside port, the enemy used the shallop they had seized to get ashore at Gabarus within view, so, on May 9 I sent a detachment of 20 soldiers under M. de Lavallière to go by land to Gabarus, and, under M. Daccarrette, I sent 39 civilians in a rowboat to recover the shallop; the first group stayed away two days and returned to town on the evening of the 11th, and M. Daccarrette's group returned on the morning of the 12th, having had to leave the rowboat ashore just outside Gabarus.

On the 11th, at about three or four in the morning, we learned of the presence of about one hundred sails which appeared behind the islands of Dion. As the winds were coming from the northwest, these ships could be seen approaching, and I took them to be transport ships. I therefore gave the prearranged signals, but several people could not go where they were supposed to, especially those from the more distant villages, the countryside being infested with the enemy who, in fact, captured several persons heading for town.

To combat an enemy raid, I sent out immediately a detachment of eighty men and thirty soldiers under M. Morpain and M. Mesilac, who proceeded to a place just below Pointe Blanche where the enemy had begun to raid. They were able to force the enemy back into their carts, but in the meantime, the enemy had landed a greater number of troops in Corromandière Cove between Pointe Blanche and Gabarus.

Our detachment hastened over as soon as they realized what was happening, but the enemy had already landed and taken up good defensive positions. Despite this, our detachment launched an attack, but because of the enemy's greater numbers we were forced back into the woods. That incident cost us four or five soldiers who were either killed or captured, as well as four or five civilians, one of whom was M. Laboularderie. Three or four other wounded men went back to town.

After the retreat of that detachment, the enemy completed its disembarkment which, according to the last of our men to return to town, included four or five hundred men plus planks and other materials. They advanced into the countryside where we saw a great number of them—not in formation—within cannon range of Pointe Dauphine and the Bastion du Roy.

The mountains overlooking the pass were covered with people; at two P.M. the cannon on Barbette fired on several platoons which seemed to be marching toward the far side of the bay. We also noticed that there were others marching along the edge of the woods to the Royal Battery, so I ordered the entrances of the town shut, and took other safety measures including the placing of 1,100 men in defensive positions.

That evening, M. Thiery, company captain of the Royal Battery, wrote me a letter in which he stressed the poor condition of his command, pointing out that if the enemy captured it, they would have a definite advantage. He recommended that it would be in our best interest to blow it up after spiking the cannon.

Upon receiving that news, I called a council of war. M. Verrier, the chief engineer who had been summoned immediately, reported that the battery had had some of its epaulements destroyed the previous year, that the covered ways were not fortified, and that it was in no condition to resist an attack by land of three or four thousand men if only the four hundred men then inside were defending it.

This report caused the war council to decide that, for the safety of the town which lacked the proper defense, the best plan would be to take out of the battery as much ammunition and as many stores as possible, spike the cannon, and then abandon it.

I must not neglect to inform you that this same war council wanted to blow up the battery, but in the face of M. Verrier's firm opposition, did not insist.

I sent an order to M. Thiery to abandon the battery after spiking the cannon and salvaging as much food and ammunition as possible. That officer spent the evening attending to the cannon; he also arranged for the transfer of part of the supplies and ammunition, and, at about midnight, he withdrew into the town with his troops.

However, as the battery was not entirely emptied that night, I sent Lt. St. Etienne and Ensign Souvigny, the next day, with about twenty men to finish the job. This they did, leaving only some cannonballs and bombs which they could not carry.

M. Bigot and I had meanwhile decided to sink all the ships we had in port which were armed before the enemy could capture them. Accordingly, I ordered Ensign Verger along with five soldiers and some sailors to sink those which were opposite the town, and Ensign Bellemont was instructed to carry out a similar operation in the bay, and also to get the oil out of the lighthouse tower. These orders were carried out.

On the 13th, I sent out all the militia with hatchets and other tools to demolish all the houses from the Porte Dauphine to Barruchois, to bring back all the wood they could find in town which we could use to warm the garrison as we had none, and to burn whatever houses they could not demolish in order to prevent the enemy from moving into them.

These men were assisted in this operation by eighty soldiers, both French and Swiss, under Captain Deganne and a Swiss officer named Rasser.

As they were finishing and about to withdraw into town, several enemy platoons appeared at Barruchois and in some of the upper valleys. Several shots were fired by those who were nearest; none of our men was killed or wounded, but they saw two of the enemy fall.

On the 13th the enemy took possession of the Royal Battery and, the following day, fired several shots from the two cannon they had unspiked. The same day, they began to fire several 12-inch bombs weighing 180 pounds and some 9-inch bombs from a battery of four mortars which they had constructed on a rise behind the plains opposite the Bastion du Roy.

This battery continued firing from time to time as did the twelve grenade-throwing mortars which the enemy had placed there, and two other cannons in the Royal Battery which they had unspiked, but none of the firing did much damage until the 18th, neither killing nor wounding a soul.

On the 16th, I sent off a messenger in a shallop with a letter to M.

Marin, an officer from Canada, who commanded a company of Canadians and Indians in Acadia, ordering him to come immediately to Louisbourg with his detachment. This would have been a journey of twenty or twenty-five days had he been in the mines as I had been assured he was, but the company had left for Port Royal when the messenger arrived.

The messenger had to follow him there and gave him the letter. He held a meeting, and although several members of his company didn't wish to go with him, he and the rest set out in good faith. According to what I learned later, he had great difficulty in securing anywhere in Acadia the vehicles he needed to transport his group.

Finally about three or four hundred of them embarked, some in a boat of approximately 25 tons, others in about one hundred canoes. As they were weathering a promontory in the bay, they were attacked by a privateer carrying fourteen cannon and the same number of stone-cannon pierriers. Our officer held off the attack vigorously, and just as he had gotten himself into a position to board the privateer, another one of equal strength came to its aid, and M. Marin was forced to give up and make for shore.

This encounter made him lose several days, and he did not get to Isle Royale until the beginning of July, after Louisbourg had surrendered. If this company had arrived fifteen or twenty days before the surrender of the town, I am more than convinced that the enemy would have had to raise the siege by land, because they were frightened by this detachment which they thought numbered more than 2,500 men.

I should inform His Majesty that this detachment, on its way through the Fronsac passage back to Acadia after our departure, killed or captured thirteen men from an English privateer who were trying to block the way. These men, who had taken their canoes to go fetch some water, fell into the hands of our men.

On the 18th, the English generals called upon me to surrender the town with its fortresses and lands, all artillery, arms and ammunition, to Great Britain in exchange for which they promised to grant good treatment to all the subjects of my lord, the King, who were in the town, to let them keep their possessions, and to give them the liberty of moving to any part of the Kingdom of France in Europe which they desired.

To this request, I answered immediately that as my lord, the King, had entrusted the defense of the land to me, I could not listen to any such proposition until after a decisive attack, and that my only other answer would come from the mouths of the cannons.

On the 19th, the enemy began to build up a battery of seven pieces of cannon in the open plain behind a little pond opposite the Bastion du Roy. From that day until the surrender this battery rained continual fire (12-, 18-, and 24-pound cannon balls) on the barracks, on the wall of the Bastion du Roy, and on the town. In fact, this battery was by far the most dangerous one the enemy had. The balls raked all the streets as far as the Porte Maurepas and the crenelated wall; no one could stay in the town, either in the houses or in the streets.

To stop the enemy fire, I had two 18-pound cannon placed on a cavalier of the Bastion du Roy. This I did by means of two wooden chests which we filled with brush and with earth, and which formed two openings. In this way, the gunners and their assistants were sheltered from enemy fire.

At the same time, I had two openings pierced in the wall of the parapet on the right side of the bastion; there we placed two 24-pound cannon.

These four cannon were so effective that they stopped the enemy fire to the extent that only one of their cannon was functioning at the time of surrender and the others were dismantled. This was told to me by some of our people who went to look at the battery after the surrender.

On the morning of the 20th I assembled the company captains to determine whether or not to organize some sallies on the enemy. It was decided that, the town being empty, it would be a poor idea; that it was difficult enough to defend the ramparts with the 1,300 men we did have, including the 200 men in the Royal Battery.

I had the Porte Dauphine blocked up, as well as the two adjoining posts, with a thickness of some eighteen feet of freestone, faggots, and earth. Without this protection the enemy could have gotten into town right after firing from the battery of Francoeur, the gate being no stronger than that of a porte-cochère—the walls were only three feet thick. Nor were the sides of the gate protected—the only defense consisted of some battlements on the posts which we couldn't even use once we had reinforced them with earth.

I ordered the construction of embrasures made of sod and earth—there being insufficient time to make them with stone—for the four cannon of the battery of the Bastion Dauphin and for the adjoining soldiers' posts. This was in order to hamper the enemy in operations on the heights facing the gate. These instructions were carried out.

All the flanks of all the bastions in the town were supplied with cannon from privateers and any other cannon which were in the town.

The enemy, having caulked up a schooner which had sunk in the bay last year, filled it with wood, tar, and other inflammable matter and, benefiting from a dark night and a cool northeast wind, sent off this fireship toward the town on the 24th.

Everybody spent the night on the ramparts, for we were waiting for a real offensive from the enemy instead of this type of trick, and the fireship having sunk outside the town opposite the property of M. Ste. Marie, didn't have the effect that the enemy had anticipated.

The enemy had taken over the rise of Francoeur which is at the end of the glacis of the Porte Dauphine, and had begun digging communications trenches and building two batteries despite continual fire from the cannon on the barbette of the bastion Dauphin and from the right flank of the Bastion du Roy, as well as musket fire. Those two batteries never stopped firing from the 29th until the surrender. They fired cannonballs from 18s, 26s, 36s, and 42s, trying to destroy the Porte Dauphine and the right flank of the Bastion du Roy.

The enemy then began to maneuver on the other side of the bay and around the lighthouse. Lieutenant Vallé of the Artillery Company came to warn me that the enemy might be able to use several 18- and 24-pound cannon which had been put near there some ten years ago to serve as a small fortification. Several of those cannon were still serviceable, and he said he had told our governors several times that the enemy could transport them to the tower and could construct a battery to fire on the harbor island and on every ship which tried to come in.

This important piece of information and the fact that the enemy had hoisted its flag on the lighthouse tower caused me to send a detachment of five hundred local young men and others of the militia along with some privateersmen under the command of M. de Beaubassin to see if that was true and to try to surprise the enemy or at least prevent them from setting anything up there.

This detachment left in three shallops on May 27, each man with food enough for twelve days as well as the necessary ammunition which was procured from the King's stores. They went ashore at Grand Lorembec. The next day, as they were nearing the tower, they were discovered by about three hundred of the enemy.

They exchanged several volleys of musket fire and then separated. As our detachment didn't realize their own advantage, and a number of them having given up, they withdrew into the woods to burn up their stores if possible. They thought this would be an easy matter since the enemy was sleeping soundly.

Koller, the second in command after De Beaubassin, coming from St. Pierre by land several days before, had entered one of the huts in the enemy camp and had stolen a boiler without being discovered. Our detachment was now about an eighth of a league from Koller's home and he had sent out spies while waiting for night to fall; they had the misfortune of being discovered by a dozen Englishmen in the area. The enemy thus sent out a large party to attack the detachment. De Beaubassin was again forced to withdraw after a little firing, and was followed by some of the enemy. Several of the men had to get rid of their supplies in order to save themselves; they were thus without their twelve days' worth of food, and others, who were from neighboring villages deserted him and went home. The detachment found itself without supplies and too weak to resist the enemy.

Consequently, they went over to Petit Lorembec to get shallops so they could get back to town. There they found forty Indians from the colony who had killed, two or three days before, eighteen or twenty Englishmen whom they had found pillaging the place. As our men were about to embark in the shallops, a detachment of two to three hundred Englishmen suddenly appeared. The Indians joined our company; thus there were about 120 men facing the enemy.

Both sides began to fire at about two o'clock and continued for more than four hours; the English were repulsed twice and would have been defeated had they not, at the start of the fighting, sent word to their men at the Royal Battery and at the tower which meant that at nightfall, considerable reinforcements arrived and surrounded our men.

Seeing that resistance was futile and that ammunition was scarce (some men had completely used up their powder) the detachment withdrew as far as Miré and crossed the river. This encounter cost us two deaths and twenty men either wounded or taken prisoner. M. de Beaubassin was among the wounded; a bullet got him in the leg and after an hour and a half of combat, he withdrew. Koller continued the fight to the end. De Beaubassin, who came back to town as an extra passenger in a canoe a few days later informed me what had happened to his detachment, saying that the remainder had taken refuge in Miré where they were under the command of Koller, and that there was a lack of both food and ammunition.

On hearing his news, I sent out a boat with twenty quarts of flour, other food and ammunition for M. Marin's detachment which I was expecting every day, as well as for the Indians. Koller and his men were found, but not M. Marin or the Indians, the latter having returned to their villages.

Koller returned to town on June 14 in a shallop with his men and some others who were at Miré; he had trouble getting through at night because of enemy ships which were cruising between Gabarus and

Escartary. We learned after the surrender from a reliable source that the enemy had suffered 150 deaths and had had 90 men wounded during the encounter at Petit Lorembec.

As the cannon of the Porte Dauphine and those on the right flank of the Bastion du Roy didn't hit the battery which the enemy had constructed at Francoeur too well, we made three embrasures in the curtain through which we meant to fire on the back of the enemy. These three embrasures, in which we placed 36-pound cannon, were made on May 30 and gave wonderful results. On the first day we unseated one of their cannon, and their embrasures were all demolished; this still didn't prevent constant fire from the enemy, and as for the battery, whatever we tore down during the day, they rebuilt again at night.

The same day at three o'clock, we saw a large ship chasing a snow, and later it engaged in a fight with the snow and with a frigate, about four leagues from the fort toward the southeast. At the same time three enemy ships which were between Cap Noir and Pointe Blanche bore down on them. The large ship, after a long fight, sailed off—probably when it saw the others coming after it—and we heard cannon fire until about nine or ten o'clock at night. Subsequently we learned that that ship was the *Vigilant*.

I gave the order to take out from the powder magazine all the powder that there was and to transport it beneath the little door in the curtain between the Bastion du Roy and the Bastion de la Reine. As the enemy had cut down the chains of the drawbridge with cannonballs from the Francoeur battery, I gave the order to destroy the bridge.

The enemy's cannon at the Francoeur battery were doing a great deal of damage to the right flank of the Bastion du Roy, particularly to the embrasures, so I had other embrasures made in the front wall of the Bastion Dauphin, and there I placed two cannon. This operation, carried out despite musket fire from the enemy, was completed successfully, and our cannon were used against the enemy's as effectively as could be hoped.

The enemy had also constructed a battery of five cannon on the heights of Mortissans, and started, on June 2, to fire 36- and 42-pound cannonballs on the Bastion Dauphin and on the buttress. The turret lookout tumbled as did a part of the salient on the same day. The buttress of the Porte Dauphine was also knocked down at the height of its embrasures, which had already been repaired several times as well as could be expected with freestones and bags of earth.

On the same day, the enemy fleet was increased by the arrival of a ship bearing about forty or fifty cannon, and we spotted in the fleet a disabled ship which we later learned was the one we had seen fighting on May 30.

On the 5th, at about two A.M., the enemy sent from the Royal Battery a fireboat which landed at Frédéric drydock and burned up a schooner. It did no other harm although it was loaded with inflammable matter and bombs which exploded. Meanwhile, the enemy batteries firing constantly, and all this time our men were, as usual, stationed along the ramparts facing the fire with great courage.

On the night of the 6th, a general alarm came from the harbor island; the enemy, wishing to capture the battery there, embarked one thousand strong in thirty-five boats, followed by eight hundred reinforcements. The night was dark and shrouded in mist. The first group went ashore—some at Pointe à Peletier, others opposite the barracks—and the rest at the landing of the island. On disembarking, the enemy began to cry "hurrah"; they even placed about twelve ladders against the embrasures hoping to scale the walls, but M. d'Aillebout, commander of the battery, gave them quite a reception! The men on the island made excellent use of their cannon and musketry, all the boats were destroyed or sunk, and firing was continuous from about midnight until three A.M.

M. d'Aillebout and his lieutenant, M. Du Chambon, as well as his ensign, M. Eurry de la Perrelle, were the first to climb up on the embrasures and fire on the enemy to give their soldiers an example. The soldiers made their officers come down from the embrasures several times, saying that they shouldn't expose themselves but should give them orders and they themselves would bring things to an end. Finally the enemy had to ask for mercy. The eight hundred reinforcements had not dared to approach and left. We took 119 prisoners, several wounded men died the same day, and the enemy had more than 250 killed, drowned, or wounded. According to our prisoners who were in the Royal Battery, the only ones who escaped got into two barges which could hold about thirty men, and among those there were several wounded men.

As the enemy could attack the town by landing in barges at the pier, I ordered that a breakwater barricade of masts be built from the buttress of the Bastion Dauphin as far as the *pièce de la grave* [artillery covering the shore]. This breakwater was finished on June 11. The enemy, who had noticed this operation, fired continually on the workers from their batteries, but to no avail.

The enemy was meanwhile continuing to work on the lighthouse tower despite heavy fire from the battery on the harbor island. We decided that it was necessary to protect the barracks and the bakery on the island, but as we were lacking wood for that purpose, we had to demolish M. Daccarrette's store.

Constant enemy fire had demolished the embrasures on the right flank of the Bastion du Roy where we had six 18- and 24-pound cannon which were always in use, but now these cannon could not be used, so I ordered the construction of more fortifications and wooden embrasures. This work was carried out with speed and completed on June 19. The cannon continued firing but the embrasures were smashed by the enemy cannon.

Since the construction of the Mortissans battery, these cannon had not stopped battering the Porte Dauphine and the buttress. The latter had been smashed and repaired several times as I mentioned above; the embrasures which held the cannon were dismantled by that battery and the Francoeur battery, and no one could stay behind the wall of the pier which had been riddled through and through by 24-, 36-, and 42-pound balls.

On the 18th, the English generals sent me an officer with a flag and a letter from Mr. Warren, fleet commander, and another from M. de la Maisonfort, ship's captain. In the first one, the General complained of the cruelties which our Frenchmen and Indians had inflicted on his compatriots, and said that if in the future such things happened, he couldn't prevent his men from doing the same.

M. de la Maisonfort informed me of his capture on May 30, and said that he had every reason to be satisfied with the treatment he and his officers and men were getting.

I answered Mr. Warren that there were no Frenchmen among the Indians who were guilty of using such cruelty—as, in fact, there were not—and that he could rest assured that I would make every effort to put an end to the Indians' cruelty insofar as I could communicate with them, etc.

To M. de la Maisonfort I answered that I would try to prevent the Indians from using further cruelties the next time I communicated with them, that there had been no Frenchmen with them when they had used their tortures, etc. The officer left with those letters forthwith.

On the 21st, the battery which the enemy had constructed at the lighthouse tower and which had seven cannon and a mortar began to fire on the harbor island with 18-pound balls and a 12-inch mortar weighing 180 pounds. The firing from that battery didn't let up until the surrender of the town, despite continuous fire from the island battery.

The enemy batteries were causing great damage in spite of shooting from our cannon on the Bastion du Roy, the Bastion Dauphin, and the Shore Battery, as well as musket fire from the breach in the Porte Dauphine and adjoining posts. I ordered M. Verrier, the engineer, to build an entrenchment in the Bastion Dauphin from which to defend the assault which the enemy might make through the breach. This construction, which stretched from the pier to the parapet of the front of the Bastion Dauphin, was ready on the 24th; much of the work had been carried out at night.

On the same day, four ships met together—two carrying sixty cannon, one with fifty, and the third with forty—including those blocking the harbor. As soon as these ships had fired signal shots, they assembled, and after conferring, sailed toward the bay of Gabarus.

On the following day, thirteen enemy ships dropped anchor in line toward Pointe Blanche about two leagues away from the harbor of Louisbourg. Both then and on the next day, the enemy built three piles of wood for signaling purposes on the heights which are to the west of the port.

At this point, I must tell His Majesty truthfully that all the enemy's batteries—mortar and cannon—were firing constantly and had been since the day they were constructed. The same was true of the musket fire from the Francoeur battery. All the houses in the town were demolished, riddled with holes, and not fit for habitation. The flank of the Bastion du Roy was destroyed, as were the wooden embrasures which we had improvised. A breach had been made in the Porte Dauphine and in the adjoining fortification which was passable for the enemy who had been gathering faggots for two days and taking them to the Francoeur battery. The buttress joining the officer's post to the Porte Dauphine was completely dismantled as were the embrasures along the pier. This all happened in spite of continuous firing from all our cannon, mortars, and musketry, which we used to the best of our abilities during this entire time.

There is sufficient proof of this in the fact that, of the 16,000 pounds of powder with which we started the siege, there remained only 47 kegs in town on June 27, and this low supply absolutely forced capitulation. We had used up all our 12-inch bombs and nearly all of our 9-inch bombs.

I would like to give credit to all the officers of the garrison, to the soldiers, and to the civilians who defended the town; they all put up with the fatigue of this siege with great courage during the 116 days that it lasted. This included spending every night in the casemates of the Porte Dauphine ever since the enemy began battering there, helping the workers who took the debris off the ramparts and to the gates to which they were assigned, without sleeping at night and, during the day, not daring to lie down anywhere lest the enemy cannon, which could aim everywhere in the town, fire upon them.

Consequently, everyone was exhausted from much work and no sleep, and out of the 1,500 people which we had at the start of the siege, 50 had been killed, 95 had been too severely wounded to give further assistance, several had succumbed to utter exhaustion, and the ramparts which had only measured 5 by 5 feet at the beginning of the siege were all broken down by the 26th of June when the inhabitants of the town handed me a petition. This stated that since the enemy force both on land and on sea was increasing daily, whereas we obtained no aid and were not strong enough to defeat the enemy, they would like me to surrender with the generals so that they could keep the little that remained to them.

This request, Monseigneur, touched me to the very quick of my soul. On one hand there was the town of Louisbourg, which had been most costly to the King, about to be captured by an enemy which had done enough damage to the fortifications to be able to storm them, and in addition, had a blockade of ships which had been there for two days.

On the other hand, a large number of the townsfolk all with families would, if they perished, lose the fruit of all their labors since the beginning of the Colony.

Finding myself in such a delicate situation, I informed M. Verrier, chief engineer, of the condition of the fortifications, and M. de Ste. Marie, captain in charge of artillery, of the status of our ammunition. Each man submitted a report to me; I then held a council of war which decided unanimously that, in view of the force of the enemy and the condition of our own fort, it would be better to capitulate.

After the council, I wrote a letter to the English generals asking for a truce for the time I would need to draw up the conditions under which I would hand over the town.

M. de Laperelle, Jr., who delivered the letter, brought me back their answer the same night. They allowed me until eight o'clock the following morning and said that if, during that time, I decided to give myself up as a prisoner of war, I could be assured of receiving the most generous possible treatment.

I was not expecting such an answer, so on the 27th (the next day) I sent M. de Bonnaventure with the articles of surrender and a second letter in which I asserted that the conditions mentioned the previous day were too rigorous for me to accept, and that I would hand over the town only under my new conditions.

The generals did not modify these propositions, but sent back a separate answer by M. de Bonnaventure in which they granted me some of the conditions I had requested. But the most important clauses, which pertained to leaving the fort with the honors of war, arms, baggage, drums beating, and flags unfurled, were not included. I immediately wrote two more letters, one to the squadron commander and another to the army general saying that I could not consent to let the troops leave the fort without these honors; that they were those due troops which had done their duty, and that once they agreed to that, I would agree to the rest.

The generals answered that they would agree, and Mr. Warren added them to the conditions for the surrender of the island and the town.

The agreement was ratified on both sides, but the English generals did not, as I did, live up to their part of the bargain, ignoring certain conditions.

In the first article, it is stated that all personal property of all the subjects of the King of France who were in Louisbourg, would remain theirs, and that they would be free to take it with them to any port of Europe under the King's rule which they saw fit.

All the boats in the harbor belonging to our citizens were part of their personal property, but the English seized them and kept them.

In general, none of our citizens who went to France could take their chests, chairs, armchairs, tables, desks, andirons, or other furniture or any large baggage, for the generals did not provide boats large enough. Our men were *not* pillaged, but as they couldn't take the few things they had for lack of ships, they had to leave them in Louisbourg, which is exactly as if they had been pillaged, unless His Majesty gets them some kind of compensation from the English court.

In addition, while I was in the colony, the English sent out, unknown to me, 436 sailors and civilians to Boston. They were embarked, as were the troops, in war ships while waiting to leave for France, but one morning, the ship in which they were received an order to leave for Boston, and they set sail.

When I was told of this, I registered a complaint only to be informed that nothing else could be done for lack of food and ships, but that they would be taken from Boston to France.

These sailors were not the only ones. I was told that after my departure the English did the same thing to families who had not been able to get on transport ships bound for France. If the English generals had wanted to, they could have used the same ships which took them to Boston to take them to France. They had food enough in store to last much longer than the crossing, but they acted in this manner to scatter the colony.

The second article concerns the ships which were in port and which they were supposed to use in case there were not enough others for transport.

I made my comments of this situation in the preceding article. It is one of the most important, all things considered, in view of the number of ships in the port which had been sunk or run aground and could have been used for that purpose. As long as our batteries were firing, the enemy could neither use them nor get them out of the harbor.

In addition, if some of the private citizens of the town had not bought ships, the English would have made use of all the items they had placed aboard as they did with the people who had not the means to buy them. These citizens would then have been forced to go to Boston, and so would others who had paid large sums to embark.

As regards the last article on the subject of arms, all the inhabitants had their own and had handed them over at the time of surrender. These arms were part of their possessions, but the enemy refused to return them. When I complained, they answered—when they sent away the 436 sailors—that they would send their arms to them. The other citizens are in the same situation.

I must also inform you, Monseigneur, that the English seized all the objects and utensils from the hospital and stores of the King. According to the terms of surrender, they are entitled only to the fortifications and batteries, along with artillery, arms, and war implements that go with them, and nothing else. However, they took everything, saying that it was the property of their King. M. Bigot's efforts to prevent them bore no fruit; he himself will give you an account of that.

M. Bigot, when he left the Isle d'Aix, was kind enough to take charge of giving you my letter of the 15th of this month with all the original papers concerning what happened at the siege of Louisbourg; I am confident that he has handed them over to you, and that after you have examined them, you will do me the justice of agreeing that I did everything possible for the defense of the town, and surrendered it only as a last resort.

I have neglected to inform you that Ensign de la Tressillière and

Ensign Souvigny, also Lopinot, the younger son, are among those who were killed during the siege.

The garrison of Canceau had been captured there on May 24 of last year. The terms were that no one should bear arms against the King for a year and a day. M. Du Quesnel freed all the officers of that garrison who were supposed to go to Boston on their word of honor, and there to spend the allotted period of time.

M. Jean Blastrick, an officer, was among them, but he broke his word which he gave last March; he was one of the leaders of the men who burned Toulouse-Port and who raided at Gabarus on May 11. He must have been general (colonel) of the Boston militia, and he entered the town at the head of this militia the day after the surrender.

APPENDIX F

Grant of Arms to Sir William Pepperrell *

TO ALL AND SINGULAR to whom these presents shall come, John Anstis, Esqr. Carter Principal King of Arms, and Stephen Martin Leake Esqr. Clarenceux King of Arms, send GREETING. Whereas Christopher Kilby Esqr. hath on the behalf of Sr. William Pepperrell, Bart represented unto the Right Honourable Thomas Earl of Effingham, Deputy with the Royal Approbation to the most Noble Edward Duke of Norfolk, Earl Marshal and Hereditary Marshal of England, that the said Sir William Pepperrell is descended from a Family of that Name in the County of Cornwall whose Father about seventy Years ago went over and settled in New England in America, where the said Sir William Pepperrell was born, and served his Country in many Honourable Stations until the year 1745 when he was appointed Commander in Chief both by Sea and land of the Forces raised by the

* Communicated by his descendant, Joseph W. P. Frost, to the *New England Historical and Genealogical Register* (October, 1950) and here reproduced through the courtesy of Mr. Frost.

several Provinces in New England, in order to attack the French Settlement on the Island of Cape Breton, which He bravely attempted and happily performed in Conjunction with His Majestys Ships sent to his Assistance in these Parts; And after a Vigorous Siege of forty-nine Days oblig'd the Capital Town of Louisburgh together with the Fortresses and Territories thereunto belonging to Surrender to the Obedience of His Britannick Majesty, for which Signal Service, His Majesty was graciously pleased to confer on him the Dignity of a Baronet of Great Britain, and likewise to give him the Command of a Regiment of Foot, raised for the Defence of the said Town and Fortresses; That by reason of the great Length of Time since the said Sir William Pepperrell's Father left England, not being able to make such Proofs of his Arms as are requisite he is therefore desirous as well to have the same confirmed by lawful Authority, as to have some Augmentation thereto that may perpetuate the Memory of the aforesaid Services to Posterity; AND FORASMUCH as his Lordship being fully satisfyed of the eminent Qualifications of the said Sir William Pepperrell to bear Arms, did by Warrant under His Hand and Seal, bearing date the twenty second Day of November 1746 Order and Direct us, to Devise, Grant and Confirm unto the said Sir William Pepperrell and his lawful Descendants such Arms Augmentation and Crest accordingly NOW KNOW YE that We the said Garter and Clarenceux Kings of Arms, in pursuance of the Consent of the said Earl of Effingham, and by Virtue of the Letters Patent of our Offices, to each of Us respectively Granted under the Great Seal of Great Britain, have devised, and do by these presents Grant and Confirm unto the said Sir William Pepperrell Baronet the Arms hereafter mentioned, to wit, Argent, a Chevron Gules between three Pine Apples Vert, together with the Augmentation of a Canton of the Second, charged with a Fleur-de-Lis of the First; And for his Crest, an Armed Arm embowed proper grasping a Staff, thereon a Flag Argent issuing out of a mural Crown proper, with three laurel Leaves between the Battlements as the same in the Margin are more lively depicted, to be born and used for ever hereafter by him the said Sir William Pepperrell, and by the Descendants of his Body lawfully begotten, with their due Differences, according to the Law and Usage of Arms, without the Lett or Interruption of any Person or Persons whatsoever. IN WITNESS whereof We the said Garter and Clarenceux Kings of Arms, have to these Presents subscribed Our Names and affixed the Seals of Our several Offices the fourth Day of December, in the twentyeth Year of the Reign of Our Sovereign Lord George the Second, by the Grace of God, King of Great Britain, France and Ireland,

Defender of the Faith, and so forth and in the Year of Our Lord God, One thousand seven hundred and forty-six.

JOHN ANSTIS, Garter
Principal King of Arms

S. MARTIN LEAKE, Clarenceux

Crest of Sir William Pepperrell, created the first native-born American baronet in recognition of his service at the first siege of Louisbourg. The crest is reproduced from his bookplate.

Originally battle flags flanked the crest but were omitted when the plate was engraved.

Emblematic of the Louisbourg victory over the French, the canton in the upper left corner shows the fleur-de-lis. The bloody left hand on the shield in the chevron is the red hand of Ulster, awarded baronets for memorable feats of arms. The motto, above and below, may be roughly translated, "By the virtue of Pepperrell you shall be guarded."

Notes and References

CHAPTER 1 Mighty Stronghold

1. The French port of Dunkerque (Dunkirk) on the English Channel was strongly fortified by Louis XIV. By the Treaty of Utrecht, which confirmed French possession of Cape Breton Island and granted the right to fortify it, the Dunkirk works were condemned to demolition. Their site was once again distinguished by the gallant evacuation of the British Army from France in the Second World War.
2. William Wood, *The Great Fortress* (Toronto: 1915), p. 5.
3. William Shakespeare, *The Tempest*, Act IV, Scene 1.

CHAPTER 2 Gage of Battle

1. The thought of John and Sebastian Cabot prompts my adaptation of the famous limerick on Boston:

   Here's to the Newfoundland waters,
   The home of great schools of the Cod,
   Where the Cabots speak only to Cabots,
   In the circumstance not at all odd.

2. J. S. McLennan, *Louisbourg from its Foundation to its Fall* (London: 1918), p. 3.
3. Francis Parkman, *A Half-Century of Conflict*, I (Boston: 1902), iii.
4. Ralph Greenlee Lownsbury, *The British Fishery at Newfoundland* (New Haven: 1934), p. 62.
5. *Ibid.*
6. *Ibid.*
7. James Johnstone, *Memoirs* (Aberdeen: 1871), p. 172.

CHAPTER 3 Pawns to the Castle

1. Marc Lescarbot, *Le Conversion des Sauvages qui Ont Baptizés en La Nouvelle France* (Paris: 1610).

2. *Ibid.*

3. Abbé J. A. Marault, *Histoire des Abenakis* (Quebec: 1866), p. 75.

4. "The Abenaki chief Bomazeen, while a prisoner in Boston in 1696, declared that the French missionaries told the Indians that Jesus Christ was a Frenchman, and that his mother, the Virgin, a French lady; that the English had murdered him, and that the best way to gain his favor was to revenge his death." Francis Parkman, *Count Frontenac and New France Under Louis XIV* (Boston: 1897), Chapter XVII.

5. William Bollan, *The Importance and Advantage of Cape Breton* (London: 1746). The Massachusetts agent in London is quoting Governor Dummer's Memorial, pp. 18 ff.

6. "While the white man drank in order to feel happy and to enjoy himself, the savage drank to get drunk, and there was no halfway business about it. When the Indian was drunk, as long as he could stand on his feet he was absolutely uncontrollable and capable of all evil, even against his own family." Edward P. Hamilton, *The French and Indian Wars* (Garden City, N. Y.: 1962), p. 58.

7. *The Jesuit Relations and Other Documents,* 65 (Cleveland: 1898), 255.

8. *Ibid.,* pp. 193 ff.

9. Lescarbot, *op. cit.,* III, 163n. "Whether the syphilis that broke out at the siege of Naples by the French in 1494-1495, and which scourged Europe through the sixteenth century, was brought from the New World by the crew of Columbus, has been much discussed. There seems to be no doubt that the disease in a milder form was rife in Brazil and the West Indies at the time of the arrival of the Europeans. On the other hand, much evidence goes to show that it existed in Europe since the time of the Crusades, though confused by the physicians of the day with leprosy. Even if this was so, however, there is no doubt that its ravages in the sixteenth century were largely caused by the form of the disease imported from America, and that in this manner the tortured Indian unconsciously took vengeance on his tormentors."

10. *Jesuit Relations,* XXXI, 25-51.

11. Parkman, *The Jesuits in North America in the Seventeenth Century* (Boston: 1867), pp. 164 f.

12. J. S. McLennan, *Louisbourg from its Foundation* (London: 1918), p. 67.

13. Marault, *op. cit.,* I, 92 f. To the Abbé's declaration, Parkman adds this sardonic comment: "French Canadians are so ungrateful that they migrate to the United States by myriads."

14. Hamilton, *op. cit.,* p. 78.

CHAPTER 4 Building a Fortress

1. Edward P. Hamilton, *The French and Indian Wars* (Garden City, N. Y.: 1962), p. 197. An instance of available but unemployed artillery is General James Abercromby's vain attempt to capture French Fort Carillon (Ticonderoga) in 1758. The British commander, leaving most of his guns in river barges, flung his troops against the French abatis and earthworks; the Black Watch Regiment alone lost more than half its strength. In 1777,

Ticonderoga's American garrison evacuated the fort when the British hauled cannon to the top of Mount Defiance to command it.

2. Lynn Montross, *War Through the Ages* (New York: 1944), p. 223.
3. All-important artillery armament was consistently neglected.
4. See Appendix B.
5. Nova Scotia Historical Society Collections. Vol. 9, 153 f.
6. Marc Lescarbot, *Adieu à la Nouvelle France,* translated by the author.
7. Albert Almon, *Louisbourg–The Dream City of America* (Glace Bay, Nova Scotia: 1934).

CHAPTER 5 Within the Walls

1. J. S. McLennan, *Louisbourg from its Foundation to its Fall* (London: 1918), pp. 92 f.
2. "One cannot but wonder if the French might not have held Canada longer if they had only been willing to drink water–certainly they would have held out longer." Edward P. Hamilton, *The French and Indian Wars* (Garden City, N. Y.: 1962), p. 99.
3. McLennan, *loc. cit.*
4. For this re-creation and for the following one, the author is indebted to F. Van Wyck Mason, *The Young Titan* (Garden City, N. Y.: 1959).
5. *Cf.*, the use of wooden cannon to drill United States artillerymen in the early training camps of the First World War.
6. Hamilton states that officers' profits on one French Canadian canteen ran as high one year as $150,000 in modern money.
7. The English set other verses to the tune, and the song then became the familiar "For He's a Jolly Good Fellow."
8. Governor Forant, in a 1729 report on the poor quality of the troops, wrote: "We would not keep a hundred soldiers if we discharged all those who are below regulation height. But, aside from stature and physique, I believe it is best to discharge invalids who are pillars of the hospital and occasion much expense, and are of no use whatsoever, as well as rascals who are incorrigible, but are even capable of leading others into vicious ways. It is better to have fewer men than to have them of this character."
9. "Chevaliers de la Table Ronde," an old French drinking song, is still a favorite in the *cafés chantants* of Paris. The translation is by the author.
10. Blankets draping sentries were probably the origin of the mackinaw coat.
11. Wrong, *The Rise and Fall of New France* (N. Y.: 1928), p. 640.
12. "Les Moines." Like the song described in Note 9, this one is still popular in Paris *cafés.*

CHAPTER 6 The Three Spectres

1. *Lettre d'un Habitant de Louisbourgh* (Toronto: 1897), pp. 15 f. This valuable document, dated August 28, 1745, is an eyewitness's account of the first siege. Its author, because of his frank strictures on the government, preserved anonymity, signing only his initials, B.L.N., and pledging the recipient of the letter to secrecy.

2. *Ibid.*, p. 34, n. 12.

3. A lack of sympathy for the plight of the troops was shown by townspeople. Wrote the *Habitant* (pp. 34 f.), "The rebels, taking advantage of the fear in which they were held, proceeded that day to the commissary's door and under frivolous pretexts such as that their money had been previously kept back, caused themselves to be paid all that they wished and to be reimbursed even for their clothing."

4. *Ibid.*, p. 35.

5. This account of the mutiny's aftermath is based on original documents in the Public Archives of Canada at Ottawa, which kindly furnished transcripts as follows:

I. M.G.1, Series 4, Vol. 28 (C11B, Vol. 27), unsigned memorandum on the mutiny, 1745.

II. M.G.1, Series 2, Vol. 170 (B82-2).
- a. President of the Navy Board to Du Barriolt, August 20, 1745.
- b. The same to the same, September 14, 1745.
- c. The same to De Karrer, September 14, 1745.
- d. The same to Du Barriolt, October 8, 1745.
- e. The same to the same, November 1, 1745.
- f. The same to De Karrer, November 1, 1745.
- g. The same to Du Barriolt, November 23, 1745.
- h. The same to De Sérigny, November 23, 1745.
- i. The same to Du Barriolt, November 26, 1745.
- j. The same to De Ste. Marie, December 8, 1745.
- k. The same to De Karrer, December 10, 1745.
- l. The same to Du Barriolt, December 10, 1745.
- m. The same to the same, December 15, 1745.
- n. The same to the same, December 20, 1745.
- o. The same to the same, December 24, 1745.
- p. The same to Bigot, December 27, 1745.

III. M.G.1, Series 2, Vol. 173 (B84-2).
- a. The same to Du Barriolt, January 18, 1746.
- b. The same to Merveilleux, January 31, 1746.

6. Washington Irving, *The Conquest of Granada*.

CHAPTER 7 Demand for Destruction

1. Francis Parkman, *A Half-Century of Conflict* (Boston: 1902).

2. *Ibid.*

3. *Louisbourg Journals, 1745* (New York: 1932), p. 2.

4. F. Van Wyck Mason, *The Young Titan* (Garden City, N. Y.: 1959), p. 439.

5. Fairfax Downey, "Yankee Gunners at Louisbourg," *American Heritage*, February, 1955.

6. Few in the expedition could match the amount of clothing and kit which Chaplain Adonijah Bidwell of the Connecticut fleet allowed himself. Considering it necesary that his appearance be consonant with his calling, he carried the following impedimenta: one hat, two coats, two waistcoats,

one watchcoat, two pairs of breeches, four pairs of stockings, two pairs of shoes, nine shirts, eleven neckbands, two caps, four handkerchiefs, three pairs of gloves, one pillowcase, four napkins, one pair of scissors, one penknife, one pocket looking glass, one brass ink case, one small bottle (contents unstated), one port mantle, one little box. *Louisbourg Journals,* Appendix V.

7. *Ibid.*, p. 3.

8. Edward P. Hamilton, *The French and Indian Wars* (Garden City, N. Y.: 1962), p. 109.

CHAPTER 8 Fortunes of War

1. *Lettre d'un Habitant de Louisbourgh* (Toronto: 1897), p. 36.

2. U. S. Naval War College, *Maritime Wars of the Early Eighteenth Century* (Newport, R. I.: 1936), p. 316.

3. Francis Parkman, *A Half-Century of Conflict* (Boston, 1902).

4. Pomeroy's *Journal* (New York: 1936) was one of many kept by Louisbourg volunteers. Numbers of them have been published; others remain in family archives.

5. *Louisbourg Journals* (New York: 1932), p. 6.

6. F. Van Wyck Mason, *The Young Titan* (Garden City, N. Y.: 1959), pp. 486 f.

7. The matter of Du Chambron's unfitness was shelved in France. A successor, belatedly appointed, had been unable to reach Louisbourg before the siege.

8. J. S. McLennan, *Louisbourg from its Foundation to its Fall* (London: 1918).

9. "Four men of Coll. Willards Company Went Ashore to get some wood. neither of 'em Carried their Guns, and while at work Were Shot Upon by A Indian and two frenchmen, and Bein Under Such disadvantages were taken Prisoners, and were Compell'd to go with 'em which was About Six Mile. But Setting down to Eat were Careless of their Guns our men, fel upon 'em and Overcame 'em But Did'ent bind 'em, and as they was in the way back One of the frenchmen took Up a Large Club and Struck one of our men on the head, and wounded him whereUpon they all fell A fighting Again But our Men Conquer'd and was going to kill the Indian but he begging for Quarter, they Granted it and he afterwards in the Scuffle got away, But the two Frenchmen they've Brought home with them, the men I knew." *Louisbourg Journals,* pp. 8 f.

10. Bourinot, quoting "a colonial writer" in "Cape Breton and Its Memorials of the French Régime."

11. George Gordon, Lord Byron, *Childe Harold's Pilgrimage.*

CHAPTER 9 By the Mouths of Cannon

1. The custom of reversing colors for the uniforms of musicians prevailed in all combat arms. It made them more easily distinguishable in the confusion of battle when they were needed to beat drum signals or, for the cavalry, to sound trumpet calls.

2. Similarly, the builders of Carillon (Ticonderoga) believed that it was impossible to bring cannon to the top of Mount Defiance to command the fort, but the British did it.

3. The *Habitant* wrote (pp. 38 ff.) bitterly of the abandonment of "the splendid battery, which would have been our chief defense had we known how to make use of it" and of "the thirty pieces, which had cost the King immense sums." "Unless it was from a panic fear which never left us again during the whole siege, it would be difficult to give any reason for such an extraordinary action. Not a single musket had yet been fired against the battery, which the enemy could not take except by making aproaches in the same manner as to the town and besieging it, so to speak, in the regular way. A reason for it was whispered, but I am myself not in a position to speak decidedly. I have, however, heard the truth vouched for by one who was in the battery, but, my post being in the town, it was a long time since I had been to the Royal Battery. The alleged reason for such a criminal withdrawal is that there were two breaches which had never been repaired. If this is true the crime is all the greater, for we had had even more time than was necessary to put everything in order."

4. *Ibid.*, p. 38. "We did not doubt that they would land there. Then it was that we saw the need of precautions we ought to have taken. A detachment of one hundred men from the garrison was sent thither quickly in command of M. Morpain, port captain. But what could such a feeble force do against the multitude the enemy was disembarking?"

5. Fairfax Downey, *Sound of the Guns* (New York: 1955), pp. 10 f.

6. F. Van Wyck Mason's *The Young Titan* (Garden City, N. Y.: 1959), pp. 524 ff., presents a graphic re-creation of the passage of the guns through the swamp.

CHAPTER 10 Battery and Counterbattery

1. Coehorns continued in effective siege action through the American Civil War—at Chattanooga, Petersburg, and elsewhere—and thereafter were invaluable in dislodging the Modoc Indians from their natural entrenchments in the Battle of the Lava Beds in California, 1872-1873.

2. William Wood, *The Great Fortress* (Toronto: 1915), p. 50.

3. *Louisbourg Journals* (New York: 1932), p. 19.

4. *Ibid.*, p. 114.

5. In time, artillerymen of all faiths would adopt Saint Barbara as their patron.

6. Usher Parsons, *The Life of Sir William Pepperrell* (Boston: 1855).

7. Wrote the *Habitant:* "On the 18th we perceived a ship carrying the French flag, and trying to enter the Port. It was seen that she really was a French ship and to help her come in we kept up a ceaseless fire from the Royal Battery. The English could easily have sunk the ship had it not been for the vigour of our fire, which never ceased, and they were not able to keep her from entering. This little reinforcement pleased us. She was a Basque vessel, and another had reached us in the month of April."

8. The *Habitant,* doubtless echoing many others in Louisbourg, believed that if the *Vigilant* with her precious stores had safely made port, it would have marked the turning point of the siege, and that she could have accom-

plished the feat as had the Basque ship had she not allowed herself to be diverted in chase of the *Mermaid*. "In France it is thought that our fall was caused by the loss of this vessel . . . In a sense this is true, but we should have been able to hold out without her if we had not heaped error upon error, as you must have seen by this time. It is true that, thanks to our own imprudence, we had already begun to lose hope when this powerful succor approached us. If she had entered, as she could have done, we should still hold our property, and the English would have been forced to retire . . . At the time there was a north-east wind which was a good one for entering. She left the English fleet two and a half leagues to leeward. Nothing could have prevented her from entering, and yet she became the prey of the English by a most deplorable fatality. We witnessed her maneuvers and there was not one of us who did not utter maledictions upon what was so badly planned and so imprudent." (P. 46.)

CHAPTER 11 Assault on an Island

1. "When Gorham's regiment first took post at Lighthouse Point, Du Chambon thought the movement so threatening that he forgot his former doubts, and ordered a sortie against it under Sieur de Beaubassin. Beaubassin landed with 100 men, at a place called Lorembec, and advanced to surprise the English detachment; but was discovered by an outpost of forty men, who attacked and routed his party. Being then joined by eighty Indians, Beaubassin had several other skirmishes with English scouting-parties, till, pushed by superior numbers, and their leader severely wounded, his men regained Louisbourg by sea, escaping with difficulty from the guard-boats of the squadron. The Sieur de la Vallière, with a considerable party of men, tried to burn Pepperrell's storehouses, near Flat Point Cove; but ten or twelve of his followers were captured, and nearly all of the rest wounded." Francis Parkman, *A Half-Century of Conflict* (Boston: 1902).

2. *Archives de la Marine. Lettre de Monsieur Du Chambon au Ministre, à Rochefort, le 2 septembre, 1745.* (See Appendix E.)

3. F. Van Wyck Mason, *The Young Titan* (Garden City, N. Y.: 1959), p. 568.

4. Fairfax Downey, *Sound of the Guns* (New York: 1955), p. 15.

CHAPTER 12 "And Great Was the Fall Thereof"

1. Nova Scotia Historical Society, IX, p. 173.

2. Usher Parsons, *The Life of Sir William Pepperrell* (Boston: 1855).

3. *Archives de la Marine. Lettre de Monsieur Du Chambon au Ministre, à Rochefort, le 2 septembre, 1745.* (See Appendix E.)

CHAPTER 13 The Victors and the Spoils

1. J. S. McLennan, *Louisbourg from its Foundation to its Fall* (London: 1918), p. 14; and William Wood, *The Great Fortress* (Toronto: 1915), p. 65.
p. 14; and William Wood, *The Great Fortress* (Toronto: 1915), p. 65.

2. Francis Parkman, *A Half-Century of Conflict* (Boston: 1902).

3. Du Chambon reported 37 barrels of powder left, an amount raised to 384 in the check by British ordnance officers, who also found some six hundred rounds of shot.

4. Parkman, *op. cit.*

5. *Ibid.*

6. F. Van Wyck Mason, *The Young Titan* (Garden City, N. Y.: 1959).

7. Parkman, *op. cit.*

8. Imposition of a stringent tax was required to cover a remaining tenth of Massuchusetts' indebtedness.

9. As yet there was only sporadic and irregular aid, by governments and communities, for bereaved families and crippled veterans. Some homes for pensioners existed. A sum was paid the Swiss government for each mercenary soldier killed or wounded.

10. Nova Scotia Historical Society *Collections,* IX.

11. Besides the victorious French Army, England was menaced by a threat on her own soil, the landing of the Pretender to the throne, Bonnie Prince Charlie. However, the uprising of the Scottish clans he led would be bloodily quelled and would later result in emigration from distressed Scotland to Louisbourg.

12. *Cf.* the influenza epidemic of World War I.

13. McLennan, *op. cit.*, pp. 173 f.

14. Edwards in Nova Scotia Historical Society, *op. cit.*, p. 178.

CHAPTER 14 Trident of Neptune

1. U.S. Naval War College, *Maritime Wars of the Early Eighteenth Century,* p. 28.

2. Nancy Mitford, *Madame de Pompadour,* pp. 16 f.

3. H. Noel Williams, *Madame de Pompadour,* p. v.

4. Bent, *Why Was Louisbourg Twice Besieged?*, pp. 11 f.

5. *Ibid.*

CHAPTER 15 Death of a Fleet

1. While accounts of the strength of the French fleet vary slightly, it was substantially as stated.

2. Albert Almon, *Louisbourg—The Dream City of America* (Glace Bay, Nova Scotia: 1934), p. 62.

3. Samuel Taylor Coleridge, "The Rime of the Ancient Mariner."

4. *Ibid.*

5. Francis Parkman, in *A Half-Century of Conflict,* II (Boston: 1902), cites authorities in notes on pp. 158-168.

6. *Ibid.*, p. 168.

7. See H. B. Jefferson's "The Day They Dug Up the Duke" in *The Atlantic Advocate,* November, 1956.

8. By Katharine McLennan, Honorary Curator, Louisbourg Museum. *Fortress of Louisbourg National Historic Park* (Ottawa: The Queen's Printer and Controller of Stationery, 1959).

CHAPTER 16 Price of Peace

1. This anonymous account is quoted in McLennan, pp. 192 f.
2. J. S. McLennan, drawing on Surlaville's papers, sums up the commandant's criticisms of the uniforms as follows: cloth too thin; badly cut and costly to make over; white bad color; stockings bad; shoes thin; paying only once a year bad; only three sizes of gaiters sent out, resulting in many misfits; hats bad; no distinguishing marks for corporals; bad linen for shirts; should have caps, and black instead of white collars.
3. William Wood, *The Great Fortress* (Toronto: 1915).
4. John Clarence Webster, *Thomas Pichon, "The Spy of Beauséjour"* (Halifax: 1937).
5. A. I. Mahan, *The Influence of Sea Power upon History, 1660-1783* (Boston: 1941).
6. *Ibid.*

CHAPTER 17 Check and Countercheck

1. Francis Parkman, *Montcalm and Wolfe*, I (Boston: 1902), pp. 118 f.
2. K. McLennan, *Fortress of Louisbourg National Historic Park* (Ottawa: 1959), p. 20.
3. J. Russell Harper, unpublished "Report on Restoration of Fortress of Louisbourg" (Ottawa: 1960). Spruce beer is made by boiling the tips of small branches of the tree until they start to disintegrate. Then the scum is skimmed off and molasses added with yeast after cooling.
4. William Wood, *The Great Fortress* (Toronto: 1915), p. 104.
5. U. S. Naval War College, *The Opening Phases of the Seven Years' War* (Newport, R. I.: 1937), pp. 34 f.

CHAPTER 18 Amphibious Operation

1. Christopher Hibbert, *Wolfe at Quebec* (New York: 1959), p. 24.
2. Interesting first-hand accounts, British and French, of the landing are quoted by J. S. McLennan in *Louisbourg from its Foundation to its Fall* (London: 1918), pp. 256-260. Other primary sources, journals of the siege, are cited by Francis Parkman in *Montcalm and Wolfe*, II (Boston: 1902), 85 f.
3. "Captain William Amherst, the commander's brother and aide-de-camp, wrote in his journal that the French who made the sortie had been well primed with brandy before they started. They came on shouting 'Kill! Kill!' " Edward P. Hamilton, *The French and Indian Wars* (Garden City, N. Y.: 1962), p. 237.
4. William Wood, *The Great Fortress* (Toronto: 1915), p. 112. The practice of assigning laundresses, usually the wives of noncommissioned officers, to military units was frequently followed. In the U.S. Army, where four were allowed each company, it persisted through the Indian Wars.

CHAPTER 19 The French Frigate

1. McLennan, *op. cit.*, p. 274 and n. 2.
2. *Ibid.*, pp. 275 f. "Drucour felt that he could not accept this offer. The buildings which might have been used on Battery Island were in ruins, and to detach a ship, as a hospital, would apparently weaken their naval force. His own view was that the ship was useless as she was, but that this could not be thought possible by the English commanders. So the civilians, nearly four thousand in number, the soldiers off duty, the sick and the wounded, as well as the combatants, all in a town, the area of which was about 600 yards in one direction, and about 400 across, had to undergo the fire of the besiegers from the lighthouse, which reached as far as the citadel, and from Wolfe's new batteries. In two days, the 6th and the 7th, 125 or 130 shells and 60 or 70 shot had fallen in the town. The purpose of the enemy seemed in the early days of the bombardment rather to destroy the buildings of the town than its defence."
3. Edward P. Hamilton, *The French and Indian Wars* (Garden City, N. Y.: 1962), p. 236.
4. *Ibid.*

CHAPTER 20 Ring of Iron

1. Veterans of the First and Second World Wars will remember the methodically timed German fire on crossroads and other targets, fire so regularly delivered that it could be anticipated and avoided, or the danger area passed between shell bursts.
2. Francis Parkman, *Montcalm and Wolfe,* II (Boston: 1902), 71 f.

CHAPTER 21 Fall into Oblivion

1. Quoted in Louis Barcroft Runk, *Fort Louisbourg* (Philadelphia: 1911).
2. Quoted in William Wood, *The Great Fortress* (Toronto: 1915), p. 121.
3. *Ibid.*, p. 122.
4. Runk, *op. cit.*
5. Pp. 126 f.
6. C. Ochiltree Macdonald, *The Last Siege of Louisbourg* (London: 1908).

CHAPTER 22 Rack and Ruin

1. C. Ochiltree Macdonald, *The Last Siege of Louisbourg* (London: 1908), p. 118.
2. Prov. 25:28.
3. *Canadian Magazine*, 42 (1913-1914).
4. Francis Parkman, *Montcalm and Wolfe,* II (Boston: 1902), 55 f.

5. Quoted in Albert Almon, *Louisbourg—the Dream City* (Glace Bay, Nova Scotia: 1934), p. 80.

6. Antoine de la Mothe Cadillac (1658-1730) founded Detroit, served at Port Royal and Quebec, and became Governor of Louisiana.

7. In Royal Society of Canada *Proceedings and Transactions,* 2nd Series, VIII (1902). Translation from the French by the author.

8. Macdonald, *op. cit.*

POSTSCRIPT

1. Edwards. Nova Scotia Historical Soc. Colls., *op. cit.*

2. McLennan, K., *op. cit.,* p. 29. Miss McLennan long served as the museum's director.

3. *Atlantic Advocate,* September, 1958. The once only practical approach to Louisbourg by sea today is supplemented by a fine motor highway.

4. *Ibid.*

5. Russell J. Harper, unpublished "Report on Restoration of Fortess of Louisbourg" (Ottawa: 1960).

6. Rudyard Kipling, "The Palace."

Bibliography

Almon, Albert, *Louisbourg, The Dream City of America.* Glace Bay, Nova Scotia, 1934.

Amherst, Jeffery, *The Journal of Jeffery Amherst.* J. Clarence Webster, Ed. Toronto: The Ryerson Press, 1931.

Babeau, Albert, *La Vie Militaire Sous l'Ancien Régime*, 2 vols. Paris: Firmin Didot, et Cie, 1890.

Baker, Henry M., *The First Siege of Louisbourg,* 1745. Concord, N. H.: The Rumford Press, 1909.

Belknap, Jeremy, *The History of New Hampshire*, 3 vols. Boston, 1791.

Bent, Samuel Arthur, *Why Was Louisbourg Twice Besieged?* Boston: Society of Colonial Wars, 1895.

Bollan, William, *The Importance & Advantage of Cape Breton.* London: John & Paul Knopton, 1746.

A Boston Merchant (James Gibson) in 1745. Boston: Redding & Co., 1847.

Bourinot, J. B., *Historical and Descriptive Account of the Island of Cape Breton.* Montreal: W. Foster Brown & Co., 1892.

Bradley, A. G., *The Fight With France for North America.* New York: E. P. Dutton & Co., 1901.

Bradstreet, Lieut. Dudley, *Diary during the Siege of Louisbourg.* Cambridge, Mass.: John Wilson & Son, 1897.

Brady, Cyrus Townsend, *Colonial Fights & Fighters.* New York: McClure, Phillips & Co., 1901.

Brebner, J. Bartlet, *Canada, A Modern History.* Ann Arbor: University of Michigan Press, 1960.

Burrage, Henry S., *Maine at Louisbourg in 1745.* Augusta: Burleigh & Flint, 1910.

Callwell, Col. C. E., *Military Operations and Maritime Preponderance.* Edinburgh & London: William Blackwood & Sons, 1905.

Canada & Its Provinces, *New France,* Vol. I. Toronto: Publishers Association of Canada, 1914.

Chapin, Howard Millar, *New England Vessels in the Expedition Against Louisbourg, 1745.* Boston: New England Historical & Genealogical Register, Jan. & April, 1923.

DeForest, Louis Effingham, Ed., *Louisbourg Journals, 1745.* New York: Society of Colonial Wars of New York, 1932.

Dickens, Admiral Sir Gerald, *The Dress of the British Sailor.* London: Her Majesty's Stationery Office, 1957.

Downey, Fairfax, "For Joy of Living." In *The Atlantic Advocate's Holiday Book.* Fredericton, N.B., Canada: Brunswick Press, Ltd., 1961.

———, "Yankee Gunners at Louisbourg." *American Heritage,* Feb. 1955.

———, *Sound of the Guns.* New York: David McKay Company, 1955.

Drake, Samuel Adams, *The Taking of Louisbourg, 1745.* Boston: Lee & Shepard, 1890.

Eaton, Evelyn, *Restless Are the Sails,* N. Y.: Harper & Bros., 1941.

Edwards, Joseph Plimsoll, *Louisbourg, an Historical Sketch.* Halifax: Nova Scotia Printing Co., 1895.

Fairchild, Byron, *Messrs. William Pepperrell: Merchants at Piscataqua.* Ithaca, N. Y.: Cornell University Press, 1953.

Fiske, John, *New France & New England.* Boston & N. Y.: Houghton, Mifflin & Co., 1902.

Frégault, Guy, *La Guerre de la Conquête.* Montreal & Paris: Fides, 1955.

———, *François Bigot,* 2 vols. Ottawa: Les Études de l'Institut d'Histoire de l'Amérique Française, 1948.

Frost, Joseph W. P., *Sir William Pepperrell, Bart.* New York: The Newcomers Society in North America, 1951.

Guizot, M., *A Popular History of France,* 8 vols. N. Y.: John W. Lovell Co., 1892.

Hamilton, Edward P., *The French & Indian Wars.* Garden City, N. Y.: Doubleday & Co., 1962.

Harper, J. Russell, Unpublished report on Restoration of Fortress of Louisbourg. Prepared for National Historic Sites Division, Dept. of Northern Affairs & National Resources, 2 vols. Ottawa, 1960.

Harney, D. C., *The French Regime in Prince Edward Island.* New Haven: Yale University Press, 1926.

Hibbert, Christopher, *Wolfe at Quebec.* London, New York, Toronto: Longman's, Green & Co., 1959.

Huidekoper, Frederic Louis, *The Sieges of Louisbourg in 1745 and 1758.* Washington: Society of Colonial Wars, 1914.

Irving, Washington, *Conquest of Granada*, N. Y.: George P. Putnam, 1852.

Jefferys, Thomas, *Natural and Civil History of the French Dominions.* London, 1760.

Jesuit Relations & Other Documents, Reuben Goldthwaites, Ed. Cleveland: The Burrows Bros., 1898.

Johnson, James Gibson, "A Neglected Chapter in Our Colonial History." *Harper's Magazine*, v. 108 (1903-04).

Johnstone, James, Chevalier de, *Memoirs*, 3 Vols. Charles Winchester, Trans. Aberdeen, Scotland: D. Wullie & Son, 1871.

Kennedy, J. H., *Jesuit & Savage in New France.* New Haven: Yale University Press, 1950.

Knox, Capt. John, *An Historical Journal of the Campaigns in North America for the Years 1757, 1758, 1759 and 1760;* 3 Vols. Toronto: The Champlain Society, 1914.

LeClercq, Father Chrestien, *New Relation of Gaspesia.* Toronto: The Champlain Society, 1910.

Lescarbot, Marc, *History of New France*, 3 vols. Toronto: The Champlain Society, 1911.

Lettre d'un Habitant de Louisbourg, George M. Wrong, Eng. Trans. Toronto: University of Toronto Studies (Second Series, Vol. 1), 1897.

Longfellow, Henry Wadsworth, *Evangeline, a Tale of Acadie.* Boston: William D. Ticknor & Co., 1848.

———, *"A Ballad of the French Fleet."*

Louisbourg Journals, L. A. de Forest, Ed. N. Y.: Society of Colonial Wars, 1932.

Lownsbury, Ralph Greenlee, *The British Fishery at Newfoundland, 1634, 1763.* New Haven: Yale University Press, 1934.

Macdonald C. Ochiltree, *The Last Siege of Louisbourg.* London: Cassell & Co., 1908.

McLennan, J. S., *Louisbourg from its Foundation to its Fall, 1713-1758.* London: Macmillan & Co., 1918.

McLennan, Katharine, *Fortress of Louisbourg National Historic Park.* Ottawa: The Queen's Printer & Controller of Stationery, 1959.

Mahan, A. T., *The Inflence of Sea Power upon History, 1660-1783.* Boston: Little, Brown & Co., 1941.

Mante, Thomas, *History of the Late War in North & South America.* London: W. Strahan & T. Cadell, 1772.

Marault, Abbé J. A., *Histoire des Abenakis.* Quebec: Gazette de Sorel, 1866.

Marquis, Thomas Guthrie, *The Jesuit Missions.* Toronto: Glasgow, Brook & Co., 1916.

Mason, F. Van Wyck, *The Young Titan.* Garden City, N. Y.: Doubleday & Co., 1959.

Massachusetts Historical Society Proc., 2nd series, Vols. 11 & 14. Boston: University Press, 1896-97, 1901.

Mitford, Nancy, *Madame de Pompadour.* N. Y.: Random House, 1953.

Montross, Lynn, *War Through the Ages.* N. Y.: Harper & Brothers, 1944.

Pargellis, Stanley, Ed., *Military Affairs in North America, 1748-1765.* N. Y.: D. Appleton-Century Co., 1936.

———, *Lord Loudoun in North America.* New Haven: Yale University Press, 1933.

Parkman, Francis, *The Jesuits in North America in the Seventeenth Century.* Boston: Little, Brown & Co., 1867.

———, *A Half-Century of Conflict,* 2 vols. Boston: Little, Brown & Co., 1902.

———, *Montcalm & Wolfe,* 2 vols. Boston: Little, Brown & Co., 1902.

Parsons, Usher, *The Life of Sir William Pepperrell.* Boston: Little, Brown & Co., 1855.

Pepperrell, Sir William, *The Journal of Sir William Pepperrell, Kept during the Expedition against Louisbourg, March 24-August 22, 1745.* Worcester, Mass.: American Antiquarian Society, 1910.

Pemberton, Ebenizer, *A Sermon Preached to the Ancient & Honourable Artillery Company in Boston, New England, June 7, 1756.* Boston: Edes & Gill, 1756.

Pepperrell Papers. Massachusetts Historical Soc. Colls. Sixth Series, Vol. 10. Boston: The Society, 1899.

Peterson, Harold L., *Arms & Armor in Colonial America, 1526-1783.* Harrisburg, Pa.: The Stackpole Co., 1956.

———, *The Treasury of the Gun.* N. Y.: Golden Press, 1962.

Pomeroy, Seth, Journals & Papers, Louis Effingham de Forest, Ed. N. Y.: Society of Colonial Wars, 1926.

Porier, Pascal, *Louisbourg en 1902,* in Royal Society of Canada, Proc. & Trans., 2nd series, Vol. VIII, 1902.

Reboul, Col. C., *L'Armée.* Paris: Marcel Sebeur, 1931.

Rich, Louise Dickinson, *The Coast of Maine.* N. Y.: Thomas Y. Crowell Co., 1962.

Runk, Louis Bancroft, *Fort Louisbourg: Its Two Sieges & Site Today.* Phila.: Society of Colonial Wars in the Commonwealth of Pennsylvania, 1911.

Stanley, George G., and Harold M. Jackson, *Canada's Soldiers.* Toronto: Macmillan Company of Canada, 1954.

Stevens, William Oliver, and Allan Westcott, *A History of Sea Power.* N. Y.: George H. Doran Co., 1920.

Trowbridge, W. R. H., *A Beau Sabreur, Maurice du Saxe, Marshal of France.* London: T. Fisher Unwin, 1909.

U.S. Naval War College, *Maritime Wars of the Early Eighteenth Century.* Newport, R. I., 1936.

Vetromile, Rev. Eugene, *The Abnakis.* N. Y.: James B. Kirkes, 1866.

Webster, John Clarence, *Thomas Pichon, "The Spy of Beausejour."* Halifax: Public Archives of Nova Scotia, 1937.

Williams, H. Noel, *Madame de Pompadour.* London & N. Y.: Harper & Brothers, 1925.

Wood, George Arthur, *William Shirley, Governor of Massachusetts, 1741-1756.* N. Y.: Columbia University, 1920.

Wood, William, *The Great Fortress.* Toronto: Glasgow, Brook & Co., 1915.

Wrong, George M., *The Rise & Fall of New France,* 2 vols. N. Y.: The Macmillan Co., 1928.

Index

About the Author

Fairfax Downey, born in Salt Lake City, Utah, has traveled in Canada, Europe, Asia and Africa. A free-lance writer, he now makes his home in New Hampshire.

His books on battles, sieges and artillery, stem from his military ancestry and his own army service.

After graduating from Yale University in 1916 he served as an artillery officer in the American Expeditionary Forces in World War I. He was awarded a Silver Star for his gallantry in action at Belleau Wood.

In World War II he rejoined the artillery and saw service in North Africa. He is now a lieutenant colonel, U.S. Army Reserve, retired.

Mr. Downey's thirty-eight books include: *Indian-Fighting Army; The Guns at Gettysburg; Clash of Cavalry; Texas and the War with Mexico.*